Celebrating Your New
Jewish Daughter

Celebrating Your New
Jewish Daughter

Creating Jewish Ways
to Welcome Baby Girls into the Covenant—
New and Traditional Ceremonies

Debra Nussbaum Cohen

Foreword by Rabbi Sandy Eisenberg Sasso

JEWISH LIGHTS Publishing
Woodstock, Vermont

Celebrating Your New Jewish Daughter: Creating Jewish Ways to Welcome Baby Girls into the Covenant—New and Traditional Ceremonies

© 2001 by Debra Nussbaum Cohen

Library of Congress Cataloging-in-Publication Data

Nussbaum Cohen, Debra, 1964–
 Celebrating your new Jewish daughter : creating Jewish ways to welcome
  baby girls into the covenant : new & traditional ceremonies / Debra
  Nussbaum Cohen
       p.   cm.
 Includes bibliographical references (p.).
 ISBN 1-58023-090-3 (Pbk.)
  1. Brit bat. 2. Judaism—Customs and practices. 3. Brit bat—Prayer-
books and devotions. I. Title.
 BM706 .C64 2001   296.4'43—dc21
                                                         00-012492

Page 233 constitutes a continuation of this copyright information.

10 9 8 7 6 5 4 3 2 1

Manufactured in the United States of America

Published by Jewish Lights Publishing
A Division of LongHill Partners, Inc.
Sunset Farm Offices, Route 4, P.O. Box 237
Woodstock, VT 05091
Tel: (802) 457-4000   Fax: (802) 457-4004
www.jewishlights.com

To Jacqueline Ruth Nussbaum,
my mother and teacher

To Aliza Shira Nussbaum Cohen,
my daughter and delight of my soul

CONTENTS

Part One
*An Introduction to Contemporary Jewish
Welcoming Ceremonies*

Part Two
Welcoming Everyone

Part Three

Preparing for Your Daughter's Welcoming Ceremony

Part Four

Creating Your Daughter's Welcoming Ceremony

A NOTE ON THE TRANSLITERATIONS

Just as Jewish welcoming ceremonies vary, so do transliteration systems. The prayers, blessings, and rituals in this book come from many different sources, and thus some of their transliterations vary in spelling.

FOREWORD

Rabbi Sandy Eisenberg Sasso,
author of God's Paintbrush

A small group of rabbinical students is sitting around our friends' living room welcoming our friends' new daughter into the covenant of the Jewish people. It should be nothing out of the ordinary, but it is. It is 1970 and such a ceremony has never been done before. We don't think of ourselves as making history, but as making holy a moment that has long yearned for sanctification. What is more amazing than our living room ritual experiment is that some thirty years later covenantal ceremonies for daughters are being enacted in living rooms and synagogues across the country. What was once an innovation, an alternative expression of Jewish life born out of a deep yearning for inclusion, has now become "tradition."

Today, as families name their daughters amidst the poetry of ritual, the embrace of community, and the joy of song, they touch the personal with the transcendent. They bless a moment in time with the sacred gifts of memory and eternity.

In the past three decades, the unwritten narratives of women's lives, newly spoken, have shaped the contours of religious renewal. To the hundreds of blessings Judaism teaches us, we have added a blessing for the birth of a daughter, holy words for her naming, sacred ritual to cradle her as she enters the covenant of her people. We celebrate her as an heir to her people's heritage, as a divine witness, and as a potential agent in the world's redemption. We wrap our daughters, as we have our sons, in the swaddling cloth of prayer, song, and symbol, that both affirms who they are and obligates them to become all that they can be in solidarity with a community of holy travelers. As parents and loved ones carry a new daughter in their arms, ritual is a reminder that this new life carries the promise and hopes not only of a single family, but of the people of Israel.

The story is told that when Picasso presented his portrait of Gertrude Stein, a critical viewer commented, "But it doesn't look like Gertrude Stein," to which Picasso responded, "It will." As we celebrate our daughters' birth, we are Picassos creating new ritual expressions. We revitalize old forms and give affirmation to new spiritual yearnings, allowing the past to resonate with the present. To the comment that it doesn't look like tradition, we may respond, "It will."

Good ritual honors both the individual and communal, tradition and change, the repetitive certainty of established acts and words and the refreshing spontaneity of improvisation. It gives expression to our innermost longings and deepest fears. It is both sacred affirmation and holy challenge. The power of the birth ritual is in its ability to call forth joy at new life, but also to evoke awe at the responsibility we have to raise our daughters to Torah, *chuppah,* and good deeds. Ritual works when it is able to connect us to something beyond ourselves and place us in a community and tradition to which we are accountable and for which we are responsible.

Our generation has not only created new ritual, it has transformed the ways in which we enact it and, in turn, build community. Women have taught us that religious revelation comes not only vertically, from outside and above us, but horizontally, from within and among us. Ritual is not simply handed down, it is shaped within community. It is not just acted out upon us, but we are the active participants in its drama. As one young mother commented to me after a ceremony for her new baby daughter, "Thank you for letting me speak. At the naming of my last child, I was silent. Now I feel included."

Celebrating Your New Jewish Daughter helps us find our voice. It reverently and gently teaches the sacred forms of Jewish ritual, and with courage allows our own breath to blow through their hallowed vessels. It enables us to imagine how the transcendent might move through our body and soul by asking us to be both descendants, honoring the tradition we inherit, and ancestors, creating the tradition for a new generation.

ACKNOWLEDGMENTS

*T*hank you, first of all, to the many dozens of fathers and mothers and rabbis of all religious perspectives, from all over the Jewish world, who responded to my request for your ceremonies. Thank you for sharing with me your joy, your wisdom, and your creativity by sending me the rituals you have created and conducted to welcome your daughters and the daughters of people you care about. Your work is inspiring and enlightening. It has been an honor to witness Jewish tradition as it is being transformed through your ceremonies. I hope that it feels good to see your work adapted and adopted in these pages, and put into the hands of so many more parents. If there are errors, however, they are mine alone.

For helping me to get the word out all over the print and electronically linked universe of Jews, thank you to Rabbi Nina Beth Cardin, Rabbi Lori Forman, Rabbi Sue Ann Wasserman, Leonard Fein, Susan Weidman Schneider and Naomi Danis of *Lilith* magazine, Lisa Hostein of The Jewish Telegraphic Agency, and Marlene Schwartz.

For providing information and wisdom, thank you to Rabbi Marc Angel, Rabbi Carie Carter, Rabbi Steven Dworken, Rabbi Yechiel Eckstein, Rabbi Eliezer Finkelman, Rabbi Zevulun Lieberman, Rabbi Jack Moline, Rabbi Rona Shapiro, Rabbi Michael Strassfeld, Mary Gendler, Sally Gottesman, Arthur Magida, Toby Fishbein Reifman, and David Rosen.

For providing inspiration and sound advice, thank you to Rabbi Debra Orenstein, Blu Greenberg, and Elisheva Urbas. The work of Rabbi Nina Beth Cardin deserves special mention. I have kept her book of prayers for the married Jewish woman, *Out of the Depths I Call to You*, near to me throughout my pregnancies and relied upon it often. And it was while I was thinking about her last book, *Tears of Sorrow, Seeds of Hope* (Jewish Lights, 1999), which is devoted to contemporary Jewish ritual responses to pregnancy loss and infertility, that I had the idea for this volume. She has contributed much of importance to the growing bookshelf of Jewish religious literature by women, and is an inspiration to me.

Thank you to my personal Jewish communities, at the Park Slope Jewish Center and at the Hannah Senesh Community Day School, where Jewish life is vibrant, my fellow congregants and parents are engaged and thoughtful Jews, and where everyone has been enthusiastically supportive of this project. They are places that strongly value creative spiritual exploration and growth, and where I always feel that I have found my Jewish home. Thank you especially to Joan Warner, who has championed the idea of welcoming new Jewish daughters in our shared community.

Thank you to my colleagues at *The New York Jewish Week*, where I am privileged to have a professional home, for being such a fun bunch to hang around with, however intermittently I make it in to the office. Thank you, too, to *Jewish Week* publisher Gary Rosenblatt and editor Rob Goldblum, for extending to me the scheduling flexibility I needed to finish this book.

Thank you to all those at Jewish Lights Publishing who have been so devoted to the idea of this project, and whose professionalism has been of immeasurable help in getting it where it belongs—into the hands of parents everywhere. Thank you to Sandra Korinchak, vice president of editorial and my indefatigable liaison to Jewish Lights and guide to the intricacies of publishing. Thank you to my editor, Donna Zerner, whose ability to see clearly both the big picture and the critical details has made this into a far more useful book than it was before she took her red pencil to the manuscript. Thanks to Martha McKinney, Emily Wichland, Susan Tarolli, and Jon Sweeney for making this book as beautiful and readable as it is. And thank you to Stuart Matlins, publisher of Jewish Lights, who knew immediately that the time for this book was right and enthusiastically put his resources behind it.

Most importantly of all, thanks to my family. Thank you Aryeh Lev, for being everything in a first child that a mother could ever want, and a source of deep pride and great pleasure. Thank you for teaching me how to be a mother. Thank you to Aliza Shira for bringing us such joy. Thank you too to Elana Miryam, our third child, who has arrived just as this book goes to press, and, in the two days she has been with us so far, has brought us great delight. Above all, thank you to my partner, whose unstinting love and support make possible anything I manage to accomplish in life as a writer, as a wife, and in my most important role, as a mother. Thank you, sweet Shepsi, for being the most loving father that anyone could hope to have as her partner in parenting, and for being such a wonderful husband. You are the foundation and the spark.

INTRODUCTION

Mazel tov! You've had a baby girl! Or you've learned through pre-natal testing that you're going to have a daughter. Perhaps you or someone you love has a strong feeling that it's a girl growing inside. Maybe you're the new mother, or mother-to-be, looking at his book. Perhaps you're her partner, or her parent, sister, aunt, uncle, or dear friend. Whatever the relationship, if you're reading this book it's clear that you will have an important role to play in this little girl's life.

While you've already welcomed this girl into your heart, you're now thinking about how you can welcome her into your extended family and into your community, and about how you can mark her arrival in a way that formally celebrates her membership in the Jewish people.

You've come to the right place.

When a son is born, every Jewish parent knows what ceremony will welcome him into the community and signal his membership in the Jewish people—the *brit milah*, the circumcision ceremony. It is not as clear what to do to welcome a daughter, and that is both our challenge and our opportunity.

It's always easier to do something when there's a fixed formula, like a set of blessings or a ritual, to rely on and that doesn't require any work, thought, or creativity on our part for participation. We can ask our rabbi to lead us or we can open a prayer book, and there it is for us to follow. Where there is no fixed liturgy, as there is not with welcoming ceremonies for our daughters, opportunities are wide open. It's a wonderful opening to do something personal, creative, and individual to welcome your daughter. It can also seem overwhelming, in the crush of the new experiences and exhaustion that follow a birth, to try to create something from scratch. This book is here to help.

I hope that you will find things to take from this book no matter what your degree of knowledge or level of engagement with Jewish life, whether you grew up Jewish or are new to the community, and whether you regard yourself as Orthodox, traditional, Conservative, Reconstructionist, Reform, unaffiliated, or something else altogether.

In these pages you will find prayers, blessings, poems, and pieces of prose that will appeal to you no matter what your orientation is toward the idea of a welcoming ceremony. They are here for you to borrow and make your own by combining the elements that appeal most to your sensibilities.

If you are traditionally minded at heart, you will find a rich offering of the customary blessings in Hebrew and in English with which you can build your daughter's ceremony. If you have a more contemporary orientation, there are plenty of offerings for you as well. There are readings from almost every imaginable source: from the Book of Psalms and others of Judaism's core texts, but also from popular poets and liturgists.

Celebrating Your New Jewish Daughter is divided into four sections. Part One provides the background and history of welcoming ceremonies for Jewish girls, as well as a discussion of the idea of covenant as it applies to our daughters today. Part Two, which is devoted to the practical aspects of setting up a welcoming ceremony, will help you get started as you think about what kind of ceremony you want for your daughter and how you will pull it together. Part Three addresses the needs of modern Jewish families—whose configurations don't always fit into our old notions of how families look—with concrete ways to make everyone feel welcome. Part Four is the heart of the book. It tells you exactly what format welcoming ceremonies generally take, and it offers hundreds of elements to consider incorporating, in an easy-to-follow menu of options. Part Four also includes complete sample ceremonies, each one created to appeal to a family with a different perspective on Judaism. You may choose to use one of the sample ceremonies as-is to welcome your own daughter, or you may elect to borrow elements and combine them with other ideas in the book, or with selections that you find in other sources.

The idea for *Celebrating Your New Jewish Daughter* came, naturally, after the birth of my own daughter, Aliza. How I had hoped—even secretly prayed—for a daughter. I adore my son Aryeh, who is five years Aliza's senior. He is teaching me how to be a mother, and I'm glad that he is our first child. At the same time, part of my heart also always yearned for a girl.

When I was pregnant with Aryeh, and unsure of whether I would have a girl or boy, I began collecting *simchat bat* (celebration of a daughter) ceremonies, hoping one day to have a need for them. I gathered together what existed in print in 1994, which wasn't all that much. From the National Council of Jewish Women I purchased a slim collection of ceremonies photocopied from different contributors. From the Conservative movement I purchased a lovely presentation folder with a couple of articles and sample ceremonies. And somehow I came across what may be the very first collection of such ceremonies, a booklet put out in the early 1970s by the original feminist Jewish group, Ezrat Nashim. (See page 228 for a full list of resources.)

Then Aryeh was born, and of course he had a *brit milah*. The core requirements of the *bris* are immutable and the traditions that go with it are lovely. But I wanted to do more to make the ritual marking the arrival of this boy—who was the first grandchild on my side of the family and the first great-grandchild for my Holocaust survivor grandmother—more personal. I wanted Aryeh's *bris* to be about very literally marking his, and our, ties to the covenant we received at Sinai, but I also wanted to make more explicit what his arrival meant not only in the chain in the generations of the Jewish people, but also for us as a family.

And so, inspired by the innovation in the *simchat bat* rituals I'd collected, we expanded the ceremony around Aryeh's *bris*. Standing at the front of our synagogue early that Sunday morning as golden sunlight streamed in through the 100-year-old stained glass windows were Ari's direct ancestors. Wrapped in my *tallit* (prayer shawl), Aryeh was carried into the sanctuary by my mother, who then placed the little bundle into the arms of my grandmother, who had survived the Holocaust with her husband and young son and sister, but had lost everything else—her parents, her cousins, her aunts and uncles, her friends, her community, and her life as a Jew in Germany—to Hitler's plan.

Oma said a few words, her voice breaking, about what Aryeh's arrival meant to her, and then passed him to my husband's father, who passed him to my father, then into my husband Marc's arms, each of them speaking briefly about the meaning, for them, of our son's arrival. With Ari back in my arms, I gave a *d'var torah*, or sermon, based on the Torah portion corresponding to the week of his birth. From there on in, the *bris* was pretty straightforward (though I didn't realize how overwhelmed I would be with anxiety while the actual cutting was taking place).

In the intervening five years, I attended several *simchat bat* ceremonies held by friends who had given birth to or adopted little girls. The rituals seemed to be growing in popularity, and they varied widely in their form and substance. Like most people interested in this new rite of passage, I took home a copy of each program handed out and stuck it in a file cabinet. The ceremonies themselves and the parties that followed certainly ranged from simple to lavish, and from the ritually traditional to the wildly innovative.

Then, finally, after waiting and hoping, miscarrying and waiting again, came Aliza. Round and dark, with a rosebud mouth and a full head of hair. What a deep and sweet joy. A week later, when I was home alone with her on the second night of Passover, she had three seizures, which turned out to be her body's way of telling us that she had had a stroke.

I had intended to welcome her with a special ceremony, but I hadn't prepared anything in advance of her birth because I see wisdom in the Jewish custom of waiting until a baby's actual arrival before setting up the crib and taking out the baby clothes. After a traumatic miscarriage and through a complicated pregnancy with Aliza, I had a new appreciation for that practice, particularly at the moments when it seemed as if the pregnancy might not come to full term. Now, of course, planning her welcoming ceremony was on hold as she went through test after test while in the pediatric intensive care unit.

A week later, with a diagnosis in hand and a future full of uncertainty and therapies and more tests and medical appointments, Aliza was released from the hospital. She was medically stable, though I was afraid she would have more seizures, and no one could tell us what her future might hold. We didn't know whether she would be developmentally impaired or whether she would recover fully. What we did know was that Aliza's life, and my own, would for the time being be built around her six therapy appointments each week.

Life felt precarious for Aliza, yet I was as hopeful as I was anxious about her future. I was also eager to put the medical difficulties of her first few weeks in the past as much as possible, and to formally celebrate what I prayed would be the beginning of a normal life for my daughter. After the stress of being with her in intensive care while we also juggled caring for our son, whose school was closed for Passover vacation, I was eager for normalcy. And so, about two weeks after she was released from the hospital, we welcomed Aliza into our community and into the family of Jews with a ceremony that was particularly tender, since everyone in our home that day knew what she, and we, had just been through.

For the same reasons that many others have experienced, I had a hard time putting the service together. Even though I am an engaged Jew, have learned a lot about Judaism as an adult, and, as a writer, know how to do research, I struggled mightily to compose our ceremony. I was uncertain about where to begin, where to end, what should be included in between, and in which order. Confronting the task made me feel Jewishly ignorant and overwhelmed. I consulted with my congregational rabbi and looked over the other welcoming ceremony booklets I'd collected, but still felt lost as I sat down to compose our own.

Eventually I managed to put things together in a reasonable order. On the advice of Debbie Friedman, a popular Jewish singer who has written many prayer-songs that have become part of liberal Jews' religious lives and who was generous enough to come sing for us, we began and ended Aliza's welcoming ceremony with music. It was a strong way to start and to close this emotionally powerful morning, which, despite the presence of a lot of people—about eighty of our nearest and dearest crowded into the first floor of our house—felt very intimate.

It was a glorious Sunday morning. Buoyed by the love of the people who had come to share in our *simcha,* by the purpose of our coming together, and by the pleasure I felt when I looked at the new daughter in my arms, I felt elevated and filled with intense joy. It was, indeed, a holy experience, and it marked a dramatic boundary between the fear about Aliza's well-being in which we had just been immersed and a place of great happiness and peace.

Aliza was carried into our living room by my dear friend Helen, her godmother, who recited a simple line from Psalms comparing her radiance to the moon's. Starting with a song that Debbie Friedman played while our son, Aryeh, helped her lead the singing, we welcomed Aliza.

We then spoke about the woman for whom she is named and the other women in the family who didn't live to see her arrival but would have celebrated it if they had. Marc and I read some prayers

I'd copied out of the Conservative rabbis' manual. Then my parents and Marc's brother and sister each took a corner of my *tallit* and folded it around Aliza as they recited a line from Psalms. Marc and I recited another prayer or two, thanked everyone for coming, and once again, Debbie Friedman sang for and with us. Her offering Aliza a *mishebeyrach*, a blessing that asks for God's protection and that is often invoked in times of danger or poor health, was particularly poignant.

We herald the birth of every child, boy and girl, because with each comes new hope. A new chance to do better for them than perhaps we feel we received. A new chance to mold them into the kind of person we wish we could be. Each child is another opportunity for redemption. And at birth, when the particular gifts and challenges of this individual child have not yet been revealed, everything feels possible. With the arrival of a daughter—who is born with all of the eggs inside her she will need to create her own children—those hopes have been put in particularly clear relief for me.

As this book goes to press, Aliza is a deliciously sparkle-filled toddler who shows no sign, physically or developmentally, of her stroke. And I am grateful.

Soon after the acute stage of Aliza's medical crisis had quieted, I was thinking about prayer and sanctification, and reflecting on a book I had relied on for comfort at moments when I wasn't sure my pregnancy with her would be sustained. I had turned many times to *Out of the Depths I Call to You: A Book of Prayers for the Married Jewish Woman*, by Rabbi Nina Beth Cardin. Thinking, too, about the new book Rabbi Cardin was writing, *Tears of Sorrow, Seeds of Hope* (Jewish Lights, 1999), which is devoted to Jewish prayers and rituals around pregnancy loss and infertility, I realized that there is a magnificent library of Jewish women's literature being published today. Prayers and rituals, some resurrected from ancient manuscripts and traditions, and others being created for the first time are available to us today to serve the needs of contemporary Jewish women. Most of this work by Jewish women is now being published in articles, in books, and in Internet discussions, and it reveals the rich bounty of fruits from Jewish women's religious creativity. Perhaps all of the thousands of new rituals to welcome our daughters that have been created over the past three decades should be considered together to be like *Bereishit*, the Book of Genesis—which is about beginnings—in this new women's Torah.

Putting together Aliza's *simchat bat* made me sharply aware that each of us has had to start from scratch each time we wanted to honor the arrival of our new daughters with a Jewish ritual—and that it has been a struggle for many—because there has been no comprehensive, easily available resource to help us. And since parents and rabbis have been creating welcoming ceremonies for Jewish girls for nearly thirty years, it seemed clear that the time had come to gather the best and most interesting practices and make them available to a wider audience than might otherwise have access to such rituals.

The birth of a daughter is one of those moments when the desire to express joy and gratitude in a Jewish way is most profound, even as it's a time of new-parent exhaustion. It is one of those moments—like weddings and funerals—when people who otherwise aren't interested in observing rituals want to do something spiritual, and to do it in a Jewish way. If only they—if all of us—had the tools easily accessible, it might feel easier to accomplish, and might permit more people to begin the lives of their daughters in this important way.

For all of these reasons the time is right for *Celebrating Your New Jewish Daughter*. I hope that you find this volume helpful. It has been a pleasure to create.

PART ONE

An Introduction to Contemporary Jewish Welcoming Ceremonies

CHAPTER ONE

The History of This New Tradition

*T*here's a reason why the time is ripe for a book on this topic. It's because we're ready. We're ready as a Jewish people, as Jewish women, as people who love Jewish women, and most of all, as people who love the little Jewish girls who are being born into our lives and community. While there has been much focus in recent times on creating naming ceremonies for girls, we know that it's time to honor their arrival with the same depth of ritual and praise of God with which we honor our sons.

Those who have preceded us in welcoming their daughters for the past quarter-century have been busy inventing, discovering, unearthing, and adapting rituals and compiling them into their own unique ceremonies. Several important works have preceded this book—articles, the first of which was published in 1973, and booklets and chapters about *simchat bat* in books about Jewish ritual. The earliest published collection dates back to 1977, when the New York Jewish feminist group Ezrat Nashim published their booklet of welcoming ceremonies. Since then, welcoming ceremonies for girls have gained acceptance in almost all Jewish circles, and are increasingly popular. Creative ceremonies are to be found in all but the most right-wing circles of the Orthodox community, and among liberal Jews of every denominational affiliation.

There is growing interest as well among new parents who want

to welcome their daughters with Jewish ritual, but who don't necessarily belong to a synagogue or know quite where to turn for assistance. So much has been written by thoughtful, creative Jews to
welcome their daughters that thousands upon thousands of such
ceremonies are circulating, most of them from one pair of hands to
another. Enough has been developed so that it's no longer necessary for each Jewish parent of a new daughter to reinvent the wheel.
There is a level of egalitarianism around *simchat bat* ceremonies
unlike that around any other Jewish ritual, probably because so few
of us, no matter what our denomination or level of Jewish involve-
ment, grew up seeing rabbis lead welcoming ceremonies for girls. We
don't feel so much that we are breaking from a Jewish tradition as
much as we are building on it, extending it, creating the next chapters of our prayer books. The fact that we are all, essentially, begin-
ners in creating this ritual of celebration and sanctification for our
daughters has permitted a great unleashing of liturgical creativity. By
gathering together the elements of these ceremonies, this book provides a single comprehensive resource from which to plan the most
important new ones—yours.

   In collecting welcoming ceremonies from Jews all over the
world, I discovered a curious thing: Common threads of structure
and liturgy run through most of them. They are shaped along similar lines, with a parallel order, and share several oft-used blessings
and lines of beautiful verse from the Torah that are particularly well
suited to the occasion. While the Reform, Reconstructionist, Conservative, and even centrist Orthodox movements have published
sample prayers and welcoming ceremonies for girls in their rabbis'
manuals and in the Reform movement's book of home-based rituals,
Jewish religious authorities have not codified a single *simchat bat* or
brit bat rite.

   The *brit milah* ceremony for boys is a single ritual of prayers,
blessings, and the physical act of cutting the foreskin, which is universally practiced. It is fundamentally the same whether the ritual is
being performed at the hands of a Chasidic rabbi in Brooklyn or a

Reform *mohelet* (female circumciser) in Georgia. We have no such single practice for our girls. It is too new a ceremony, still being tried on and shaped by every pair of parents that welcomes their daughter this way. That means there is no set liturgy, that each time the responsibility for what we are to do is in our hands. That is our challenge and our opportunity.

Jewish religious practice is, and always has been, an evolving, organic process, reflecting the needs of an individual Jewish community at a particular point in time and influences from the cultures in which we have lived. As feminist Jewish theologian Judith Plaskow has written, the boundaries of what is religiously acceptable evolve over time in the context of changing circumstances.[1] The newness and innovative nature of *simchat bat* extends to each of us the opportunity to compose the ceremony that feels best suited to our family's needs. What will feel right to one family in the *simchat bat* they create for their daughter might feel awkward or foreign to another.

But these ceremonies work best, too, when they are rooted not simply in modern poems and songs, reflections of the popular culture of the moment in which we are living, but in what have become elements of classical Jewish liturgy. The religious evolution reflected in the popularity of welcoming ceremonies for Jewish girls does not mean a break with the past. Instead, it means an adaptation of tradition and continuity, bringing some of the same precepts that we apply to the ritual welcoming our sons into consonance with our contemporary sensibilities. This evolution illustrates the vitality of contemporary Judaism and its centrality in our lives.

I found, in reviewing the hundreds of ceremonies sent to me from Jewish communities around the world, that there has already been a process of organic codification, that certain prayers and poems and rituals are emerging in many, though far from all, of the ceremonies as the elements that seem right to most of the parents. So while there has been no rabbinic seal of approval designating a single ceremony as the only suitable one, there has been, in fact, a process turning experiment into accepted liturgy all the same. And, as befits this egalitarian age, when the power to determine the level of Jewish engagement we and our children will have is up to our will alone, this process has been in the hands of the people.

The first contemporary welcoming ceremonies for Jewish daughters were held in the early 1970s by people involved in the then-nascent *havurah* movement, whose goal it was to take the power of Judaism out of the sole purview of the rabbinate. They wanted to go beyond rabbis and cantors performing rituals for their congregants, empower the laity to take on those tasks and commitments themselves, and create a renewed sense of intimacy and community in Jewish life.

One of the earliest published daughter's welcoming ceremonies was that created by Rabbi Michael and Sharon Strassfeld for their daughter Kayla in 1973.[2] They were central figures in the movement now known as Jewish Renewal and edited the groundbreaking Jewish Catalog series of books, which put do-it-yourself Judaism literally into people's own hands. It was about that time that two Reform rabbis published a new ritual called *kiddush peter rechem* (sanctification of the womb's opening) to mark the arrival of a first child of either sex, in an egalitarian parallel to the traditional *pidyon ha-ben*, or ceremonial redemption of a one-month-old firstborn son from service in Jerusalem's holy Temple.

In an article in *Response* magazine in the summer of 1973, Rabbi Sandy Eisenberg Sasso discussed a welcoming ceremony she and her husband, Rabbi Dennis Sasso, had created for the birth of a daughter of a colleague, and offered an outline of that ritual; the article also explained the rationale behind the creation of this new kind of ceremony.

Excitement and ferment about these emerging modern welcoming rituals for girls were also spawned in 1973 at the first Conference on Women and Judaism. "Thirty years ago nobody even asked the question of whether a girl should have a ceremony," says Rabbi Nina Beth Cardin. "There is a huge awareness that has developed over a relatively short span of time, and it has bubbled up from the bottom. These ceremonies were a very radical expression back then, and nowadays they're not," she said.[3]

The very notion of welcoming daughters in a religiously significant way is rooted in an egalitarian concept of what Judaism should be: different, perhaps, for females and males, but equal nonetheless. It is an idea born out of feminism and the then-astonishing idea that women have a voice within Judaism that deserves, and needs, to be heard. Today these ceremonies are held by people who regard feminism in all sorts of different ways—with enthusiasm, with suspicion, or with indifference. Like so many of the benefits enjoyed by contemporary women and men, even if they are embraced by people who would describe themselves as anti-feminist, they are rooted in feminism nonetheless.

But welcoming ceremonies have also grown beyond the ideological confines of what feminism may be. Today they are embraced, as one modern Orthodox woman wrote in her own daughter's welcoming ceremony, as "women's Torah."

Orthodox Jews have, by definition, historically been less open to ritual innovation than more liberally inclined Jews, but it didn't take long after the very first contemporary welcoming ceremonies were created and publicized for Orthodox Jews to adapt the idea to their own theological and liturgical perspectives, probably starting with the ceremony Joseph and Sharon Kaplan created to welcome their daughter, Micole, in the winter of 1974.[4] Until then, traditionally observant Jews had welcomed their daughters with the standard blessings in synagogue and, sometimes, a festive kiddush reception after services.

Three years later Orthodox Rabbi Yechiel Eckstein and his wife, Bonnie Eckstein, held a contemporary *simchat bat* for their daughter Tamar in Riverdale, New York. Rabbi Eckstein's mother had said before the baby arrived that if it was a boy, family members would travel to New York for the *brit milah*, but if the new baby was a girl, they wouldn't come to meet her until later. The inequity of her statement spurred the Ecksteins to create something ritually significant for their daughter, and so they held their welcoming ceremony at home, weaving together several traditional sources by reciting psalms and the *shehechiyanu*, the prayer of thanksgiving. Bonnie Eckstein said the *gomel* prayer of thanksgiving for having come through a dangerous passage, and then recited the prayer of Chana, in which the previously infertile biblical figure gives birth after heartfelt petition to God and then says "My heart exalts to *Hashem*." Rabbi Eckstein said at the time that "all rabbis, including the Orthodox, agree that women share equally with men in the covenant with God. So as I see it, if women share equally, it is not only permissible to devise an appropriate symbol for girls entering the covenant, it is a religious obligation. The technical problem is how to put together a ceremony."[5]

Today we've mastered that technical problem of how to put together a ceremony, though the details and approach are still being worked out, as one family at a time creates the ritual that best reflects its personality and perspective on Judaism.

Today we are creating the rituals that our own children, we hope, will build on when the time comes for them to welcome our grandchildren. Perhaps by that time, when the contemporary *simchat bat* has been employed by a second generation, there will be some sort of codified ceremony used by, and adapted from, Jews the world over. It's likely to take more time than that and, unlike with the *brit milah*, there will probably not be a sole core welcoming ceremony for girls employed by Reform, Reconstructionist, Conservative, and Orthodox Jews in our lifetimes. There will probably always be a great range of variation, reflecting the attitudes and interests of people approaching Judaism in many different ways, each, perhaps, an aspect of the seventy faces of Torah described by our ancient sages.

We are now at the time that borders the end of the first generation of feminist Jewish women and men who created the very idea of a contemporary ritual with which to welcome their daughters, and the beginning of the next. We're at the cusp of an epochal moment, when the very first girls who were welcomed by their parents in inventive contemporary rituals are becoming old enough to welcome their own daughters. As we move forward with our daughters' celebrations today—creating, experimenting, trying things on, and seeing which aspects fit and which don't—it's important to be familiar with that which has gone before, and to anchor our rituals in as much of Jewish tradition as we can. The notion that we should welcome our daughters with a serious Jewish ritual was a revolutionary idea when the first parents did it. But by basing their daughters' ceremonies on traditional sources and forms of prayer, they acknowledged a truth we should continue to keep in mind today: The most effective ritual is evolutionary, rather than broken off from its roots. Drawing on our own tradition links us to the generations who went before, as we welcome the generation that will succeed us.

On a fundamental religious plane, two streams of thought have emerged about the role of a daughter's welcoming ceremony. One, the more traditional view, is that girls are born into the covenant that God made with the Jewish people and do not need the "finishing step" of *brit milah* that boys are obligated to undergo to fully be part of it. The ceremonies of people who have that view are generally titled *simchat bat* or *zeved habat* and focus on celebration through recitation of prayers of thanksgiving, psalms, and blessings, and a traditional form of ritually naming their daughter.

The other view is that girls, like boys, must go through a ritual transition in order to be entered fully into the covenant. (See chapter 3 for a further examination of this issue.) Though Jewish tradition reserves *milah* (circumcision)—the commanded physical manifestation of the covenant—for males, those who share this attitude believe that all Jews must actively enter into the covenant. They generally include the word *brit*, for covenant, in the title of their welcoming ceremony, and integrate into it a ritual of transition, often using a small representation of a *mikvah* (ritual bath), footwashing, or a *tallit*.

Welcoming ceremonies for our daughters are rituals in their

purest sense. Communal rituals capture in symbols the emotions that go with an important life transition.[6] They enhance our lives psychologically, socially, and spiritually, and help us appreciate our connection to our religious culture and heritage. Rituals also mark the liminal experience of moving from one spiritual state of being into another, of crossing thresholds. For some people, holding a welcoming ceremony for their daughter marks the transition from individual baby into covenanted Jew. For others it denotes the transition from her being the new baby in one particular family into her being a member of the larger family of Jews. For all of us who give our daughter the gift of a *simchat bat,* the ritual marks the transition from individuals into parents and child, and the moment of crossing the boundary between one stage of our lives into the next—a stage full of joy, trepidation, and hope as we are charged with the responsibility of raising this new life.

Our contemporary welcoming ceremonies are also a *midrash,* a commentary, on this moment in time. For this is an age in which the power to make of our Jewish futures what we wish is in our hands, and our hands alone. Because of an inadequate or absent Jewish education we may be coming to the task with empty hands, with the only thing clear to us being a sense of our own limitations. But the power is within us: to learn, to integrate, to claim a Jewish future as our own. And what better time to begin, or confirm, that commitment than by ritually marking the birth of our daughters, for whom all things are possible.

CHAPTER TWO

Traditional Ways of Welcoming Jewish Daughters, from Cultures around the World

T here have always been ways in which Jewish families welcomed their daughters—some with more festivity than others, but almost always with less of a party and certainly less of a significant religious ritual than the ways in which they've welcomed their sons. When today we want to build on, or expand on, the kinds of welcoming rituals that have been conducted throughout history or even that are currently done in more traditional religious circles, it's nice to incorporate traditional elements. Rather than break totally free of our Jewish past, we can let it give us roots to grow.

Sephardic Jewish communities and some Ashkenazic ones have had special ways in which to welcome their baby girls. The current tradition among traditional Ashkenazic Jews (those of Central and Eastern European descent) has been spare. On the first day that the Torah is read after his daughter is born (a Monday, Thursday, or Saturday), a new father is called up to recite the blessings over the Torah. The rabbi will say a blessing for the new daughter, incorporating an announcement of her name, and the father will say a prayer petitioning God for his wife's safe recovery from the birth. In some Orthodox communities today, including some Chasidic communities like Lubavitch, women are permitted to say the blessing known as *gomel*, thanking God for having been brought safely through a dangerous passage, in a public fashion by standing up in the women's section of synagogue at the appropriate time during services.

In Orthodox, Ashkenazic-based communities, the blessing *hatov v'hameitiv*, which is said when something good has happened for the benefit of the Jewish community, is recited only for boys. Traditionally, the father of a newborn daughter goes to synagogue on the first day the Torah is read after her birth—often before the mother and her daughter are able to attend—and recites the *shehechiyanu* blessing, which is said when something good has happened to an individual.

In liberal synagogues the practice of recent years has been for the new family to be called up to the Torah together on the first Shabbat that the mother has felt well enough to go. They have a joint *aliyah*. Then prayers naming this child, expressing gratitude for her arrival, and for her and her family's well-being are recited by the rabbi.

In Sephardic (Jews of Spanish, Middle Eastern, or North African heritage) and Italian communities there is a long tradition of welcoming girls with a *zeved habat*, or celebration called "gift of the daughter." The name for the ceremony derives from the Book of Genesis, in which the matriarch Leah states, following the birth of Zevulun, *"Zevadani Elohim oti zeved tov,"* or "God has granted me a gift." The lavish kiddush, or Sabbath meal, that follows it is called the *sebet habat*, using the Arabic term for "Shabbat of the daughter," according to Rabbi Zevulun Lieberman, a rabbi in the tight-knit Syrian Jewish community of Brooklyn, New York.[1] In his congregation, on the first Shabbat after a girl is born, usually with the baby and her mother in attendance, her father is called to the Torah along with his father and father-in-law. The father recites the blessing over the Torah twice—once in his own merit and once in honor of his daughter—and the grandfathers each have an *aliyah* as well. The rabbi offers the family congratulations on their new arrival and offers a blessing for the girl's well-being, a prayer known as a *mishebeyrach*.

Then the words *avi habat,* or "father of the daughter," are called out. That's the congregation's cue to start singing traditional songs for welcoming girls, songs based on poems known as *pizmonim* dating back to fourteenth- and fifteenth-century Spain. Women and men join in together. Afterward there's a kiddush of extreme gastronomic proportions. Tables in the synagogue social hall groan under platters of *helweht*, which means sweets in Arabic, many of them dripping with honey and loaded with almonds and pistachios. The reception usually lasts two or three hours and typically attracts 250 to 300 people.

Interestingly, *brit milah* ceremonies for baby boys in his community aren't generally followed by such lavish parties, Lieberman says, though there is a social opportunity for the family the night before the circumcision, when people come to visit them at home and "protect" the baby from evil spirits—a custom practiced today both by Chasidim, who are usually of Ashkenazic descent, and by those in the Sephardic community.

A complementary practice for welcoming girls—*Las Fadas*—dates back to medieval Spain before the expulsion in 1492, but is rarely practiced today in America. When it is celebrated, it is generally by families of Turkish and Balkan heritage.[2] It is a ceremony that was employed the night before a baby boy's circumcision, as well as for baby girls.[3]

About two weeks after the baby's birth, when her mother felt up to having company, the family would invite family and friends to their home for *Las Fadas.* The rabbi would make a speech and then the guests would each take a turn holding the baby, offering blessings and speaking about their hopes for this new life. It was based on a medieval folk custom among Spaniards in general, not just Jews, though the Jews turned it into a community and family celebration. The ritual was rooted in a popular folk tale about bad fairies from the underworld *(Las Hadas)* feeling upset that they weren't invited to celebrate the new child, and doing harm.[4] Passing the baby from person to person was designed to fool the bad fairies into thinking that good fairies were protecting the baby by blessing him or her.

In Turkey it was customary at *Las Fadas* for the mother and daughter to have an embroidered silk veil placed over their heads. It was lifted after the naming, and the mother would continue to wear it until she gave it to her daughter to wear at her wedding ceremony.[5] In more recent years, some Sephardic Jews in Italy, Holland, the Balkans, Turkey, and parts of Morocco would invite family and friends for a similar ceremony on the thirtieth day of the girl's life.

Orthodox Yemenites officially welcome new babies into the congregation on the first *Simchat Torah* after their birth, on the autumn holiday that celebrates the conclusion of the year-long cycle of reading the entire Torah and beginning it anew. The father or grandfather usually "buys" a *hakafa*, or dance with the Torah, in the baby's honor, with the infant leading the procession around the block or the neighborhood.

Debbie Meline Sapir married into a traditional Yemenite Jewish family and was living in Israel when her children were born. Her Yemenite mother-in-law cracked a raw egg on the doorstep of her house the first time her new grandchildren, first a boy and then a girl, were brought in. A Yemenite aunt of her husband put salt in the baby carriage the first time they took the baby to synagogue, to keep away the evil eye. Her daughter and son were both honored with dances celebrating the Torah on the first *Simchat Torah* after their births, said Meline Sapir, though "I am pretty certain that my father-in-law paid more for my son's honor!"

The Sephardic naming prayer for daughters, from the Spanish and Portuguese traditions, is particularly beautiful. (See chapter 10, Complete Sample Ceremonies.)

In Southern Germany, Bavaria, the Rhineland, and Alsace, the cradle ceremony greeted the birth of both girls and boys in Jewish homes.[6] Children would surround the baby's specially decorated cradle and raise it three times while shouting "*Hollekreisch, Hollekreisch!* What shall be this child's name?" (Scholars are uncertain about the origin and meaning of the word *"Hollekreisch."*) Several passages would be read from the Torah and the baby's name would be announced, and then the ritual concluded with cakes and drinks. By the 1650s urban Jews had ceased the cradle ceremony and it was practiced only in small towns and rural areas, but the custom spread to Alsace and the Rhineland, to southern Holland, and to the Jewish communities in what is now Switzerland, and has continued until modern times for the naming of girls. An elderly German-born aunt of my father exclaimed, after my own daughter's welcoming ceremony, "That is like *Hollekreisch!*" She had attended such rituals as a child but couldn't recall what, exactly, was involved.

In late sixteenth-century Poland a couple went to synagogue on the first Saturday morning after a woman recovered from the birth of a daughter, echoing the biblical duty to offer a Temple sacrifice after having a baby.

The Jews of Greece had no particular customs to welcome their daughters, according to Nikos Stavroulakis, founder and former head of the Jewish Museum of Greece, in Athens.[7] He is now director of the newly restored Etz Hayyim synagogue in Hania, Greece, which rose in 1999 from the ashes of 1944. "In Ioannina it was not very well received [to have a girl] in general, as a daughter usually meant getting together a dowry and also finding a husband—which was not always easy there, and the poor had to resort to offering up daughters to husbands from other communities," he said. "The name Stamata, which occurs occasionally among Greek-speaking Jews, was given when there had been several girls born in the family, and this nickname, which literally means 'Stop It!,' was supposed to break the pattern."

But the Jews of India welcome their daughters by decorating their homes with flower blossoms floating in water.

CHAPTER THREE

Understanding
Covenant and Dedication

*T*he concept of honoring covenant is central to all *simchat bat* ceremonies, though some parents include it as an implicit element, while others feel it important to make explicit. Covenant refers to the eternal contract between God and the Jewish people, who at Sinai promised to keep God's laws (the Torah), as God promised to keep the Jews close and to reward them with the Land of Israel and fertility, among other things.

Inherent in the covenant is the idea that each Jew, by birth or by conversion, belongs to it, and that being part of the covenant is not so much a statement of belief (as baptism is for Evangelicals and other Christians) as it is, simply, a state of being. Whether we follow the laws of the Torah or not, each Jew belongs to the tribe, to the Jewish people, making us connected to one another and interdependent. On its simplest level, perhaps, the experience of being part of a shared covenant is felt in that sense of connectedness to other Jews even when we are meeting them for the first time, whether they are from our own community or a country on the other side of the globe. When referring to covenant in the context of our daughters' welcoming ceremonies, it is to all these things that we refer—the responsibilities the Israelites took upon themselves when they accepted God's offer, as well as the ways in which we feel connected to Judaism and to other Jews.

The covenant between God and the Jewish people belongs to all of us—male and female alike. Yet it has only been discussed explicitly in traditional Judaism as something quite literally between God and man. Woman was so implicit, perhaps, that she became an afterthought in many aspects of traditional Jewish liturgy and religious practice. That's the generous view, of course. Others would ascribe the absence of woman in this discussion to the androcentrism, or even misogyny, of the Talmudic rabbis. For boys, being born to a Jewish mother makes a baby a Jew, but it does not necessarily enter him into the covenant, which must be marked by specific action. And while the Torah tells us to circumcise each son on the eighth day, a daughter's entry has historically been effected by her father, who would go to synagogue to have her blessed and named—generally without the baby or her mother present.

But this is a different time than any that has preceded us in Jewish history. Feminism has prompted us to look at the spaces where women's voices are not heard in our texts and in our traditions. Ours is an egalitarian era, one in which men and women share roles that were historically divided between the genders. We see it in the workplace, in the home, and in our religious lives as well, in every religious movement in Judaism, from the most liberal to the Orthodox. This is an era and a culture in which we value each child—male and female—as equally precious. And so, in *simchat bat* rituals we make clear the covenantal bond, this obligation, and this privilege on the part of our daughters, through the readings, blessings, and rituals that follow.

The covenant between God and the Jewish people is dynamic. We received it, but we also accepted it. The covenant is God's promise to us, yet it requires our active participation in the practices that are integral to Jewish life. We are partners with God in every aspect of daily existence, the great and the commonplace. The active acceptance of our side of this partnership helps to elevate what is mundane to the realm of the holy.

This is also an era when Jewish identity is, almost paradoxically, at once strong and fragile. It is strong for those of us who are deeply engaged with what it means to be a Jew today, who integrate a living Judaism into our lives. But, in the big picture, Jewish identity seems almost fragile when we consider the number of people who are not actively engaged in Jewish practice. The birth of a daughter provides the perfect opportunity for us to consider what we want our daughter's connection to Judaism to be. It also gives us the chance to affirm our commitment to Jewish life no matter how we interpret that bond.

Until fairly recently this was done in most—but not all—Jewish communities for boys alone, in the rite of *brit milah* and the parties and rituals that preceded and followed it. The Torah tells us that God instructed Abraham to circumcise himself as a sign of his dedication to the covenant between him, as the first Jew, and the Creator.

Brit milah is today, as it was then, an act between father and son. The rite stipulates that it is the father's responsibility to circumcise his son, and though today through reciting a Hebrew formula the father generally appoints a *mohel* to act as his agent, the point is made in the ritual's liturgy that the charge still belongs to the father. I can understand why. The mother has had the experience of carrying this new being inside her for forty weeks, felt him cause her all sorts of back pain and muscle cramps, and had the thrilling sensation of feeling him move inside her. Then she has brought him forth in struggle and pain and blood, and knows on the deepest level possible that this child is connected to her, that this tiny, needy new creature is hers to take care of.

The *brit milah* draws the father to the son in a psychologically and emotionally powerful experience, marking the beginning of parenthood. The father is obligated to take his tender new child and cut him on the body part that is most like him, the part that created him to begin with, and he is obligated to draw blood. *Brit milah*, our most primal religious act, may also be our most difficult ritual, as a painful physical procedure that we are compelled to perform as a sign of our commitment to the covenant and to our child's being part of the Jewish people. In this way it binds the child to his father, to his grandfathers before them, and to the generations of Jews that he himself will one day father.

Perhaps the rabbis of old didn't develop some sort of ceremony for girls because daughters were less valued in the culture of the time. They didn't hesitate to express the fact that a daughter was viewed as less desirable than a son. It is written in the Talmud that "There are three things a man would rather not have: grass in his standing grain, vinegar in his wine, and a female among his children. Yet all three were created for the world's need" *(Tanhuma, Hayyei Sarah)*.

But the question of why boys are ritually entered into the covenant, and not girls, was discussed by the rabbis of the Talmud. In *Masechet Nidah* the rabbis say that it is as if women have already had a *brit milah*. In the *Genesis Rabbah* it is written that "Whatever was created during the six days of creation needs further perfecting. . . . Every man needs finishing."

Rabbi Avi Shafran, a spokesman for the ultra-Orthodox organization Agudath Israel of America and the father of six daughters and three sons, articulated the traditionalist view that "*Brit milah* might just be something that men need and women don't, spiritually as well as physically. *Bris* is a connection to the divine, a consecration of a person to the divine, even a sacrifice to come close to the divine. Simplistically, there's a certain closeness to God that comes from taking this step and establishing this bond. Women do tend to be more spiritual, more easily connected to things that are not physical. It could symbolize that men have to make a greater effort toward being spiritual," he said.[1]

That's a view that some readers may find sensible and others offensive—or both at once. Either way, we know that to celebrate our sons' arrival with a ritual, and not our daughters', would be wrong. It would send the message that we value our boys in the deepest religious ways, but not our girls.

As a Jewish act circumcision goes back to ancient times. Yet it is not ours alone. Indeed, it is the most widely practiced surgical operation known, according to an article written by Mary Gendler and published in 1974 in *Response* magazine. She wrote that it has been estimated that the rite is observed, in one form or another, by between two and three hundred million people throughout the world—among the most primitive aboriginals and the most sophisticated technocrats alike. Gendler, in the *Response* article, created quite a stir when she proposed ritual hymenotomy for girls as an equivalent ritual act to circumcision. She proposed creating a new ritual in which a baby girl's hymen would be gently ruptured by a woman using a sterile instrument. No one, according to Gendler and others, actually went through with it.

Instead, in the nearly thirty years since Gendler's article, something else has developed—the modern *simchat bat*, or welcoming ceremony, for girls. Perhaps we are adapting, much as the synagogue service replaced animal sacrifice once Judaism had to adjust to being without the Second Temple in Jerusalem. But, like the raw physical ritual it replaced, synagogue worship can lack the drama and the psychologically transformative power that ritual offering of animal sacrifice surely had in Temple times.

Simchat bat ceremonies can suffer the same problem. They are lovely, usually moving, and always important rituals. But they can lack the fundamental drama present at every *brit milah*. That's not to suggest that we try and find another way to make a physical mark on our daughters. We don't need to. After all, Jewishness itself is not conferred on boys by their circumcision. Though *brit milah* is the commanded sign of the covenant, the Jewishness itself is a gift of birth—which can also be attained, of course, by choosing to join the Jewish people through conversion. And the goal of our ceremonies isn't to leave a physical manifestation of the fact that a new daughter is a member of the Jewish people.

Creators of contemporary ceremonies have, over the past generation, developed several uniquely female ways to mark our daughter's entry into the covenant—from dipping her briefly into a miniature *mikvah*, to washing her feet, to walking her between two halves of the community, to wrapping her in a *tallit*. All of them are described to you later in this book. Only time will tell which rituals the Jewish community more widely adopts and, in the process, codifies into a standard part of the liturgy of welcoming a daughter.

The traditionally minded reader may feel that including an explicitly covenantal ritual in a welcoming ceremony is contrary to *halacha*, or Jewish law, since there is no commandment in Torah for such a change in status. In that view, a girl's inclusion in the covenant is implicit and complete without rite. The person with that perspective would also likely feel that it is forbidden to add to, delete from, or alter in any way the blessings and prayers codified by previous generations of rabbinic authorities. Those who feel this way may simply choose to focus on the celebratory and naming aspects of the ceremony that they can compose from the selections offered in this book to create an expression of welcome for their daughter that is uniquely theirs. They should also refer to the second sample ceremony provided in chapter 10, which was created by an Orthodox family.

For those who do not feel bound by such traditional understandings, however, there is great room for creativity and flexibility.

The goal of our ceremonies is to recognize that our daughter's arrival is worthy of celebration, to greet her with the same kind of marriage of seriousness and joy with which we welcome our sons, and, perhaps most of all, to remind ourselves that this new person provides another possibility for the ultimate redemption of the world. It is also to recognize this child as the female she is, with elements of the ceremony created to reflect her gender. Our goal isn't to copy the *brit milah* ceremony minus the physical aspect. It is to create something rooted in tradition but something contemporary, too, something that is both Jewish and female.

It is also to reinforce, through our acts of dedicating our daughters to being part of the Jewish people, the value of performing "public" rites and passages for that half of the Jewish people that is female. Something important comes with the repeated act of welcoming daughters with a Jewish ritual. Each ceremony we attend—even more so, each in which we participate—adds on another layer to the psychological and spiritual foundation that anchors our own Jewishness.

As you explore the options you have in creating a ceremony to welcome your daughter, keep in mind that this is a good time to consider, in a more literal sense, the Jewish community that you and your daughter will be part of. To enter your child into a covenant is a beginning, a symbol of continuing participation as part of a community; and it's important to think about how your family will connect with that community—whether it takes the form of a synagogue, a *havurah* group, or a Jewish Community Center, for example—through the years ahead.

Jewishness is a state of being, of course, and for most of us it is something we inherit with our birth. But to live as a Jew today requires something more, something deep inside that compels us to engage with it. That something, that anchor, is something we may have to seek out and build for ourselves as adults. If we were lucky, it is something that our parents established for us in the way they lived their lives, in the things we saw them do, and in the ways they taught us to live Jewishly.

If we want our own children to love the fact that they are Jews, it is something we must establish inside of them from their very first moments, along with self-confidence and a sense of security and worth. It is something we can begin establishing for them in the way we welcome their arrival. Circumcision is clearly a dedicatory act. And that is what we are now creating for our daughters—a way to express our dedication to raising them, joyfully, as members of the Jewish people.

PART TWO

Welcoming Everyone

CHAPTER FOUR

Involving Non-Jewish Loved Ones in Your Welcoming Ceremony

*T*oday there is a good chance that someone special in your life who isn't Jewish will be at your daughter's welcoming ceremony. It might be a dear friend, a beloved aunt or uncle, a grandparent, or even a non-Jewish parent of the little girl who has committed to raising her in a Jewish home. They can, potentially, feel uncomfortable at her Jewish welcoming ceremony, uncertain about what to expect or their role in the ritual. Since, of course, it is important that everyone feels welcome, you can alleviate those feelings by explaining to them in advance what will take place, and even take it a step further by making sure that they have an important place in your daughter's rite of passage. There are several ways in which they can be included with roles integral to the ceremony.

According to Rabbi Yoel Kahn, acknowledging the history and community of the family can include the explicit recognition of a non-Jewish parent's heritage. "If the parents have already made a commitment to raise the child as a Jew and maintain a Jewish home, we are not undermining the Jewish family if we acknowledge that the child has two heritages which have shaped her parents' values and lives."[1] Kahn recalled a ceremony held by one family in his former synagogue, San Francisco's Congregation Sha'ar Zahav, at which their child wore the handmade christening gown that had been passed down as a family heirloom for several generations. While that might seem out of place at a Jewish ceremony to some, the public acknowledgment of this mother's non-Jewish heritage helped make it possible for her to fully commit to raising her children as Jews because her own past was not being rendered invisible.

If this new little girl has non-Jewish grandparents, her welcoming ceremony may be one of the very first Jewish rituals in which they're being involved. A grandchild's birth can be a time of great healing, but it's also a time fraught with intense emotion. As painful as the marriage of their presently or formerly non-Jewish child to a Jew may have been for them, even that may not have had the sense of permanence as does a ritual making clear that their grandchild will be raised as a Jew.

While the birth of a child can be a very healing time for family relationships, it can also highlight the stress points in relationships. If there are non-Jewish grandparents who feel ambivalent about this new child being raised as a Jew, those feelings may well come up during the planning of her welcoming ceremony. Be prepared to handle their feelings with compassion and sensitivity. You don't want difficult feelings to get in the way of a joyous celebration of your new daughter's arrival.

At the same time, if you and your spouse have made a commitment to raising her as a Jew, then there isn't room for the birth-related rites of passage, like baptism, of another faith. You must be empathetic but firm, and hold fast to your commitment to starting out your daughter's life with a Jewish celebration of her arrival, which would be undermined and devalued if another faith's ritual were performed as well. This is an opportunity for non-Jewish relatives to see the beauty of the religion to which you have committed your family, and also an opportunity to involve them and, in the process, demonstrate that choosing a Jewish life for your children does not mean severing family ties with them.

Still, there are other ways of including non-Jewish loved ones in your welcoming ceremony. Above all, be sure to take a few minutes before the day of the ceremony to talk through with them what you'll be doing, telling them what to expect, and discussing what role they will feel comfortable taking. While they were surely at your wedding, they may have had no formal role to play in the wedding ceremony itself, and could, on this occasion, feel intimidated and excluded by the ritual of another faith. But there are plenty of points in any *simchat bat* in which they can be involved. The simplest way to involve non-Jewish loved ones, particularly grandparents, is to invite them to offer personal thoughts about what this baby's arrival in the family means to them.

Particularly pertinent to the grandparents' role is speaking about the person for whom the baby has received her English name, if she has different English and Hebrew names and if the person was from their side of the family. They can speak extemporaneously or put pen to paper before the ceremony, which would permit their thoughts to be included in the program distributed to everyone in attendance.

You can also ask your non-Jewish loved ones to read aloud something during the ceremony to welcome the baby. It might be a contemporary poem, a prose passage from a favorite book, or even a section of text from the Bible translated into English, like one of the psalms. Another way to engage them is to ask them to offer your new daughter a favorite poem or reading that they select themselves, as long as it doesn't refer, implicitly or explicitly, to another faith. A wide range of selected readings is included in chapter 9.

The birth of a baby has a marvelously healing effect on relationships, and it is the right time to be as inclusive as possible. At the same time, this is a Jewish child being welcomed with a specifically Jewish ritual, and so there are roles that are appropriate only for Jews to fill, like reciting Jewish prayers and Hebrew blessings.

Another way to incorporate note of the non-Jewish culture that may be part of your daughter's heritage is to include a relevant song or prose selection from that tradition. Or you could include food from the culture of her non-Jewish relatives at the party following the ceremony. It is certainly possible to make kosher or vegetarian Italian, Irish, African, and Asian foods, for example, or to add some symbol of the other culture to your decorating scheme for the day, like using red tablecloths, a color that in China represents good fortune.

A further way of thoughtfully including non-Jewish relatives, particularly grandparents, is to express your appreciation to them as you close your welcoming ritual by saying something like, "We thank Patrick's parents for lending their love and presence to this holy moment in the life of our baby and their grandchild."

CHAPTER FIVE

Especially for Adopted Daughters

When your daughter has come to you through adoption it is wonderful to weave into your welcoming ceremony special ways of acknowledging her route to you. A Jewish welcoming ceremony is also a meaningful way to close this part of the long journey—emotionally, spiritually, often medically, and sometimes physically—that you have taken to get to the place where you have this girl in your arms.

A welcoming ceremony should come after she is converted to Judaism, as most adopted infants must be, since few were born to Jewish birth mothers. A *simchat bat* is no substitute for conversion. It is a wonderful complement.

One unmarried Orthodox woman who adopted her daughter wrote of her experience: "In many ways, the months I spent waiting for my daughter's adoption to come through were analogous to the nine months of pregnancy. While I experienced no physical cramps or labor pains, the emotional stress of waiting was indeed a burden. When I finally held my one-year-old daughter in my arms, I realized that the effort I had put in to adopt her allowed me to immediately feel she was my own. I wanted to welcome my daughter into the community in a special way. As she was born into a non-Jewish family, she first had to undergo a conversion. Following the conversion ceremony we celebrated her 'rebirth' with a *simchat bat* celebrated by family and friends. The juxtaposition of the conversion and *simchat bat* was extremely meaningful, as it truly symbolized her entering into the Jewish community. Following the *tefilla* (prayer) at the *simchat bat*, I announced my daughter's name. . . . At the *seudat mitzvah* (celebratory meal) guests showered my daughter with their own personal blessings. . . . When I feel daunted by the task of raising her alone, I look back at her *simchat bat* and find comfort in the fact that she was not only welcomed into my family, but into the larger family of *klal Yisrael* (the Jewish people)."[1]

Adoption is an ancient practice mentioned often in the Bible. Moses was rescued from death by the Pharaoh's family and raised as a non-Jew, only to become the redeemer of his people from slavery. Mordechai raised his niece, Esther, and rabbinic literature documents the positive views of adoption voiced by ancient rabbinic commentators. As it says in *Exodus Rabbah* 46:5, "He who brings up a child is called 'Father,' not he who merely begot him."

Just about any of the songs, prayers, and blessings that follow in upcoming sections of this book would be appropriate to use in your adopted daughter's welcoming ceremony. But there are elements you can add to the ceremony in order to make special note of her origins. First, in the context surrounding the welcoming ceremony itself, you can add reminders and aspects of your daughter's birth culture, like foods made in the style of her ethnic heritage.

Adina Kalet, who, with her husband Mark Schwartz, adopted a daughter from Colombia, wore a beautiful rust-colored stone and gold necklace during Sara's welcoming ceremony. It was a necklace they had bought together when they went to get their new daughter from the orphanage.

Suspended from it is a gold representation of a Colombian fertility goddess.

If your child is African-born or comes from an African-American birth heritage, that can be honored by holding up a piece of kente or other African-patterned cloth as a *chuppah* over her and her parents during the covenantal ceremony, or by wrapping her in a *tallit* fashioned from such cloth or simply in a length of such fabric.

Ciel Gordon, who, with her husband Corey Gordon, adopted their daughter from China, clothed the baby in a dress Ciel made during a batik class she took at her local Jewish community center while they waited for their daughter's arrival. The Gordons carefully selected a name for their daughter, Lian, which has meaning in both Chinese and Hebrew. In the language of her birth it means graceful willow, and in Hebrew it is a word for joy, according to the name dictionaries they consulted.

You can also add elements reflecting your daughter's origins to the decorations for the day of her welcoming ceremony—like selecting a red tablecloth and flowers for a Chinese baby, since in the culture of her birth red signifies good fortune.

If you have photos developed from when you traveled to pick up your new daughter, particularly if you went overseas, it might be nice to have them displayed or to pass them around during the party.

You can acknowledge your new daughter's origins in your remarks, like these said by Adina Kalet at the *simchat bat* for her daughter, Sara Gittel Kalet-Schwartz. Here is what Kalet said just before she and her husband explained Sara's names:

This little girl came into our family after a bit of a journey ...

After a few years of longing and wanting ...

After many a visit with doctors and nurses and the help of talented scientists and compassionate and spiritual friends ...

After too many trips to the operating room and some very dark moments ...

Finally we were led to a beautiful place in the mountains of war-torn Colombia to our daughter, who we needed very much and who needed us as well.

She is gentle and full of love, she wakes up singing and has a deep and throaty giggle which she mostly reserves for her brother. We thank God the Creator of all things and our community of loving family and friends, especially our parents and siblings, who have helped us get to the other side of that *Mitzrayim*—narrow place—that we have passed through to open up so many new possibilities for our family.

There are also ritual ways in which to acknowledge your daughter's beginnings. Here is a prayer meant to be said upon bringing the baby home for the first time, whether from the hospital or from an airport, but that seems particularly well suited to bringing home an adopted child for the first time.[2]

מַה־טֹּבוּ אֹהָלֶיךָ, יַעֲקֹב, מִשְׁכְּנֹתֶיךָ יִשְׂרָאֵל!

Man-tovu ohalecha Ya'akov, mishk'notecha Yisrael!

How lovely are your tents, O Jacob, your dwelling places, O Israel!

May our home always be a small sanctuary, O God, filled with Your presence. May this home be your sanctuary, child, a place where loving arms will cradle you, hands uphold you, and eyes delight in you. Let this home be filled with love. Here let the hearts of parents and children be ever turned to one another. Here may the bonds of trust and caring keep us together as a family.

בָּרְכֵנוּ, אָבִינוּ, כֻּלָּנוּ כְּאֶחָד בְּאוֹר פָּנֶיךָ.

Barcheinu, Avinu, Kulanu K'echad b'or panecha.

As a loving parent, bless all of us together with the light of Your presence.

This naming prayer is to be recited following the child's conversion in a *mikvah*[3]:

May God who blessed our ancestors Abraham, Isaac, and Jacob, Sarah, Rebecca, Rachel and Leah, bless _____ and _____ and the daughter who has recently come into their lives as a blessing from God.

Let her be known among the people Israel as _____, daughter of _____ and _____.

We pray that she will grow in the love of Judaism and find blessing as a member of the Jewish people. May she offer her willing heart and hands to all those in need, and strive to perfect the world in accordance with Jewish tradition. May her parents be privileged to raise their child to womanhood and may _____ enjoy the blessings of Torah, *chuppah,* and *ma'asim tovim,* good deeds. And let us say: Amen.

Here is a beautiful poem written for the welcoming ceremony of Bonnie Lauren Schwartz[4]:

Not flesh of my flesh
Nor bone of my bone
But miraculously my own
Never forget for a minute
You didn't grow under my heart
But you grew in my heart!

Our Harvest

AUTHOR UNKNOWN

We did not plant you,
True.
But when the season is done,
When the alternate prayers
For the sun and for rain are counted,
When the pain of weeding
And the pride of watching are through,
We will hold you high.

A shining leaf
Above the thousand seeds grown wild
Not by our planting,
But by heaven.
Our harvest.
Our own child.

The following song was written by Rabbi Geela-Rayzel Raphael shortly after she, her husband, and their son adopted their daughter and sister, Hallel Margalit Nesya Angel Robin Raphael.

On My Knees

RABBI GEELA-RAYZEL RAPHAEL

Through the tears and the longing
through the grief and the pain
We have held our hearts open
Waiting for this day.
It was a miracle to find you
Like a puzzle's missing piece
Hope was our companion
Now our joy can be released.

CHORUS:
On my knees I will hold you
On my knees I will care
On my knees I will love you
I'll always be right here.

As our father Yaakov
lay his hands upon their heads
Calling forth the blessing
this is what he said:
Let God who has been my shepherd
all my many days
and the angel who redeemed me
bless you many ways. CHORUS.

Mother Michal was a beauty
wore *t'fillin* every day
yet her heart yearned for children
so deeply did she pray;
When her sister passed on over
leaving five little ones alone
Just as Michal took them in
we welcomed you home. CHORUS.

May you do good deeds among us
study Torah all the while
May we all live to know the moment
when you walk down that aisle;

Be all that you can be
Your curiosity never cease
May you seek the cause of justice
and work for the planet's peace. CHORUS.

Our mothers and fathers
and all who have gathered here
open their arms to embrace you
and wipe away your tears.
As we walk with you on your journey
through life's twists and turns
May we be the kind of family
Where love is what you learn.

FINAL CHORUS:
In our arms we will hold you
In our hearts we will care
With our souls we will love you
We will always be right here.

Prayer for an Adopted Child

RABBI SANDY EISENBERG SASSO

We have been blessed with the precious gift of this child. After so much waiting and wishing, we are filled with wonder and gratitude, as we call you our daughter. Our daughter, our child, you have grown to life apart from us, but now we hold you close to our hearts and cradle you in our arms with our love. We welcome you into the circle of our family and embrace you with the beauty of a rich tradition.

We pledge ourselves to the creation of a Jewish home and to a life of compassion for others, hoping that you will grow to cherish and emulate these ideals.

God of new beginnings, teach us to be mother and father, worthy of this sacred trust of life. May our daughter grow in health. May she be strong in mind and kind in heart, a lover of Torah, a seeker of peace. Bless all of us together within Your shelter of shalom.

CHAPTER SIX

Especially for
Gay and Lesbian Parents

*T*his is a short chapter, essentially because there is not much that is ritually or liturgically different about a daughter's welcoming ceremony in a gay family than there is in a straight one.

There are only two overtly evident differences between a gay family's baby-naming ceremony and that of a straight family. The most obvious difference is in who is present—two parents of the same gender. One of the mothers or fathers of the baby might make a few comments reflecting the nature of their family, or how their daughter arrived to them—whether it was through artificial insemination and pregnancy, adoption, surrogacy, or a loving arrangement with a good friend of the opposite sex—but that is generally as far as any kind of special notice of the parents' sexual orientation goes.

The other change that might be made in the welcoming ceremony for the daughter of a gay or lesbian couple is in the heightened sensitivity to language, which may be adapted from traditional prayers and blessings to better reflect the values of these particular parents. Melanie Schneider and Marla Gayle, lesbian partners in Manhattan who have two daughters, Sasha and Eliana, slightly altered the language of a blessing they said during their girls' welcoming ceremonies. Instead of speaking of bringing them to the marriage canopy, the mothers spoke of "bringing them to loving relationships." Because of their status as a lesbian couple engaged in

Jewish life, and their acute sense that homosexual Jews face deep dis-
crimination in the Jewish community, "We also spoke more about
tikkun olam, and wanting our daughters to work for justice," Schneider said.

Though there are few explicit differences between the welcoming ceremony for a daughter of a heterosexual couple and that of a
homosexual couple, there is much that is implicit. The very picture
of a female or male couple standing at the front of their synagogue
sanctuary or living room before their assembled loved ones as they
welcome their new daughter is in and of itself a strong, affirmative
statement. There is no time in history before the present when such
families—as rarely as they existed—could step up, metaphorically
as well as physically, before their community and claim their place
as a family.

Yet there remain great challenges, some of them presenting
heartache, for gay and lesbian Jewish parents. Disapproving relatives,
particularly a grandparent or aunt or uncle of the new baby, may
refuse to attend, and that absence may be very painful for the partner
whose family member it is. On the other hand, even if a close family member had been deeply disapproving of the couple's choice of
partner beforehand, the arrival of a new baby may present an opening for them to come back into your life. Be sure to let everyone—
even those who may have been estranged—know about your
daughter's arrival. Nothing is as healing to family relationships as the
arrival of a new child. If a relative who had not been in close touch
before your daughter arrived is able to heal that breach around her
arrival, her welcoming ceremony is a wonderful time to honor that
relationship and the role that you hope this relative will play in her
life in the coming years. You can ask that relative to pick a prayer,
blessing, poem, or passage of prose to recite, or to speak about the
person for whom your daughter is being named.

Today there remain many ways in which gay and lesbian families
are isolated—in general and in the Jewish community—struggles
they endure, and special considerations that they will have to make

as they raise their daughter—like how they will prepare her to answer the question from other children of why she has two mommies or daddies, or where they will find a school where she will not feel that she is the only child with a family like hers.

But in terms of how she is welcomed into their family and into the Jewish people, in practice today there are no significant distinctions made between her welcoming ceremony and any other. The fact that there is no special reading or prayer that has been developed, even at the largest gay and lesbian synagogue in the world, New York City's Congregation Beth Simchat Torah, is an astounding comment on how ordinary such occasions have become. Prayers are written, and new rituals like a girl's welcoming ceremony itself are created, when there is an absence. They develop in opposition to that void. What a wonderfully remarkable fact of life it is today that it is unexceptional for a gay or lesbian Jewish couple to welcome their daughter with a Jewish rite of passage. After all, as Melanie Schneider says, "We want the same things for our children as anyone else does for theirs."

PART THREE

Preparing for Your Daughter's Welcoming Ceremony

CHAPTER SEVEN

Planning the Event

An Orientation, What to Call Your Daughter's Ceremony,
When to Have It, Where to Have It, Setting It Up,
How Long It Should Be, How to Handle the
Unexpected, the Program Guide

An Orientation

*T*he welcoming ritual you want to hold for your daughter is
yours. The ceremony does not belong to the rabbi, to the community, or even to tradition. It belongs to you and your daughter, and
should, above all, reflect who you are.

Before creating your daughter's welcoming ceremony, you and
your spouse should find a quiet time to discuss what you want it to
be. Talk over a few key questions and clarify for yourselves what you
hope the day will mean to you and your family, and for your daughter. What you decide will help you shape the day as you begin your
planning. Ask yourselves what you want to accomplish with this day.
Is it to welcome your daughter into the community of your family
and the family of Jews? Or is it also to welcome her, explicitly, into
the covenant between God and the Jewish people? Do you want your
ritual to be focused on the meaning of this girl's arrival in your particular family, or more oriented toward her role as another link in the
chain of Jewish history and peoplehood? Do you want her ceremony to feel traditional or modern? How comfortable are you with
innovative rituals? Do you prefer to stick to prayers and blessings that
have long ties to Jewish tradition? A rabbi can help you think through
what you want to include in the ceremony, and can also suggest

prayers and blessings that will help you create the balance that you want.

Before you sit down to talk, leaf through the prayers, blessings, readings, and sample ceremonies that come later in this book to give you an idea of what you can consider incorporating. What role do you want other family members to play? This may be a time you wish to honor the elders of your family with special roles like readings and blessings. Is there friction in family relationships that should be considered before you assign responsibilities? Also, are your other children old enough to participate in a meaningful way in the welcoming ceremony, or do you think that they're likely to freeze up when they look at the crowd around them?

If you are observant in your approach and Jewishly literate, then you may choose to hold your welcoming ceremony largely in Hebrew and based primarily on traditional prayers, blessings, and text. If you are not so well versed in Hebrew but want to sanctify this moment Jewishly in your and your daughter's lives, you may want to create a welcoming ceremony that is almost entirely in English. If you believe that the generations of sages before us have codified what is authentic and valid in Judaism, you may elect to stick to traditional formulations of often-used prayers and the more traditional translations of their meaning, along with a focus on the role of your daughter within the community of the Jewish people, *klal Yisrael*. If you feel unfettered by history, you may instead choose modern renditions and reconceptions of Jewish prayers and blessings, like those by Marcia Falk, and focus more on contemporary readings and the meaning to you personally and to your family of the arrival of this new little girl. In the end, the welcoming ceremony that you create may fall somewhere in between these poles. As long as it reflects the uniqueness of your family, it will be perfect.

One of the many empowering aspects of the *simchat bat* is that there is no leader designated by tradition. At a *brit milah* the *mohel* generally runs the show, and in many Jewish rituals the rabbi is the leader. While you can choose to have your rabbi lead your welcoming ritual, it is not necessary. This is one of those moments that presents an opportunity for parents to lead the rituals of their Jewish life directly, rather than having them performed by proxy. And, Jewishly educated or not, sophisticated or simple in your tastes and religious background, you can make this ceremony reflect exactly who you are as a family. Many times, it makes for a stronger and more personal welcoming ceremony when the parents, or a close and Jewishly knowledgeable friend, lead it—though you may want to invite the rabbi and ask him or her to read significant prayers, and you should feel free to ask the rabbi to be the primary leader of your ceremony if that would make you feel comfortable. You may also wish to assign leadership of different sections of your welcoming ceremony to a couple of different people.

What to Call Your Daughter's Welcoming Ceremony

There are dozens of different names for the ceremonies of welcome and covenant that in this book, for ease of reference, I call by one Hebrew name—*simchat bat*. To some, *simchat bat*, which means rejoicing in a daughter, is a kind of catchall term for the types of ceremonies included in this book.

For others, the specific term used to name the ceremony is very meaningful. Some feel that the term *simchat bat* doesn't sufficiently indicate the fact that they are having a ceremony to publicly celebrate that their daughter is entering the covenant between God and the Jewish people. And so they use the Hebrew word for covenant, *brit*, as part of what they call the ceremony. They prefer terms like *brit bat*, covenant of the daughter; *hachnasat habrit*, entry into the covenant; *simchat brit bat*, celebration for the daughter's covenant; or simply *brit*.

There are also people who are concerned that this ceremony not imitate, or even derive from, the *brit milah* that welcomes Jewish boys into the covenant. Such folks, who are traditionally oriented and often Orthodox, embrace the idea of welcoming a daughter into their families and community with a celebration, but do not want it to be confused with the Torah-based *mitzvah*, or obligation, of *brit milah*, and so they specifically choose not to use the word *brit* to describe it. They are more likely to employ the term *simchat bat, zeved habat*, a day of blessing, or, simply, a naming ceremony.

Names used for welcoming ceremonies include

- *Brit Bat*—Covenant of the Daughter
- *Brit Banot*—Covenant of Daughters
- *Brit Banot Israel*—Covenant of the Daughters of Israel
- *Brit Kedushah*—Covenant of Holiness
- *Brit Chayim*—The Covenant of Life
- *Brit Bat Tzion*—Covenant of the Daughter of Zion
- *Chag Hachnasat Labrit*—Celebration for Entering the Covenant
- *Seder Hachnasat Bat Labrit*—A Ceremony of Welcome for a Daughter to the Covenant
- *Brit Mikvah*—Covenant of Waters
- *Brit Nerot*—Covenant of Candles
- *Brit Melach*—Covenant of Salt
- *Shalom Bat*—Peace of a Daughter
- A Day of Blessing

When to Have Your Daughter's Ceremony

The time for a boy's *brit milah* is fixed at eight days, unless he is ill, in which case it is postponed until he is well. Even when the eighth day falls on Shabbat or Yom Kippur, a *brit milah* is performed. Being so soon after the birth, it's not always easy for the parents to pull the accompanying party together, but at least in the case of a son, there is a fixed ceremony that they can expand on to some degree if they wish, but also simply rely on and not have to worry too much about what surrounds it.

When it's time to welcome a girl, we don't have that fixed ritual in place. We do have basic ceremonies in the rabbis' manuals published by each of the religious movements, but when putting together the ceremony for a daughter, parents often want to do something more. With a daughter, there's time to plan it. A welcoming ceremony for your new daughter can, but does not have to, replace the traditional custom of going to synagogue the first week of her life and being called to the Torah to bless her and name her.

There are several intervals of time after the baby is born that have strong ties to Jewish tradition and custom, as well as dramatic impact to consider in planning the date of the welcoming ceremony. Some of the meaningful points after your daughter's birth are:

- **The eighth day,** to parallel the *brit milah*. Parents of a twin son and daughter might elect to hold their daughter's welcoming ceremony at the same time as their son's *brit milah*. You will want to hold rituals and readings welcoming your daughter into the covenant before your son's ritual circumcision gets under way, since you will want to be able to devote your attention to comforting him after the *bris*.

- **The fifteenth day,** which marks the end of the traditional two-week period of *niddah*, or being in a ritually impure state after the birth of a daughter, according to traditional Jewish texts and some rabbinic interpreters. The period of ritual impurity after the birth of a boy lasts for one week, according to these sources. Rather than seeing it as a label of physical impurity, the state of being in *niddah* can be considered a time of separation from the possibility of giving life, and a sanctification of women's natural monthly cycle. Some contemporary Orthodox interpreters say that the length of *niddah* is twice as long after the birth of a daughter because, with her arrival, a mother sees the next link in the chain of creation more clearly than she does after the birth of a son. The awareness of the power of creation is so deep and profound that more time is given for the mother to integrate it.

- **The twenty-first day,** which marks the end of that two-week period plus the seven "clean" days a woman must count before immersing herself in a *mikvah.*
- **The thirtieth day,** to parallel the day on which a boy, if he was the firstborn child into a family that is not of the priestly class, would have his *pidyon ha-ben,* his ritual redemption from service in Jerusalem's Temple. Thirty days is also the period after which a Jewish child was historically counted in a census.
- **The thirty-first day,** because it is the first day of full viability, according to the rabbis of the Talmud. (*Talmud Shabbat* 135b)
- **The eightieth day,** which is the end of the period of *niddah* after the birth of a daughter observed by some traditional Jewish communities.
- **On *Rosh Chodesh,*** the beginning of a new Jewish month and traditionally a minor holiday specifically for women during which they are supposed to suspend work. There are other uniquely female echoes in choosing *Rosh Chodesh* as the time for your daughter's welcoming ceremony. The Jewish calendar is based on the phases of the moon, as are the tides of the sea, and the moon is also said to govern women's monthly cycles. So by extension, we see that the start of a new moon's cycle relates to female fertility, which in Jewish tradition is connected to the waters of the *mikvah,* the ritual bath in which observant Jewish women immerse themselves at the conclusion of each month's cycle.

I have heard of people holding naming ceremonies for their daughter as late as her first birthday. Waiting that long would seem to diminish the dramatic element, but if she hasn't yet been given a Hebrew name, then her first birthday party is a lovely occasion on which to announce and explain it.

Then again, you can choose to hold your welcoming ceremony on the first convenient Sunday, as we did. Holding it on a Sunday, rather than Shabbat, means that even the most religiously observant members among your family and friends will be able to travel to join you.

If that's not an issue for you, then holding your daughter's welcoming ceremony on Shabbat is also nice, particularly if you hold it in synagogue. That way her ceremony can incorporate an element of the most traditional observance, which is having the family called up for the honor of an *aliyah* to bless the Torah before it is read. That's the time in synagogue during which the rabbi will say a blessing asking that God protect and care for the baby and her family, and at which one of her parents can take a few moments to explain the meaning of her name. If you do it this way, you can celebrate at a festive kiddush following services, perhaps with the addition of a special cake you've ordered in your daughter's honor, and your whole community can celebrate with you.

I've also seen ceremonies held at the conclusion of Shabbat. This way it can begin with the lovely *havdalah* ceremony that marks the end of the holy Sabbath and re-entry into the week of work. See the section on Rituals to Welcome Your Daughter into the Covenant (beginning on page 105) for examples of this type of ceremony. This way, too, it's a Saturday night party and people who are Sabbath observant can come but just arrive late. Of course, most infants like to be headed toward a quiet bedtime when *havdalah* time comes, but it is another option.

Rabbis Sandy Eisenberg Sasso and Dennis Sasso suggest Shabbat as the ideal time because it is the day set aside to recall the covenant God made with the Jewish people, just as we are celebrating this girl's entrance into that same contract. The Sassos note that "The Sabbath, even though a covenantal sign of the whole community, embraces special feminine imagery and may be symbolically adopted to mark the female covenantal commitment."[1] The traditional imagery used in the poems and songs to welcome the day of rest heralds the Sabbath as a queen, and kabbalistic sources speak of the divine energy of the day as manifestations of God as *Shechina*, a feminine term.

There are just two periods of the Jewish year when it would be appropriate to consider *not* holding your daughter's welcoming ceremony—two intervals of collective mourning for the Jewish people during which we recall tragedies that befell our people earlier in our history. One is the seven-week period between Passover and *Shavuot*, a time of modified mourning to commemorate the deaths of 24,000 of Rabbi Akiva's students from the plague during the second century. The Talmud says that they died because they failed to treat each other with respect, and that the plague ceased on *Lag B'Omer*. Modern scholars believe that the period commemorates their deaths in battle, since Rabbi Akiva supported a Jewish warrior's rebellion against Rome and it was likely that his students were among his soldiers. During this time traditional Jews hold no weddings. The more observant also abide by other limitations on their behavior during this period, refraining from swimming, cutting their hair, and even, among some, listening to live music. *Lag B'Omer* is the one day of joy and jubilation during this period, thirty-three days after the start of Passover, when the rabbis allow marriages to take place, and your daughter's welcoming ceremony might take place then, too.

The other period during which it would be sensitive to refrain from scheduling your daughter's welcoming ceremony is during the three weeks that fall in the summertime between the seventeenth of the month of *Tammuz*, on which day it is traditional to fast to commemorate the Romans' invasion of Jerusalem in 70 C.E., and the ninth of *Av*, in Hebrew known as *Tisha B'Av*, on which day they burned down the Temple. No marriages are scheduled by traditional Jews during the entire three weeks, but the restrictions intensify for the last nine days, between the first and ninth of *Av*, during which Jews are not supposed to cut their hair or shave, drink wine, or eat meat except on Shabbat, when drinking wine and eating meat are considered obligatory by some as a way of celebrating the day.

Since we have flexibility when it comes to scheduling our daughters' welcoming ceremonies, it would be appropriate to consider celebrating it either before or after these periods. Honoring our history in this way is a fitting way to start your Jewish daughter's life. If you would have ordinarily held her *simchat bat* during one of those periods but instead did it sooner or later to be sensitive to these times, you can make note of that in your remarks and printed program and in that way elevate the level of Jewish awareness of everyone joining you.

Where to Have Your Daughter's Welcoming Ceremony

You can have your *simchat bat* just about anywhere. I've attended them in synagogues and catering halls, but most often, and most intimately, in the parents' living room.

I attended one *simchat bat*, held in a large hall attached to a synagogue, that was more lavish than most bar mitzvahs and even some weddings. That affair (organized and paid for by the thrilled new maternal grandmother) was sumptuously catered, with an enormous buffet island groaning under dozens of different fancy foods reflecting the little girl's Syrian heritage, dozens of large tables festooned with beautiful table linens, and lavish centerpieces fashioned of flowers and balloons in pink and white.

That was a lovely celebration, but most welcoming ceremonies are far simpler affairs. Having the welcoming ceremony in your home is the most intimate and personal choice. The only potential downsides are that your house or apartment may not be able to accommodate all the people you'd like to have celebrate with you, and it has to be cleaned, which may be too difficult to accomplish when you've just had a baby. If you're feeling overwhelmed, call in family and friends to lend a hand. They'll likely be eager to pitch in, which will enable them to feel a greater sense of connection to the celebration as well. If the weather is temperate you can hold a daytime ceremony outside.

Just make sure that the mother or other person holding the baby during the ritual has a place to sit if she wants it.

I heard about one welcoming ceremony held in the sunny climate of northern California that went on all day. Friends came throughout the afternoon and evening to celebrate with the new parents, who spent time outside and in, with food distributed around the house and yard, all of it enhanced by lots of group singing.

Setting Up Your Daughter's Welcoming Ceremony

If you're having your daughter's *simchat bat* in synagogue, you'll probably want to use the sanctuary for the ceremony, with the participants standing in front of, near, or on the *bimah* (pulpit) and the ark holding the Torah scrolls. For greater intimacy, you can also hold it in a chapel or library, if they're available in your synagogue. The party will in all likelihood be held in the synagogue social hall.

If you're having your daughter's welcoming ceremony at home, it's best to hold it in your living room. Push aside the sofa, tables and chairs if they're usually positioned in the middle of the room to make a clear staging area with the parents, baby, and officiant standing in the visual front. Be sure there are seats for them, if any of those leading the ceremony want to sit down. Have one or more chairs ready as seats of honor, in recollection of Elijah and Miriam the prophets. They can be as simple as folding chairs draped in beautiful fabric or something more intricate, like a regally upholstered, throne-like seat of honor or a wooden chair hand-painted with special motifs in honor of this occasion.

Make sure there's plenty of seating for guests. Friends are happy to lend folding chairs if you don't have enough. Some folks will stand during the ceremony if they can't find a chair, but most will sit wherever there's room—on furniture, cross legged on the floor, even on the staircase.

It is traditional to have a festive meal to honor the *mitzvah* you've celebrated, much as one does after a *brit milah*. The party food can be set up already, buffet style, in your kitchen and dining room, but left covered so that people know that the eating comes afterward. If you're holding your welcoming ceremony in the morning and in your home, it's nice to set up a coffee urn and let people know that they can help themselves to drinks before things begin. The meal can consist of foods as simple as egg, tuna, and whitefish salads set out with bagels and beverages, and served on disposable plates. It's easiest on the parents if platters of salads and spreads are ordered and picked up in advance, or delivered. Preparing food for your party is also a great way for family and friends to pitch in. If the weather is good, invite people to enjoy their festive meal outside, where you have set up extra seating.

Be sure to have a challah and a kiddush cup with wine, and give someone special the honor of making the blessings over the wine and bread, the kiddush and *ha-motzi*, before everyone digs in. You may choose to end the party with everyone singing *birkat ha-mazon*, the blessing of food that is recited by observant Jews after eating.

How Long Your Daughter's Welcoming Ceremony Should Be

Having attended many *simchat bat* and other welcoming ceremonies for new baby girls, I can say one thing for sure: Keep yours to thirty minutes, or forty minutes at the outside. It's tempting to put everything we can into our welcoming ceremony. After all, we want to capture every important element of this new little girl's arrival in what we compose. But it's not a good idea to make it too long. Longer than about a half hour and the attention span of people attending—even the people who love you the most—flags. Children start making more noise. And the ceremony loses dramatic steam and emotional force.

Ask those who will be speaking extemporaneously to keep their remarks to just a minute or two. Be selective about what you choose from the liturgical elements that follow later in this book. Keep in mind that old résumé-writing dictum: if you want to keep people's attention, you don't have to show them everything you've ever done, just the things that will help you get the job. So, to make your daughter's welcoming ceremony memorable, keep it concise. That way people can feel deeply involved in the emotional peaks you want it to contain.

How to Handle the Unexpected

Something unforeseen is bound to happen. The baby may start wailing in the middle of her ceremony, for instance. To prevent hunger from triggering her complaints, be sure your daughter has been fed before the guests arrive. It's common before a *brit milah* for the mother to stay in seclusion in a bedroom, feeding and soothing the baby until the ceremony actually begins, and to leave the task of welcoming guests to the baby's father and other immediate relatives. The same can be done before your daughter's welcoming ceremony, especially if she tends to be sensitive to noise and crowds, as many newborns are. Not to worry—there will be plenty of time after the ceremony ends and the party begins for the baby to be shown off to each and every cooing guest. At that point she may well have fallen asleep, as many infants do when they feel overwhelmed, but all of your nearest and dearest will still get to see—and tell you—how beautiful she is. If she begins to cry hard during the ceremony, though, it's best not to stop the ritual in the middle, keeping in mind your guests' attention spans and the flow of the *simchat bat*. Instead, one of the parents or a grandparent can walk the baby into the next room, hoping to calm her down and perhaps nurse her or give her a bottle for a few minutes. You can always quickly amend the order of your welcoming ceremony and hold off the part in which she is a central player until the end, allowing others to go ahead with their readings and blessings.

Of course, your new daughter might not be the one making the noise that day. Her older siblings will understand the important nature of the day through the preparation they've seen you undertake. It's also a good idea to talk through with them what will happen that day and what they should expect. Another way to keep them interested and cued in to the ceremony is to give them each roles to play throughout. Still, your daughter's older siblings or other children, like cousins and friends, may not be able to sit still long enough for you to finish your daughter's *simchat bat*, and they may start zooming around the house and distracting adults. It's best, before the day of your welcoming ceremony, to ask another adult— someone not directly involved in the ritual, like a friend or neighbor—to be the semiofficial child-minder. He or she can be in charge of corralling wayward children into another room or the back yard if they get too noisy. You can also consider hiring a teenager to babysit the children in a different part of the house while the ceremony is under way, though I feel that the presence of children is integral to a *simchat bat,* and of course, it's also an opportunity for them to witness and learn about one of Judaism's most beautiful life-cycle rituals.

The Program Guide for
Your Daughter's Welcoming Ceremony

It's nice—and a part of most welcoming ceremonies today—to distribute a kind of personal program guide to those attending. Make sure you pass out copies of your ceremony to everyone before it begins so they can read along and take home a keepsake of your beautiful celebration. Even the youngest guests are up to handing out booklets and will feel proud if they are put in charge of the task. Don't fret too much about making it a fancy booklet. A simple way to do it is to write out the English language text on your computer, leaving space for the Hebrew. Then you can either cut and paste the Hebrew prayers and text from the source you're using, or handwrite them in. You can type it up on a Hebrew word processor if you're really well set up, but if not, don't worry. Half the beauty of these booklets is their homemade look.

A useful element to include is a brief list at the top of the program guide of the participants—the baby's parents, grandparents, siblings, and anyone else who will have a speaking role. This way everyone joining you, even if they haven't met your extended family before, will be able to appreciate the loved ones' roles in your daughter's life when they are speaking. Another nice touch is to include photocopied pictures of the people for whom your daughter is being named.

Another meaningful element is, as a last page, a family tree composed either by hand or on a computer, showing your daughter's roots. Include the place and date of each birth if you know them, along with the names of her forebears. You can highlight or underline the relatives after whom she is being named.

Another special addition to the program can be letters written to your new daughter from her great-grandparents, grandparents, aunts or uncles, and other loved ones, particularly if they are not able to join you at her welcoming ceremony. You may choose to read some out loud if time and your guests' attention spans permit, or you may instead simply attach them at the end of the program to make them a meaningful part of your daughter's keepsake.

On the cover of the program, include in large letters the name of your daughter, the title you're giving to her welcoming ceremony, the date, and the city. Include Hebrew, handwritten or via computer, if you can. If you know what birth announcement you're going to use, or have already sent it out, it's nice to repeat its decorative motif on the welcoming ceremony program guide cover.

Giving the cover a different color paper or different stock altogether is another simple way to dress it up. To decorate the cover,
most word processing programs have some basic border clip art,
and you can select something pretty to put around the opening page.
You can create something more ambitious if you're feeling adven-
turous, have access to fancier Jewish clip art, or have a friend who is
artistically gifted.

Take the program guide to the nearest copy shop and run off
enough photocopies for all the guests you're expecting. Be sure to
have the copy shop collate and staple the program. If you're feeling
pressed for time, ask a friend to take care of this errand.

The program for her welcoming ceremony will be a beautiful
keepsake to add to your daughter's baby book. It's also something
to send, along with a photo of your new arrival, to friends and family members who can't make it to her welcoming ceremony.

Examples of Welcoming Ceremony
Program Covers

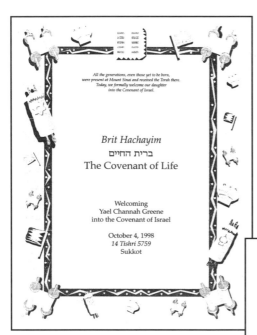

All the generations, even those yet to be born,
were present at Mount Sinai and received the Torah there.
Today, we formally welcome our daughter
into the Covenant of Israel.

Brit Hachayim
ברית החיים
The Covenant of Life

Welcoming
Yael Channah Greene
into the Covenant of Israel

October 4, 1998
14 Tishri 5759
Sukkot

A Ceremony for the Naming of

TALIA LILYAN SCHNUR

Daughter of Michael Schnur & Jody Comins

August 15, 1999/3 Elul 5759

Talia's Hebrew name is Talia Leah. She was named for Jody's paternal
grandmother, Lilyan, whose Hebrew name was Leah. In the bible, Talia is
the angel that escorts the sun from dusk 'til dawn. The English translation for Talia is dew.

Sally G.

Simchat Bat
of

Jessica Sloan
Shayna Yehudit

שֵׁינָה יְהוּדִית
בַּת יָפָה וְאֶלְעָזְרָה

January 22, 2000
Tu B'Shvat 5760

We dedicate today's celebration to Jessica's great-grandmothers.
To Helen and Mary, who are with us always, and to Ida and Bea,
who could not join us today. Jessica is truly blessed to have come
from such love, beauty and strength.

Simchat Brit Bat Ceremony

ADIEL KEREN SCHMIDT
born July 15, 1994
נולדה ז' אב תשנ"ד

She is
more precious
than rubies and all
that you desire cannot be
compared to her
(Proverbs 3:15)

Simchat Bat

April 23, 2000   18 Nisan, 5760

Naming Ceremony for

Sara Gittel Kalet-Schwartz
שרה גיטל

מאתה היתה זאת היא נפלאת בעינינו

She is a gift from God and a wonder in our eyes

Born: September 8, 1999 in Medellin, Colombia
Adopted: January 18, 2000

Named in honor of her great-grandmothers:
Sally, Sonia, and Gertrude

CHAPTER EIGHT

Sanctifying
Your Surroundings

*T*he day you welcome your daughter with a Jewish rite of passage is, of course, a deeply special day. You are by now probably sufficiently recovered from her birth to be able to focus on the spiritual and emotional experience of being surrounded by those who love you most—perhaps some who have come from great distances to be with you—and of having your precious new daughter in your arms. The things around you will doubtless reflect the joy and importance of this day. Fresh flowers may adorn your fireplace mantle or dining room table. Lovely decorations, perhaps made by your daughter's older siblings or cousins, may festoon the walls and doorways. Balloons may greet your guests as they walk in.

Just as important, though, are the Jewish ways in which you will set apart this day. A fundamental component of your daughter's welcoming ceremony will be the ritual objects you choose to incorporate as integral parts of the rite. You may also choose to plant a flowering tree—see the section below—as a way of echoing an ancient Jewish practice, and as a beautiful manifestation of the ways in which you hope to see your daughter grow and blossom.

Significant objects are central to ritual in all religious practice, in all faiths. Every religion uses special tools in its rituals, from the incense censers swung during Eastern Orthodox Christian church services to the rugs on which Muslims kneel for prayer. These specially designated objects are an extension of our intention, physically embodying and representing the actions we take to mark the boundaries between secular and holy. At the end of Shabbat, observant Jews bid farewell to the day of rest by performing the *havdalah* ritual. While we could pop open a plastic container of cinnamon from the spice cabinet, hold the braided *havdalah* candle in our hands, and drink the wine or grape juice from a plastic cup, the ritual is enhanced by using a specially crafted box to hold the fragrant spices, a specially designated holder for the candle, and a kiddush cup used just for ritual purposes, all of them artistically adorned. Using these special items, even preparing for the ritual with them in advance, helps us to transition from the mundane into a holy space and time.

Special religious objects serve the same purpose in a *simchat bat*. When welcoming our daughters, we may use objects that are newly created or purchased and designated as hers to use as she grows up, or things that we have used in other significant life-cycle ceremonies and that recall those sanctified moments of our lives as we use them again to honor the arrival of this new girl. They can be set up, or placed ready for use, near where the parents and baby will be standing during the *simchat bat*.

Some suggested Jewish ritual objects to incorporate into your daughter's welcoming ceremony:

◆ A *chuppah* to stand beneath or wrap around your daughter. Using the wedding canopy under which this baby girl's parents stood is a beautiful way of linking these deeply tied life-cycle events. Gail Eisenstein said during her daughter's welcoming ceremony, "The canopy, the *chuppah*, which we stand beneath today was lovingly made for us five years ago by Brad's mother and her dear friends. The *chuppah* represents a Jewish home, and five years ago we stood beneath it for the first time as we exchanged our wedding vows. Today we return to our *chuppah*

as we hold our precious daughter in our arms to welcome her
into our home."

◆ A *tallit,* prayer shawl, in which to wrap your daughter. The *tallit*
may be used as a central element in the covenantal part of her
ceremony, or you may choose to simply wrap your daughter up
in one beforehand as a visual reminder of being enfolded within
Jewish heritage. The *tallit* may be a family heirloom, inherited
from a beloved grandparent or parent, it may belong to one of
the parents of the new girl, or it may be purchased as a gift for this
new daughter of Israel, to be put away after her welcoming ceremony until it is given to her at the time of her bat mitzvah.

◆ A **kiddush** cup from which to drink during your daughter's welcoming ceremony. If you have the kiddush cup from which you
drank at your wedding, when this girl was no more than a twin-
kle in your eye, it is beautiful to use that. If not, use the kiddush
cup you use at Shabbat and holiday meals, or one specially purchased for this momentous day that will become hers when she
gets old enough to sit at the table and sing along as the wine is
blessed on special occasions.

◆ **Ritual candlesticks** that you may want to incorporate into your
daughter's welcoming ceremony. Several ways to do this are
described later in the book.

◆ An **Elijah's chair.** The prophet Elijah is "invited" to every *brit
milah* and can be invited to every welcoming ceremony for girls
as well. The *kiseh shel Eliyahu,* or Elijah's chair, has been a customary presence at *brit milah* ceremonies since the Middle Ages.
At Passover we invite Elijah into our homes and talk about his
return as a harbinger of the messianic era. He is also known as
the guardian of young children.

◆ Adding a **Miriam's chair,** or replacing Elijah's chair with one
for Miriam, is a new interpretation of this tradition. In the Bible,
Miriam is the sister of Moses and Aaron, the quick-thinking girl

who saved the life of her younger brother by arranging for their mother to be his wet nurse once the Pharaoh's daughter plucked Moses from his reed cradle in the Nile. Popular interest in Miriam has recently blossomed as feminist Jews look to unearth female role models from Jewish history and to expand understanding of these foremothers' roles. Just as a place for Elijah is a symbol of our hope for future redemption, a symbol of Miriam—a cup or a chair—represents our faith that the Creator will nurture and take care of us in the present. And what greater reminder is there of God's work in the world than the birth of a new baby?

Elijah's and Miriam's chairs can be as intricate and unique as specially decorated or hand-painted chairs crafted by a loving friend or purchased from an artisan. They can be as simple as folding chairs over which a nice length of cloth has been draped. You can also take the two most ornate chairs in your house, or from the *bimah* in your synagogue, and place them in the front of the living room or sanctuary. One position of honor at the welcoming ceremony is the *kvatterin*, usually the baby's grandmother, who will carry her in and place her in the arms of the person who will hold her for the rest of the ceremony. An honored guest—a grandparent, aunt, or someone else—can hold your daughter in her arms as she sits in the chair as the *sandeket*, a parallel to the *sandek*, the honored guest who holds a baby boy during his *brit milah*. Two other honored guests can also stand on either side of the chair as *shomrot*, or watch-women, like spiritual protectors. Alternatively, you may choose to have three chairs at the front, much as a Jewish bride at a traditional wedding is accompanied on one side by her mother and on the other side by her mother-in-law. The mother might sit in the middle chair holding her new daughter, with the baby's grandmothers on either side, one each seated in *kiseh Eliyahu*—Elijah's chair—and *kiseh Miriam*—Miriam's chair.

During Passover seders it is becoming increasingly common to place a Miriam's cup alongside the cup we have on our table for Elijah. One of the miracles connected with Miriam in Torah was that a well of fresh spring water followed her as she journeyed with the other Israelites for forty years in the desert, providing her fellow travelers with drinkable water. So into the Miriam's cup on our seder tables we place water from rain or a spring to reflect our faith in God's presence in our lives. The same can be done at our daughter's welcoming ceremony, with the cup placed on a fireplace mantel in our living room or on a handy side table, and pointed out and explained during the course of the *simchat bat*. Water collected outside or simply spring water poured from a bottle can be used.

♦ A **ceremonial pillow** on which your daughter will be held during the ceremony, much as a boy is placed on a pillow during his *brit milah*. The pillow may have a lace-decorated case or a plain one that may already be, or can be when time permits, embroidered with the baby's name, her birth date, and the date of her welcoming ceremony, along with any decorative elements that room and the embroiderer's talents permit.

♦ **A wimple.** It used to be customary, going back as far as sixteenth-century Germany, to wrap a boy at his *brit milah* in a cloth that would later be used to make a wimple, the belt that holds a Torah scroll closed between readings. The cloth would be carefully cleaned and then cut into four pieces, sewn together, and embroidered, sometimes simply, sometimes ornately, with a blessing and themes that related to the boy's name, like the image of a lion if his name meant lion in Hebrew. It would typically be presented to the synagogue on or around the boy's first birthday, when the Torah portion corresponding to the week of his birth was read. This is a custom that can easily be adapted to the birth of a girl, particularly if there is a talented seamstress or artistic needleworker who is close to the family. *The Second Jewish Catalog* (The

Jewish Publication Society of America, 1976), compiled and edited by Sharon Strassfeld and Michael Strassfeld, offers detailed instructions on making a wimple.

◆ **Planting a tree.** The Talmud tells us of a custom in ancient Israel in which parents would plant a tree—a pine or cypress tree for a daughter and a cedar tree for a son. The tree would not be cut until the child was ready to marry, when its branches would serve to hold a *chuppah.*[1] It is a lovely custom to adapt for today by planting a beautiful tree near your home in honor of the birth of your daughter. Do not feel bound to plant a cypress; instead, select a tree that is appealing and well suited to your climate.

If you plant a tree as part of your daughter's welcoming ceremony, be sure to have the preparations set up before your daughter's *simchat bat* begins: a hole dug in the ground for the tree's roots, with the tree placed right next to it; the burlap removed from around the tree's roots, if that is required; several shovels available; and a few hand towels available so that afterward people can wipe their hands clean of dirt.

The tree's planting can be a central feature of your daughter's welcoming ceremony. Or, if the season isn't right or the climate intemperate, a tree can be planted later in her first year, as part of a smaller family ritual. If you like the concept but can't actually plant a tree, consider donating to the Jewish National Fund so that one or more trees are planted in Israel in your new daughter's honor. If that's the route you choose you might want to note it as part of the welcoming ceremony program.

Treasure Cohen wrote about the tree-planting her family did in honor of her son and then his three younger sisters around the time each was born.[2] "All of our children cared for and about their trees," wrote Cohen. "In their own small way, they became *shomrei adamah*, guardians of the earth. It became a yearly custom in our house to have a *Tu B'Shvat* birthday party when the children would invite their friends over to decorate their trees with bows and streamers. When we planted the trees we were aware that, as with any living organism, there was a chance that the tree would not live out the length of its days. And although we intended the parallel between trees and children to reflect celebrating life with life, not every tree we planted survived."

In its fifteenth year, her daughter Shira's peach tree died. After mourning its loss, they knew that they had to replant and so they did, to celebrate Shira's sixteenth birthday. This time, Shira planned the ceremony, inviting her closest friends and siblings to read poems of their choice about trees. She included the poem that her grandmother, now deceased, had written for her at her welcoming ceremony and first tree planting. She also let her father read what he had written for her so long before. "Our eyes brimming with tears, we saw how much of our prayer had already come to fruition," wrote Cohen. "We softly said our own *shehechiyanu*, and I added my own blessing for our almost-grown daughter."

If you want to make planting a tree part of your daughter's welcoming ceremony, the best place for it in the ceremony is probably near the beginning, after an introduction but before the covenantal and naming rituals, or at the end, after them, as a closing rite. Wherever in the welcoming ceremony you do it, the following two blessings are an appropriate way to begin. The first is the blessing traditionally recited upon witnessing a natural wonder, such as a sunrise, a vast desert, or a shooting star, and the second is the blessing recited at reaching a new or momentous occasion.

בָּרוּךְ אַתָּה יהוה, אֱלֹהֵינוּ מֶלֶךְ הָעוֹלָם, עוֹשֶׂה מַעֲשֶׂה בְּרֵאשִׁית.

Baruch Atah Adonai, Eloheinu Melech ha'olam, oseh ma'aseh vereshit.

Blessed are You, Adonai our God, Ruler of the universe, who continually does the work of creation.

בָּרוּךְ אַתָּה יהוה, אֱלֹהֵינוּ מֶלֶךְ הָעוֹלָם, שֶׁהֶחֱיָנוּ וְקִיְּמָנוּ וְהִגִּיעָנוּ לַזְּמַן הַזֶּה.

Baruch Atah Adonai, Eloheinu Melech ha'olam, shehechiyanu v'kiyemanu v'higgiy'anu la'zman hazeh.

Blessed are You, Adonai our God, Ruler of the universe, who has kept us in life, preserved us, and enabled us to reach this season.

The parents might then say something like what Rebecca Schwartz and her husband did when they welcomed their daughter, Alyssa Rose:

We plant a tree in our daughter's honor to celebrate life with life, and mark the importance of this occasion in our lives. In ancient Israel a tree was planted when a child was born. As children grew up they cared for their own trees, and when a couple married they stood under a canopy made of branches cut from the trees that had been planted in their honor years before. This, the Jewish tradition, formed a strong bond between birth and marriage, and helped to develop a love for trees and a sensitivity to the wonders of nature.

We say that the Torah is a Tree of Life, and the mystics saw the universe in the image of a tree. Our family is also a tree, whose roots reach back into history, and whose branches are carried forward with Alyssa's birth.

Dear God, we stand in awe before You as we witness these miracles of Your creation—this young tree and our new baby. Both are unique and original, unlike anything that ever was before or will be. Each began with a single seed, miraculously growing in beauty and complexity with each passing day. Help us to nourish and nurture this tree and our child so that they may both mature and prosper, fulfilling to the greatest possible extent the potential for which God placed them on earth.

Then plant the tree. The parents should put in the first two shovel-fuls of dirt, then the grandparents, and so on, until each guest has had the chance to contribute to the planting. Those who feel moved to do so might offer their blessings and prayers for the new baby immediately before adding their dirt to the tree.

PART FOUR

Creating
Your Daughter's
Welcoming Ceremony

CHAPTER NINE

How to Use This Guide, and the Order of a Contemporary Welcoming Ceremony

*T*here is no fixed liturgy for a Jewish girl's welcoming ceremony. And that is both our challenge and our opportunity. Though it is certainly not the role of this book to decide how, precisely, the ritual should be composed, common threads quickly emerged from among the more than 250 Jewish daughter welcoming ceremonies I explored from all over the world. Though each was an original creation, most shared the same internal structure—it's one that makes common sense—and many shared a few of the same poems and prayers that are deeply resonant with the occasion and have been widely circulating from one family to the next in recent years. Some have been published in articles and chapters of books devoted to parenting.

The purpose of this book is to serve as a guide to inform what you do. Remember—a *simchat bat* does not have a fixed liturgy. Use what you find in the sections that follow as a template, a base on which to build a ceremony that reflects who you are. Feel free to innovate, if that is your bent, or, if you are traditionally oriented, to pattern your daughter's welcoming ceremony closely on traditional formulations.

When it comes to the *simchat bat*, liturgical history is still being written. While it seems clear that the *simchat bat* ceremony is here to stay, its final form has not yet been canonized. All those who use these rituals are partners in their creation.[1]

What you will find in this chapter are twelve sections that contain many examples of the blessings, prayers, poems, songs, and readings that you will want to choose from for your daughter's welcoming ceremony. You may elect to use them exactly as they are presented here or to adapt the language and wording to your own sensibilities. That's fine. Please also consider integrating readings and selections of prayers and Torah text that you find elsewhere, or writing your own poems and prose as inspired by the birth of your daughter. The possibilities are wide open, and you should include in your daughter's ceremony what will be most meaningful to you and your loved ones.

Another aspect to consider adapting to your own approach to Judaism is the way God is addressed in the prayers and blessings presented in these pages. Most of the language included is traditional, that is, "Blessed are You, Lord our God, King of the universe." If that doesn't feel quite right to you, consider terminology like "Blessed are You, Fountain of life," or "Blessed are You, Creator of the universe," or even "Blessed are You, *Shechinah,* Mother of all that lives." If you choose to go this route, consider adapting the Hebrew form of the blessings, as well as their English translations.

If you decide to go with the format presented in this book for your daughter's welcoming ceremony, you will want to incorporate just a couple of elements from each of the following twelve sections and assemble them in the order that they are presented, i.e. readings from the first section, followed by readings from the second section, followed by readings from the third, etc. The first thing you should do is peruse this chapter and note which readings strike you as personally meaningful. Revisit them later for a more serious consideration, but initially just let your eye and heart wander over the possibilities. Each of the sections offers you many different prayers, blessings, and readings from which to choose. Ultimately you may elect to use several readings or blessings from one section and none from another. The form and content of your daughter's ceremony is wholly up to you.

The sequence in which the following sections are presented is that most often found in welcoming ceremonies for Jewish daughters. It's a form that lends both a sensible liturgical structure and a nice rhythm and flow to welcoming ceremonies. It also leaves a great deal of room for choosing the elements that best suit your family and most accurately and beautifully reflect your feelings on this meaningful occasion. Of course, if you feel strongly that certain sections should be reversed or omitted, then go right ahead and tailor the ceremony's organization to what fits your own sensibilities.

As an alternative, chapter 10 offers five samples of complete ceremonies, each composed from a different orientation toward Judaism. You may choose to use one of these ceremonies almost exactly as it is presented, or you may use them as guides, templates, to inform the ceremony you want to create from the ground up.

In this chapter I outline the structure used most often. Feel free to adapt and build on it as you wish—but remember: Everyone, including the baby and the guests, are happiest if the welcoming ceremony is kept to about thirty minutes long.

The Order of a Contemporary Welcoming Ceremony

1. A song. Singing together is a powerful way to create a sense of holy space, to distinguish the time of the ceremony from what preceded it, and to bring everyone together in fellowship. What you sing can be a Jewish traditional wordless tune, called a *niggun*, that people can chime in with, or a contemporary song, either Jewish or secular. If you want to open your welcoming

ceremony with a song, it is helpful to your guests if you distribute the lyrics. See page 74.

2. An introduction: A brief introduction from you or your daughter's other parent, welcoming everyone to your *simcha* (joyous occasion). In it, you should note the presence of honored people in attendance—rabbis, special friends and relatives, and anyone else who has had a notable role in your daughter's first weeks of life, like a midwife, labor support coach, or doula—by thanking them for being part of your day. This is also the place to briefly outline what your guests should expect from the welcoming ceremony, and to assure them that it won't last more than thirty minutes or so.

3. Hebrew welcome: The Hebrew statement "*Brucha haba-ah b'shem Adonai,*" Welcome in the name of the Creator, is recited by the person leading the ceremony or by all the assembled guests, and it welcomes the baby into the room as she is carried in by a grandmother or other adult who has the honor of being the *kvatterin*, godmother, or *kvatter*, godfather.

4. Blessings of thanksgiving by the baby's parents: Mother recites *gomel*, the prayer of thanksgiving for having come through a potentially life-threatening passage, if she hasn't done so already. This prayer is traditionally said after returning from a long voyage and after childbirth, and traditionally it is recited after blessing the Torah on the first Shabbat that the mother is up to returning to synagogue. If that hasn't happened, for one reason or another, then *gomel* can be said now. While it is conventionally said after childbirth, it can also be said today if the new baby has been adopted—particularly if her parents had to travel overseas to get her, or if the mother underwent medical intervention. See page 78.

5. Blessings and readings by the parents related to parenting and the baby. See page 83.

6. A ritual welcoming your daughter into the covenant. There are

two approaches to the notion of recognizing a Jewish girl's relationship to the covenant between God and the Jewish people. The first, the more traditionalist orientation, regards Jewish girls as being born into the covenant, and says that there is no need to welcome her into something of which she is already a part. Those with this perspective may simply choose a few of the blessings and readings starting on page 105 to acknowledge their daughter's participation in this covenant. The second approach is for those who feel that girls, just like boys, should be explicitly and overtly brought into the covenant. For those of this perspective there are several different ritual possibilities presented beginning on page 111.

Ritual, of course, is a powerful tool and brings us into an experience emotionally, psychologically, physically, and spiritually. We have that for boys in the *brit milah*. For girls we can choose from rituals incorporating the powerful symbols of fire (candles), water (*mikvah*), and being wrapped in a *tallit*. As always, the ritual and symbol that most resonate for you are the ones you should choose.

7. Explanation of your daughter's names and recitation of formal naming blessings to give her Jewish names. See page 149.

8. Presenting Jewishly meaningful gifts to the baby, like a ceremonial charity collection box, a kiddush cup, or candlesticks, from her parents, older siblings, or beloved relatives. See page 162.

9. Recitation of psalms, or lines of Jewish text assembled into an acrostic using the baby's name. See page 165.

10. Prayers, poems, and other readings of thanks, to be read or recited by honored guests. See page 172.

11. Blessings of gratitude to be said by the baby's parents. The *shehechiyanu* is recited when something good for the individual or immediate family has happened. Some might say this at the moment of their daughter's birth. The prayer *hatov v'hameitiv* is said when something good for the larger community has

transpired. Other closing prayers, like the *Sh'ma* and additional blessings, may be said as well. See page 183.

12. Another song or two to close the ceremony. See page 192.
13. Blessings over the wine and bread, and dipping the bread in honey to set apart this sweet day. See page 198.
14. The festive meal.

Most of all, remember that this is a day of joy. Take pleasure in it!

Welcoming with Songs and Blessings

Each of these songs sounds beautiful when sung unaccompanied but becomes even more spirited when led by someone playing a piano, tambourine, or guitar. Be sure to print the words to the songs you want to sing in your program guide so that everyone can join in. Select songs with simple melodies, as the best Jewish music by composers like Debbie Friedman and Rabbi Shlomo Carlebach have, so that all of your guests can participate even if they haven't heard the song before. Choose songs that you already know well. If you aren't familiar with much Jewish music, treat yourself to a few recordings from a local Judaica shop or from an online store like www.jewishmusic.com, and listen to them as you plan your daughter's ceremony. A longer list of website resources begins on page 229.

These songs are sung in Hebrew. The transliterations are provided to make it easier for everyone to participate. The translations are included so that everyone understands what they're singing.

There are also many beautiful wordless *niggunim* composed by Rabbi Shlomo Carlebach and others, which can be started by the ceremony leaders and easily picked up by those who are assembled to celebrate with you.

B'ruchot Habaot

DEBBIE FRIEDMAN

This song is sung with both the Hebrew and English words.

בְּרוּכוֹת הַבָּאוֹת תַּחַת כַּנְפֵי הַשְּׁכִינָה
בְּרוּכִים הַבָּאִים תַּחַת כַּנְפֵי הַשְּׁכִינָה.

Bruchot haba-ot, tachat kanfei haShe'china
Bruchim haba-im, tachat kanfei haShe'china

May you be blessed beneath the wings of She'china
Be blessed with love, be blessed with peace

Havah Nashira

*This simple song is beautiful when it is repeated several times
with growing strength, and perhaps at its loveliest when sung in
a round.*

הָבָה נָשִׁירָה שִׁיר הַלְלוּיָהּ.

Havah nashira, shir halleluya

Let us sing a song of praise, praise to the Creator.

Pitchu Li—Open the Gates of Heaven

*The tune by Rabbi Shlomo Carlebach set to these words from
Psalms is particularly lovely.*

פִּתְחוּ לִי שַׁעֲרֵי צֶדֶק אָבֹא בָם אוֹדֶה יָהּ.

Pitchu li sha'arey tzedek,
Avo vam odeh Yah

Open for me the gates of righteousness,
that I may enter and praise the Lord.

Gates of Righteousness

MARCIA FALK (AFTER PSALM 118:19–20), FROM *THE BOOK OF BLESSINGS*

פִּתְחוּ־לִי שַׁעֲרֵי־צֶדֶק,
אָבֹא בָם וְאוֹדֶה.

זֶה הַשַּׁעַר לַתּוֹרָה,
נָבוֹא בוֹ וּנְבָרֵךְ.

Pitchu-li sha'arey-tzedek,
avo vam v'odeh.

Zeh hasha'ar latorah,
navo vo unvareykh.

May the gates of righteousness open
that I may enter, grateful.

Here is the way before us—
let us enter, let us bless.

Halleluyah

The tune to these words, written by Debbie Friedman, is very
festive and uplifting.

כֹּל הַנְּשָׁמָה תְּהַלֵּל יָהּ. כֹּל הַנְּשָׁמָה תְּהַלֵּל יָהּ. הַלְלוּ־יָהּ:

Kol ha'n'shama t'hallel Yah Hallelu, Hallelu-Yah
Hallelu, Hallelu, Hallelu,
Hallelu, Hallelu, Hallelu-yah

(repeat several times)

We hope you will enjoy this book and that you will find it useful and use it to enrich your life.

Book title: _____

Your comments: _____

How you learned of this book: _____

Reasons why you bought this book: (check all that apply) ☐ SUBJECT ☐ AUTHOR ☐ ATTRACTIVE COVER

☐ ATTRACTIVE INSIDE ☐ RECOMMENDATION OF FRIEND ☐ RECOMMENDATION OF REVIEWER ☐ GIFT

If purchased: Bookseller _____ City _____ State _____

Please send me a JEWISH LIGHTS Publishing catalog. I am particularly interested in: (check all that apply)

1. ☐ Spirituality	5. ☐ Women's Issues	9. ☐ Caregiving/Grieving
2. ☐ Mysticism	6. ☐ Environmental Issues	10. ☐ Ideas for Adult Reading Groups
3. ☐ Philosophy/Theology	7. ☐ Healing/Recovery	11. ☐ Religious Education Resources
4. ☐ History/Politics	8. ☐ Children's Books	12. ☐ Audio Tapes of Author Lectures

Name (PRINT) _____ Phone _____

Street _____ E-mail _____

City _____ State _____ Zip _____

Please send a JEWISH LIGHTS Publishing catalog to my friend:

Name (PRINT) _____ Phone _____

Street _____

City _____ State _____ Zip _____

JEWISH LIGHTS PUBLISHING

Sunset Farm Offices, Rte. 4 • P.O. Box 237 • Woodstock, VT 05091 • Tel: (802) 457-4000 Fax: (802) 457-4004

Available at better booksellers. Visit us online at www.jewishlights.com

Henay Ma Tov

A traditional song that sounds very nice when everyone begins singing together, but can also be sung in a round.

הִנֵּה מַה טּוֹב וּמַה נָּעִים שֶׁבֶת אַחִים גַּם יָחַד.

He-nay ma-tov oo-ma-nay-im
Shev-et ach-im gam ya-chad
He-nay ma-tov oo-ma-nay-im
Shev-et ach-im gam ya-chad

Look around! How beautiful and pleasant it is
for brothers and sisters to all be together!

Oseh Shalom

TRADITIONAL

עֹשֶׂה שָׁלוֹם בִּמְרוֹמָיו הוּא יַעֲשֶׂה שָׁלוֹם עָלֵינוּ וְעַל כָּל יִשְׂרָאֵל וְאִמְרוּ
אָמֵן.

O-seh sha-lom sha-lom bim-ro-mav
Hu ya-a-se ya-a-se sha-lom
O-seh sha-lom sha-lom bim-ro-mav
Hu ya-a-se ya-a-se sha-lom
Hu ya-a-se ya-a-se sha-lom a-ley-nu
v'al kol Yis-ra-el v'im-ru a-men

God who creates peace in heaven, may You create peace for us
and for all Israel; and let us say: Amen.

Welcoming the Baby

The words *"Brucha haba-ah!"* are said—loudly and enthusiastically—as the baby is carried in by her grandmother or other adult honored with the role of acting as her *kvatterin*, or spiritual godmother.

בְּרוּכָה הַבָּאָה.

The welcome can be recited by the parents, rabbi, or other ritual leader of the *simchat bat*, or the assembled guests can be instructed to all say it together as the baby girl is carried in.

Blessing of Welcome

בְּרוּכָה הַבָּאָה בְּשֵׁם יהוה,

בְּרוּכָה הַבָּאָה בְּשֵׁם יהוה,

בְּרוּכָה אַתְּ בָּעִיר וּבְרוּכָה אַתְּ בַּשָּׂדֶה,

בְּרוּכָה אַתְּ בְּבֹאֵךְ וּבְרוּכָה אַתְּ בְּצֵאתֵךְ.

Brucha haba-ah b'shem Adonai

Blessed is she who comes in God's name

(alternatively)

Brucha haba-ah b'shem Adonai
Brucha at ba-ir u-vrucha at ba-sodeh
Brucha at be-vo-eych u-vracha at be-tseyteych

May she who enters be blessed in the name of God
Blessed are you in the city and blessed are you in the countryside,
Blessed are you when you come and blessed are you when you go

Prayers of Thanksgiving

Expressions of gratitude to the Creator are a central element in Jewish prayer. The parents' expressions of gratitude at their daughter's Jewish welcoming ceremony both anchor and elevate their feelings, and they acknowledge the absolute miracle visible in the creation of this new life.

Gomel

This prayer of thanksgiving is traditionally said after being called to bless the Torah during synagogue services, and after escaping injury, recovering from a serious illness, or returning home after a lengthy journey or other potentially life-threatening experience. After birth, it is most appropriately said by the mother, who has been through the dramatic physical experience of bringing forth life. After an adoption, particularly if they undertook an overseas journey to find their child, it might be said jointly by both parents.

If the mother has not made it to synagogue since the birth of her daughter, then *gomel* can be recited at the beginning of the baby's *simchat bat*. If, however, the mother has already said this prayer, it should not be repeated during the welcoming ceremony. Instead, another prayer of thanksgiving may be recited.

בָּרוּךְ אַתָּה יהוה, אֱלֹהֵינוּ מֶלֶךְ הָעוֹלָם, הַגּוֹמֵל לְחַיָּבִים טוֹבוֹת, שֶׁגְּמָלַנִי כָּל טוֹב.

Baruch Atah Adonai, Eloheinu Melech ha-olam, ha-gomel le-chayaveem tovot, she-gmalanee kol tov.

Praised are You, God, who rules the universe, granting favor even to the imperfect. Thank You, God, for granting mercy to me.

Alternative translation:

Blessed are You, Lord our God, Source of the universe, who in bestowing goodness upon humanity has dealt graciously with me.

Alternative translation:

Blessed are You, O Lord our God, Ruler of the universe, who bestows kindness on those who are committed, and has granted to me all kindness.

Those present respond:

מִי שֶׁגְּמָלֵךְ כָּל טוֹב הוּא יִגְמָלֵךְ כָּל טוֹב, סֶלָה.

Mi she-gemalech kol tov hoo yigmalech kol tov, selah.

May God, who has been gracious to you in your time of need, continue to favor you with all that is good.

Alternative translation:

May the One who has granted you all kindness always grant kindness to you, selah.

Prayer Said by a Mother Upon the Birth of a Girl

SHELLEY LIST AND YAEL PENKOWER

This very beautiful prayer can also be said upon the birth of a son, with a few simple changes in the gender language in English and Hebrew.

יהוה, בּוֹרֵא עוֹלָם, עוֹשֶׂה מַעֲשֶׂה בְרֵאשִׁית, שֶׁתִּפְתַּנִי עִמְּךָ בִּבְרִיאַת
חַיִּים שֶׁיָּלַדְתִּי בְּיוֹם גָּדוֹל וְנוֹרָא זֶה. לִבִּי מָלֵא שִׂמְחָה, תֵּן לְאִישִׁי
וּלְמִשְׁפַּחְתִּי לַעֲמֹד לְיָדִי וּלְהַלֵּל אֶת רַחֲמֶיךָ, כִּי לֹא עֲזַבְתַּנִי בְּצַעֲקִי
וְלֹא שְׁכַחְתַּנִי בִּכְאֵבֵי צִירַי, אֲבָל מִכְּאֵבִים אֵלּוּ חוֹלַלְתָּ שִׂמְחָה גְדוֹלָה:
וְאֶת בִּכְיִי כִּסִּיתָ בְּבִכְיָהּ שֶׁל הָרַכָּה הַנּוֹלֶדֶת הַבָּאָה לָעוֹלָם.
יְהִי רָצוֹן מִלְּפָנֶיךָ יהוה אֱלֹהַי וֵאלֹהֵי הָאִמָּהוֹת שֶׁתִּשְׁמֹר עַל חַיֵּי
הַיַּלְדָּה הַזֹּאת מִכָּל מַחֲלָה וּתְאוּנָה וּתְקַיֵּם אֶת נַפְשָׁהּ. וְאוֹתִי, אִמָּהּ,
רְפָא וְחַזֵּק לְמַעֲנָהּ. כִּי הַיַּלְדָּה הַזֹּאת בּוֹטַחַת בְּךָ לְהַחֲיוֹתָהּ וּלְשָׁמְרָהּ
כְּשֵׁם שֶׁאֲנִי בּוֹטַחַת בְּךָ לְהַחֲיוֹתֵנִי וּלְשָׁמְרֵנִי.
עֲזֹר לִי לַעֲמֹד עַל הַמִּשְׁמָר לְמַעַן בִּתִּי. מַלְּאֵנִי בְּסַבְלָנוּת, בְּצֶדֶק
וּבְיֹשֶׁר כְּלַפֶּיהָ. תֵּן לִי אֶת הַיְכֹלֶת לָתֵת לָהּ בְּגַדְלָהּ מָזוֹן, אַהֲבָה וְדִבְרֵי
תּוֹרָתֶךָ. וְיִהְיוּ פְּחָדֶיהָ כְּעָשָׁן בְּלִי אֵשׁ, כֶּעָנָן בְּלִי גֶשֶׁם וּפַזְּרֵם בְּרוּחַ
אַהֲבָתֶךָ.

Adonai, borey olam, oseh ma'aseh vereishit, shi-taftani imcha b'vriat chayyim she'yaladtee b'yom gadol v'norah zeh. Leebee maleh simcha, tayn l'ishee oo-l'mishpachtee la-amod l'yadee oo-l'hallel et rachamechah, kee lo azavtanee, b'tza'akee v'lo shechachtanee bikhayvay tzirai, aval mikayaveem eyloo cholalta simcha gedolah. V'et bichyly keyseeyta b'vichyah shel haraka hanoledet ha-ba'ah la-olam.

Yehi ratzon milfanecha, Adonai, Elohai v'Elohay ha-imahot she-tishmor al chayay ha-yaldah hazot mi-kol machalah oote'unah ootekayem et nafshah. V'ohtee, imah, rafeh v'chazek lemaanah, key hayalda hazot botachat becha le-ha-chayotah oo-leshomrah k'shem she-anee botachat b'cha le-hachayoteynee oo-leshomreyni.

Azor li la-amod al hamishmar lema'an beetee. Malehni b'savlanoot, b'tzedek oo-viyoosher k'lapeha. Ten li et hayicholet latet lah b'godlah mazon, ahavah, v'divray Toratecha. V'yihiyoo pechaday ke'ashhan bli esh, k'anan bli geshem oo-fazrem be-ruach ahavatecha.

Master of creation: You have made me Your partner in creating a new life on this great and wonderful day. My heart is filled with joy! Let my husband and family stand with me and praise Your mercy. For You did not desert me in my wailing, nor forget me in my labor, but You fashioned from this pain a great joy and covered my cries with the birth-cries of a tender infant.

May it be Your will, my God and God of the foremothers, to guard the life of this girl from sickness and accident, and to sustain her. Heal me, her mother, and give me strength for her sake: Since this girl trusts in me to nurture and protect her, I must trust in You to nurture and protect me.

Help me be diligent for the sake of my child. Fill me with patience and fairness, and let me act correctly toward her. Let me nourish her with food, with love, and with the words of Your Torah. And may all my fears be like smoke without fire, like clouds with no rain, which scatter before Your loving spirit.

I acknowledge that:

(If the pregnancy was conceived or maintained through medical intervention)

הֵבֵאתָ לָעוֹלָם אֶת יֶדַע הָרְפוּאָה שֶׁעָזַר לִי לְהַפְרוֹת אֶת רַחְמִי בְּיַלְדָּה זוֹ וּלְהַחֲזִיקָהּ בְּרַחְמִי עַד הַשָּׁעָה הַטּוֹבָה לַלֵּדָה.

Hevetah la-olam et yeda harefuah she-azar li l'hafrot et rachmi b'yaldah zo oolehachazikah b'rachmi ad hasha'ah hatovah la-laydah.

You brought into the world the medical knowledge to help me conceive this child, and to keep her in my womb until a fortuitous time for birth.

(If labor and delivery proceeded without need for medical inter-vention)

צִירַי הִסְתַּיְּמוּ בְּשִׂמְחָה רַבָּה. יְהִי רָצוֹן מִלְפָנֶיךָ שֶׁתִּשְׁמֹר עַל
בְּרִיאוּתֵנוּ.

Tzirai histaymoo b'simcha rabah, yihi ratzon m'lifanecha shetishmor al briootaynoo.

My cries ended in great joy. May You watch over our health.

(If medical intervention was necessary to save the life of the child)

הֶחֱזַרְתָּ אֶת חַיֵּי הַיַּלְדָּה הַזֹּאת אֵלַי בְּמֶשֶׁךְ הַלֵּדָה, בְּעֶזְרַת מַדָּע
הָרְפוּאָה. יְהִי רָצוֹן שֶׁתַּמְשִׁיךְ לִשְׁמֹר עַל חַיֵּינוּ.

Hechezartah et chayay hayaldah hazot aylai b'meshech halaydah, b'ezrat madah ha-refooah. Yihi ratzon shetamshich leeshmor al chayaynu.

You returned the child's life to me during labor by means of medical science. May You watch over our lives.

(If medical intervention was necessary to save the life of the mother)

הֶחֱזַרְתָּ אֶת חַיַּי לִי בְּעֶזְרַת מַדָּע הָרְפוּאָה. יְהִי רָצוֹן שֶׁתִּתֵּן לִי רְפוּאָה
שְׁלֵמָה, רְפוּאַת הַנֶּפֶשׁ וּרְפוּאַת הַגּוּף.

Hechazarta et chayay li b'ezrat madah ha-refooah. Yihi ratzon she-titen li refooah shlaymah, refooat hanefesh oo-refooat hagoof.

You returned my life to me by means of medical science. May You grant me a complete recovery of body and spirit.

יְהִי רָצוֹן שֶׁתִּפְתַּח אֶת רַחֲמֵיהֶן שֶׁל כָּל עֲקָרוֹת יִשְׂרָאֵל הַמְצַפּוֹת
לְבִרְכוֹתֶיךָ. בָּרוּךְ אַתָּה יהוה, שׁוֹמֵעַ תְּפִלָּה.

Yihi ratzon she-tiftach et rachmayhen shel kol akrot yisrael ha-mitzapot levirchotecha. Baruch Atah Adonai, shomeah tefillah.

May it be Your will to open the wombs of all the barren women of Israel who await Your blessing. Blessed are You, God who hears supplication.

Readings and Blessings for the Parents

These readings are all ideally suited to being read by the baby's parents, though the rabbi or other leader of the *simchat bat* may also be asked to read some of the following passages. Be sure to include in your program guide the words to whatever will be read out loud.

L'Dor vaDor

לְדוֹר וָדוֹר נַגִּיד גָּדְלֶךָ וּלְנֵצַח נְצָחִים קְדֻשָּׁתְךָ נַקְדִּישׁ וְשִׁבְחֲךָ אֱלֹהֵינוּ מִפִּינוּ לֹא יָמוּשׁ לְעוֹלָם וָעֶד.

L'dor vador nagid godlecha ule'netzach netzachim kedushatcha nakdish. V'shivchacha Elohaynu mi-pinu lo yamush l'olam va'ed.

From generation to generation we will tell of your greatness for all eternities. We will sanctify Your holiness. Your praise, O God, will not depart from our lips forever.

Blessing of Creation
MARCIA FALK, FROM *THE BOOK OF BLESSINGS*

נְבָרֵךְ אֶת עֵין הַחַיִּים,
מְקוֹר הַחֹשֶׁךְ וְהָאוֹר,
מְקוֹר הַשְּׁלֵמוּת וְהַתֹּהוּ,
מְקוֹר הַטּוֹב וְהָרַע,
מְקוֹר כָּל יְצִירָה.

N'vareykh et eyn hachayim,
m'kor hahoshekh v'ha'or,
m'kor hash'leymut v'hatohu,
m'kor hatov v'hara,
m'kor kol y'tzirah.

Let us bless the source of life,
source of darkness and light,

heart of harmony and chaos,
creativity and creation.

The Gift of Gratitude
MARCIA FALK, FROM *THE BOOK OF BLESSINGS*

בְּפֶה מָלֵא שִׁירָה
וּבְלָשׁוֹן שׁוֹפַעַת רִנָּה —

נְבָרֵךְ אֶת עֵין הַחַיִּים
וְכֹה נִתְבָּרֵךְ.

B'feh maley shirah
uvlashon shofa'at rinah—

N'vareykh et eyn hahayim
v'khoh nitbareykh.

Our mouths filled with song,
our tongues overflowing with joy—

We bless the source of life
and so we are blessed.

A Peek into the Messianic Age
DEBRA NUSSBAUM COHEN

To parent a baby daughter is to get a taste of the messianic age. She
is born perfect and complete, already in possession of all of the
eggs that contain her genetic half of the grandchildren she will one
day, we hope, give us. She is a look into our future where all is beauty, all is hope, all is promise.

She is pure pleasure. She is also our chance for emotional and
psychological *tikkun*, for repair and completion. She offers us the
opportunity to do well what we have never had the chance to do
before: to give without limit. To look at her is to know peace.

This Is the Day of Our Joy

יוֹם חַג הוּא יוֹם זֶה לָנוּ, כַּכָּתוּב: יִשְׂמַח־אָבִיךָ וְאִמֶּךָ וְתָגֵל יוֹלַדְתֶּךָ.

Yom chag hoo yom zeh lanoo, kakatoov: Yismach avicha v'eemecha v'tagel yoladtecha.

This is the day of our joy. As it is said: "Your father and mother will be jubilant; the woman who bore you will exult." (Proverbs 23:25)

From Every Human Being Rises a Light . . .

TRADITIONAL

From every human being there rises a light that reaches straight to heaven, and when two souls that are designed to be together find each other, their streams of light flow together and a single, brighter light goes forth from their united being.

Excerpted from
Shir HaShirim—The Song of Songs

מִי־זֹאת הַנִּשְׁקָפָה כְּמוֹ־שָׁחַר, יָפָה כַלְּבָנָה, בָּרָה כַּחַמָּה?

Mi-zot ha-nishkafah k'mo-shachar, yafah ka-levana, barah ka-chamah?

Who is she who shines through like the dawn,
Beautiful as the moon, radiant as the sun?

Excerpted from
Shir HaShirim—The Song of Songs

אַחַת הִיא יוֹנָתִי תַמָּתִי. אַחַת הִיא לְאִמָּהּ. בָּרָה הִיא לְיוֹלַדְתָּהּ. רָאוּהָ
בָנוֹת וַיְאַשְּׁרוּהָ. מְלָכוֹת וּפִילַגְשִׁים וַיְהַלְלוּהָ.

Achat hi yonati tamati. Achat hi l'imah. Barah hi l'yoladtah. Ra-ooah banot vay'ash-ruha. Melachot u-filagshim vayehalleluha.

Only one is my dove, my perfect one; she is unique to her mother, the delight of her who bore her, maidens see and praise her.

With Every Child Born

ADAPTED FROM ABRAHAM JOSHUA HESCHEL

With every child born a new experience enters the world. She encounters not only flowers and stars, mountains and walls, but a sublime expectation, a waiting for, when something is asked of you. Meaning is found in responding to the demand, meaning is found in sensing the demand.

May you remember that every deed counts, that every word has power, and that we can all do our share to redeem the world in spite of all the absurdities and all the frustrations and disappointments. Above all, remember to build a life as if it were a work of art.

You are unique, exceedingly precious, not to be exchanged for anything else.

No one will live your life for you, _____, no one will think your thoughts for you or dream your dreams.

Every Person

ADAPTED FROM MARTIN BUBER

Every person born into this world represents something new, something that never existed before, something original and unique. It is the duty of every person in Israel to know that there has never been someone like her before. For if there had been someone like her before, there would be no need for her to be in the world. Every single person is a new thing in the world and is called upon to fulfill her particularity to the world.

Planting for the Future

FROM THE *BABYLONIAN TALMUD TAANIT* 23A

The Talmud tells the story of an old man who was seen planting a carob tree. As the king rode by he called out "Old man, how many years will it be before that tree bears fruit?"

The old man replied "Perhaps seventy years."

The king asked "Do you really expect to be alive to eat the fruit of that tree?"

"No," answered the old man, "but just as I found the world fruitful when I was born because my ancestors planted for me, so I plant trees for my children and my children's children."

Holiness and Love

ADAPTED FROM THE *MIDRASH*

How are we able to perform countless acts of love as we are commanded? How can we begin to obey such a difficult charge? It is not such a mystery, really. Every lullaby, every diaper change, every smile, every sleepless night, every wordless prayer of thanks for this perfect baby—in these and the unending ways we care for and teach and protect our children, we perform countless acts of love. And the world is made holier. And so are we.

A Prayer for Parents

AUTHOR UNKNOWN

אֱלֹהֵינוּ וֵאלֹהֵי אֲבוֹתֵינוּ גַּדֵּל אֶת הַיַּלְדָּה הַזֹּאת לְחַיִּים שֶׁל שִׂמְחָה,
חַיִּים שֶׁל טוֹבָה, חַיִּים שֶׁל חָכְמָה. יְהִי רָצוֹן שֶׁתִּהְיֶה יַלְדָּתֵנוּ עוֹשָׂה
שָׁלוֹם וְרוֹדֶפֶת שָׁלוֹם בֵּין אִישׁ לְרֵעֵהוּ, וְיִזְרַח אוֹרָה מִסָּבִיב לְהָאִיר
דֶּרֶךְ לְכָל רֵעֶיהָ. חַזֵּק יָדֵינוּ לְהַדְרִיכָהּ בְּדַרְכֵי תוֹרָה וֶאֱמוּנָה, וְאַמְּצֵנוּ
לְהוֹלִיכָהּ בְּעִקְבוֹת גִּבּוֹרִים וּגְבוֹרוֹת יִשְׂרָאֵל, שֶׁמַּעֲשֵׂיהֶם זָרְחוּ לָנוּ בְּכָל
דּוֹרוֹת עַמֵּנוּ.

Elohaynoo v'Elohay imotaynoo v'avotaynoo, ga-del et hayaldah ha-zot le-chayim shel simcha, chayim shel tova, chayim shel chochmah. Yehi ratzon sheh-tehiheh yaldateynoo osah shalom v'rodefet shalom bayn ish l'rayahoo. V'yizrach orah mi-saviv l'ha'ir derech l'chol ray-eh-ha. Chazek yadaynoo lehadricha b'darchey Torah v'emunah, v'amtzenu leholicha b'eekvot giboreem vgiborot Yisrael, shema'asayhem zarchoo lanoo b'kol dorot amaynoo.

O God and God of our mothers and fathers, bring this baby into a life of joy, a life of goodness, a life of wisdom. May it be Your will that our daughter be a maker of peace and a pursuer of peace between one person and another, and let her light shine round her to illumine her companions. Strengthen our will and our strength to guide her in the ways of Torah and faithful devotion to You. Give us the ability to lead her in the paths of the valiant women and men of Israel whose actions have shone brightly in all generations of our people's history.

Adapted from
Shir HaShirim—The Song of Songs

Usually read as an ode to a lover, or more traditionally as a love song between the people Israel and God, this section can also be applied to a new daughter, particularly one born in the spring or early summer.

Winter is past,
the rains are over and gone.
Flowers appear on the land,
the time of the nightingale has come.
The voice of the turtledove
is heard in our land.
The fig tree is heavy with small green figs,
and grapevines are in bloom,
pouring out fragrance.
Rise my love, my beauty,
and come away.
My dove, you are in the crevices of the rock,
in the recess of the cliffs.
Let me see your face,
let me hear your voice,
for sweet is your voice,
and your face is beautiful.

We Thank You

ADAPTED FROM SIDNEY GREENBERG IN *LIKRAT SHABBAT*

We thank You, O God, for our family and friends and what we mean and bring to one another. We are grateful for the bonds of loyalty and affection which sustain us and keep us close to one another no matter how far apart we may be.

We thank You for implanting in us a deep need for each other, and for giving us the capacity to love and to care.

Help us be modest in our demands of one another, but generous in our giving to each other.

May we never measure how much love or encouragement we offer, may we never count the times we forgive.

Rather, may we always be grateful that we have one another and that we are able to express our love in acts of kindness.

Keep us gentle in our speech. When we offer words of criticism, may they be chosen with care and spoken softly. May we waste no opportunity to speak words of sympathy, of appreciation, of praise.

Bless our family and our community of loved ones with health, happiness, and contentment. Above all, grant us the wisdom to build a joyous and peaceful home in which the awareness of Your presence will always abide.

I Am a Father

ABRAHAM JOSHUA HESCHEL

I am a father. I have a daughter and I love her dearly. I would like my daughter to obey the commandments of the Torah; I would like her to revere me as her father. And so I ask myself the question over and over again: "What is there about me that deserves the reverence of my daughter?"

You see, unless I live a life that is worthy of her reverence, I make it almost impossible for her to live a Jewish life. So many young people abandon Judaism because the Jewish models that they see in their parents are not worthy of reverence. And so, in many cases, it is the parents who make it impossible for the young to obey the Fifth Commandment.

My message to parents is: Every day ask yourselves the question: "What is there about me that deserves the reverence of my child?"

Blessed Is the Child

AUTHOR UNKNOWN

In every birth, blessed is the wonder
In every celebration, blessed is the new beginning
In every child, blessed is the life
In every hope, blessed is the potential
In every existence, blessed are the possibilities
In every love, blessed are the tears
In every life, blessed is the love.

A Parent's Gift

AUTHOR UNKNOWN

Gold and silver, have I none
What gift, then, can I give my daughter or son?
I can endow her with a sense of worth.
I can deepen her inner security by developing self-esteem.
I can encourage natural talents and special qualities.
I can help her to develop an awareness of all life around her.
I can ignite the spark of her creativity.
I can kindle her imagination.
I can accept her new ideas.
I can appreciate her efforts.
I can give her time to dream.
I can mold her character.
I can set a worthy example for her to follow.
I can motivate her toward achieving honest goals.
I can be reverent and hold certain values sacred.
I can laugh with her when life tests us both.
I can offer her LOVE.

A Blessing

DANNY SIEGEL

May your eyes sparkle with the light of Torah,
and your ears hear the music of its words.
May the space between each letter of the scrolls

bring warmth and comfort to your soul.
May the syllables draw holiness from your heart,
and may this holiness be gentle and soothing to the world.
May your study be passionate,
and meanings bear more meanings
until life itself arrays itself to you
as a dazzling wedding feast.
And may your conversation,
even of the commonplace,
be a blessing to all who listen to your words
and see the Torah glowing on your face.

Parents' Prayer
AUTHOR UNKNOWN

Source of all life, our hearts are filled with joy for the new life which has been entrusted to us. Not with words alone shall we voice our thanks, but with our striving to rear our daughter with love and understanding and tender care.

May our child find her way in the paths of Torah and good deeds as a loyal member of her people, always faithful to the Covenant.

Give us the wisdom, courage, and faith that we as parents will need to raise our daughter to be a human and humane being, a strong and happy and loving person. Amen.

The Birth of a Child Is a Miracle of Renewal
AUTHOR UNKNOWN

We dedicate our daughter to Torah, to a never-ending fascination with study and learning.

With a book she will never be alone.

We dedicate our daughter to *chuppah*, to never-ending growth as a human being capable of giving and receiving love.

With a loving mate she will never be alone.

We dedicate our daughter to *ma'asim tovim*, to a never-ending concern for family and community, and justice.

If she cares for others she will never be alone.
We pray for wisdom to help our daughter achieve these things,
to fulfill the needs of her mind and body.
To be strong when she needs us to be strong.
To be gentle when she needs us to be gentle.
But always to be there when she needs us.
The birth of a child is a miracle of renewal.
We stand together today, awed by the miracle of our daughter,
_____.

Sing Out to God
PSALM 98

Sing out to God, all the earth,
Break forth and sing for joy.
Sing praises to God with the harp,
And with voices full of joyous melody.
With trumpets and the sound of the horn sing out to God.
Let the sea roar in all its fullness
The whole world and all its inhabitants.
Let the floods clap their hands,
And the mountains sing for joy
Before God and the nations.

A *Midrash*

The rabbis taught that there are three partners in the making of a child:
The Holy One, the father, and the mother.
The father supplies the white substances, from which are formed bones, sinew, nails, brain, and the white of the eye. The mother supplies the red substances of skin, flesh, hair, blood, and the black of the eye. The Holy One gives the child spirit, breath, beauty of features, eyesight, hearing, the ability to speak and to walk, and the power of understanding.

A Blessing for My Daughter

MYRNA RABINOWITZ

May you walk through life as a person
With other people, with other people
May you walk through life as a person
Kind and just and caring.

May you walk through life as a woman
With other women, with other women
May you walk through life as a woman
Proud and strong and sharing.
May you walk through life as a sister
And a daughter and a mother
May you walk through life as a sister
Nurturing and giving.
May you walk through life with *Shechina*
Guiding you, guiding you
May you walk through life with *Shechina*
And know the joy of living.

A Yiddish Folk Saying

No matter how many children parents have, each child is like their
only one.

Parents' Prayer

RUTH F. BRIN

You who have planted in the brain of every spider
Foresight to provide food for the child she will never see;
You who have taught every sparrow enough wisdom
To push her fledglings from the nest;
You who have created the wasp an engineer
To build a house of paper for her child;
You who make of the brown bear a patient pedagogue
To feed and teach her unruly cubs;
Teach me, too, wisdom and foresight, skill and patience

Not to use instinctively, but with intelligence;
Help me to learn what I must know to raise these,
The most beloved and delicate of all Your creatures,
my children.

Above All, Teach This Newborn Child
DANNY SIEGEL

Above all, teach this newborn child to touch,
to never stop,
to feel how fur is other than the leaf or cheek
to know through these hands diamonds from glass,
Mezuzah from anything else in the world
The same with Challah and a book.
As the baby grows,
teach this child to embrace the shoulders
of another
before sadness brings them inhumanely low,
to stroke the hair softly of one younger who is weeping,
one older who cries.
Let these hands be a gentle Yes
When Yes is the Truth
and gently, a No when No is right.
Whatever these fingers touch—
may they be for new holiness and blessing,
for light, life and love.
Amen.

Blessing the Children
DANNY SIEGEL

May you be as Sarah, Rivka, Rachel and Leah
whose names and deeds
are our inheritance;
who bore us, raised us,
guided and taught us
that a touch

is a touch of Holiness,
and a laugh is prophecy;
that all that is ours,
is theirs;
that neither Man nor Woman alone
lights the spark of Life
but only both together,
generating light and warmth
and singular humanity.

The Covenant of Creation

TIKVA FRYMER-KENSKY

God,
In my womb You formed the child (Psalm 139:13)
In my womb, I nourished it. (Psalm 139:16)
You formed and numbered the baby's limbs
I contained and protected them.
You who could see the child in my depths, (Psalm 139:15)
I who felt the kicks and turns,
together we counted the months.
Together we planned the future.
Flesh of my flesh (Jeremiah 1:5; Isaiah 49:5)
form of Your form.
Another human being upon the earth,
a home for You, God, in this, our world.

Blessing of the Children

RABBI LEAH KROLL

May you know God as Abraham our father did, and face your trials
    with great dignity.
Like our mother Sarah, may you be gracious and kind to those
    who pass your way.
May you be gentle as Isaac and as determined as Rebecca.
Like Jacob, may you be dedicated and conscientious in all you set
    out to do.

May you be blessed, as Leah was blessed, with a close and loving
    family.
And like Rachel, may you radiate warmth from your soul to
    everyone whose life touches yours.

A Wish for You, My Daughter

DONNA DARGIS

If there could be only one thing
in life for me to teach you,
I would teach you to love.
To respect others so that you may
find respect in yourself.
To learn the value of giving,
so that if ever there comes a time
in your life that someone really needs,
you will give.
To act in a manner that you would wish to be treated;
to be proud of yourself.
To laugh and smile as much as you can,
in order to help bring joy
back into this world.
To have faith in others;
to be understanding.
To stand tall in this world and
to learn to depend on yourself.
To only take from this Earth
those things which you really need,
so there will be enough for others.
To not depend on money or material things
for your happiness, but
To learn to appreciate the people
who love you, the simple beauty
that God gave you and to find peace
and security within yourself.
To you, my child, I hope I will teach all these things,
for they are love.

A Mother's Prayer

NAOMI BAR-YAM

You are the Mother of all.

You know how to weigh the needs, demands, joys, fears of all Your children. To You it is known whose cry must be heeded now and who is best able to wait.

I have only two children. Help me so that I too may know whose call to answer now—whose tears must be kissed away first— this time.

You are the Mother of all.

You know how and when to be patient, and how and when to lose patience so that Your children can be strong, independent, caring people.

Teach me too, to be patient with my children and to know the moments when impatience will teach them strength, independence, caring. Let my impatience and anger come when they will best serve You and my children—not myself.

You are the Mother of all.

You watch Your children explore the world in its beauty and wonder—its horror and despair.

They sing praises to You of its beauty, shed tears of pain and anger to You of its horror.

With love and patience You help Your children use their unique wonder and joy, fear and anger to make the world a better place.

Guide my hands and my soul to teach my children that each of us is responsible to You and to one another to make our contribution to *Tikkun Olam,* the repair of the world.

You are the Mother of all.

To You it is known how and when to encourage Your children to stretch their minds, their bodies, their souls.

Help me to give my children the physical and spiritual tools they will need to face and learn from the challenges You will set before them in their lives.

You are the Mother of all.
Help us to share with our children the joy and pain of growth.
Teach us to use and to trust the uniqueness of ourselves and
　　others in raising our children.
Guide our thoughts and our acts so that we, in turn, may guide
　　our children more wisely.
Bless us always with the knowledge of the light of Your presence.

Sh'ma: Communal Declaration of Faith

MARCIA FALK, FROM *THE BOOK OF BLESSINGS*

שְׁמַע, יִשְׂרָאֵל —
לֶאֱלֹהוּת אַלְפֵי פָנִים,
מְלֹא עוֹלָם שְׁכִינָתָהּ,
רִבּוּי פָּנֶיהָ אֶחָד.

נֹאהַב אֶת־הַחַיִּים
וְאֶת עֵין הַחַיִּים
בְּכָל־לְבָבֵנוּ וּבְכָל־נַפְשֵׁנוּ
וּבְכָל־מְאֹדֵנוּ.
יִהְיוּ הַדְּבָרִים הָאֵלֶּה
בִּלְבָבֵנוּ וּבְקִרְבֵּנוּ:
שְׁמִירַת אֶרֶץ וְיוֹשְׁבֶיהָ,
רְדִיפַת צֶדֶק וְשָׁלוֹם,
אַהֲבַת חֶסֶד וְרַחֲמִים.
נְשַׁנְּנָם
לִבְנוֹתֵינוּ וּלְבָנֵינוּ
וּנְדַבֵּר בָּם
בְּשִׁבְתֵּנוּ בְּבֵיתֵנוּ,
בְּלֶכְתֵּנוּ בַדֶּרֶךְ,
בְּשָׁכְבֵּנוּ וּבְקוּמֵנוּ.
וְיִהְיוּ מַעֲשֵׂינוּ

נֶאֱמָנִים לִדְבָרֵינוּ,
לְמַעַן יֵדְעוּ דּוֹר אַחֲרוֹן,
בָּנוֹת וּבָנִים יִוָּלֵדוּ:
חֶסֶד וֶאֱמֶת נִפְגָּשׁוּ,
צֶדֶק וְשָׁלוֹם נָשָׁקוּ.

Sh'ma, yisra'eyl—
la'elohut alfey panim,
m'lo olam sh'khinatah,
ribuy paneha ehad.
Nohav et-hahayim
v'eyt eyn hahayim
b'khol-l'vaveynu uvkhol-nafsheynu
uvkhol-m'odeynu.
Yihyu had'varim ha'eyleh
bilvaveynu uvkirbeynu:
sh'mirat eretz v'yoshveha,
r'difat tzedek v'shalom,
ahavat hesed v'rahamim.
N'shan'nam
livnoteynu ulvaneynu
undabeyr bam
b'shivteynu b'veyteynu,
b'lekheynu baderekh
b'shokbeynu uvkumeynu.
V'yihyu ma'aseynu
ne'emanim lidvareynu,
l'ma'an yeyd'u dor aharon,
banot uvanim yivaleydu:
Hesed ve'emet nifgashu,
tzedek v'shalom nashaku.

Hear, O Israel—
The divine abounds everywhere
and dwells in everything;
the many are One.

Loving life
and its mysterious source
with all our heart
and all our spirit,
all our senses and strength,
we take upon ourselves
and into ourselves
these promises:
to care for the earth
and those who live upon it,
to pursue justice and peace,
to love kindness and compassion.
We will teach this to our children
throughout the passage of the day—
as we dwell in our homes
and as we go on our journeys,
from the time we rise
until we fall asleep.

And may our actions
be faithful to our words
that our children's children
may live to know:
Truth and kindness
have embraced,
peace and justice have kissed
and are one.

To Bring a New Life into This World

CONGREGATION KOL HANESHAMA

To bring a new life into this world is the most affirmative of actions, in a time when such actions seem hardest to make. And for that reason it is so a Jewish decision, affirming life and goodness, and innocence and learning, and love and responsibility.

Choose Life

CONGREGATION KOL HANESHAMA

Reverence for life has been enjoined upon us as a fulfillment of our covenant with God, as it is written: And God said to Israel … Choose life, that you and your descendants may live. (Deuteronomy 30:19) The birth of a daughter brings us joy and hope, and the courage to reaffirm our enduring covenant with life and its Creator.

We Have Not Seen the Robin But We Know He Is There

BEN ZION BOKSER

We have not seen the robin but we know he is there
because we heard him singing through our window from the
    tree-top outside.
We have not seen God. But we have looked into a child's eyes, and
    have been overwhelmed by the miracle of unfolding life.
We have watched the trees bedeck themselves with the new garb
    of green in the Spring, and have been stirred by the miracle of
    continual rebirth.
We have looked at the stars, and have been overcome by the
    miracle of the grandeur and majesty of the universe.
We know that God exists, because we have heard the song of the
    Divine Presence from all the tree-tops of creation.

We Shall Strive

AUTHOR UNKNOWN

We shall strive to make of our home
A place where you can grow to serve God with joy
To delight in Torah
And help extend the possibilities of your people;
A place where you can become at ease in nature
And endlessly inquisitive about the world;
A place where your body can move to the rhythms of music
And understand its depth,
Where art and reading and sport,

The quiet life indoors and hearty life with others outside,
Can help you make the choices through which you will find
The image of God that is yours.
We want you to feel secure in your family, both near and far,
Loyal to your friends,
Not afraid to disagree with those you love,
More and more aware as you grow up that the world needs
      loving, caring people,
More and more able to take risks, to make commitments, to fight
      for what you believe,
We want you to know that it is dignified to be a child,
It is a special gift to be a woman.
You are special not only for what you do,
You are special not only for what others may say about you,
You are special because you are.

Each Lifetime

LAWRENCE KUSHNER, FROM *HONEY FROM THE ROCK*

Each lifetime is the pieces of a jigsaw puzzle.
For some there are more pieces.
For others, the pieces are more difficult to assemble.

Some to be born with a nearly completed puzzle.
And so it goes.
Souls going this way and that.
Trying to assemble the myriad parts.

But know this: no one has within herself all the pieces to her
      puzzle.
Like before the days when they used to seal jigsaw puzzles
in cellophane, ensuring that all the pieces were there.
Everyone carries with them at least one,
and probably many, pieces to some else's puzzle.
Sometimes they know it.
Sometimes they don't.

And when you present your piece—which is worthless to you—
to another,

Whether you know it or not,
Whether they know it or not,
You are a messenger from the Most High.

See the Resources beginning on page 229 for information on where to purchase the recorded and sheet music for the lyrics below.

Child of Mine

ESTA CASSWAY

Child of mine,
Child of mine.
Dance slowly through your spring
And bring me flowers.
One by one
Like years I press them,
Deep inside the hidden place
Where dreams are born.
And in your smiling face,
The hope and innocence of childhood
Braves a darkening world
And dares the clouds away.
May sunbeams ever shine for you my child,
Oh child of mine.
And when my winter comes,
And you look down on me,
Summer in your eyes,
Tree tall
And very wise,
The silver song that is your life
Shall soothe my days,
Oh child of mine,
Oh part of me apart.
And I shall rock you, ever gently,
And I shall rock you,
In the cradle of my heart.

Welcome to the World

ESTA CASSWAY

The songwriter based this song on Psalm 98:8 and dedicated it to her grandchildren.

Welcome to the world,
Little one.
Miracles are waiting;
open up your eyes.
See the silver moon,
Smiling down upon you.
Watch as daylight tiptoes in
And paints the sky.
You are our miracle;
You make us complete.
May you dance in sunshine.
May your dreams be sweet.

Welcome to the world,
Little one.
Raindrops on your window
Play a gentle tune
Bees and butterflies
Waving from the flowers
Birds are singing lullabies
To say hello
You are our miracle;
You make us complete.
May you dance in sunshine.
May your dreams be sweet.

Welcome to the world,
Little one.
Miracles are waiting;
Listen to their song,
Little one.

Miracles are waiting.
Mountains and hills
Shall sing before you.
Welcome to the world,

Welcome to the world,
Little one.

Rituals to Welcome Your Daughter into the Covenant

A ritual to acknowledge your daughter's entry into the covenant, or to welcome her into it, paired with her formal naming, is at the very heart of her welcoming ceremony. To introduce this section of your daughter's welcoming ceremony you may choose to explain to your guests how you plan to integrate being part of a sacred covenant into your daughter's life. For a detailed exploration of the concepts involved, see chapter 3, "Understanding Covenant and Dedication."

This section, which gives you several different ways to approach welcoming your daughter into the covenant between God and the Jewish people, is divided into three parts. The first part contains several readings related to covenant for girls and women, beginning with noting the presence of a chair that represents the prophet Elijah or a cup or chair that symbolizes the prophetess Miriam. For further discussion of these elements, refer to chapter 8, "Sanctifying Your Surroundings." Select one or all of the readings in this part to transition into the covenantal portion of your welcoming ceremony.

The second part includes several variations on general formulas for prayers to recognize your daughter's induction into the covenant, should you choose not to employ one of the more extensive rituals that follow in the third part. Choose the prayer that best suits your religious sensibilities. If you wish to recognize your daughter's transition into partnership with the covenant in a more specific way, seven types of ritual are provided in the third part of this chapter. They range widely in their level of innovation, and again, you should select the ritual to which you feel most drawn.

Part One
Transitioning into the Covenantal Part of the Ceremony

To begin this portion of your daughter's welcoming ceremony, if you are using a chair to remember the prophet Elijah, point to it and say:

זֶה הַכִּסֵּא שֶׁל אֵלִיָּהוּ הַנָּבִיא זָכוּר לַטּוֹב הִנֵּה אָנֹכִי שֹׁלֵחַ לָכֶם אֵת אֵלִיָּה הַנָּבִיא לִפְנֵי בּוֹא יוֹם יהוה הַגָּדוֹל וְהַנּוֹרָא: וְהֵשִׁיב לֵב־אָבוֹת עַל־בָּנִים וְלֵב בָּנִים עַל־אֲבוֹתָם.

Zeh ha-kiseh shel Eliyahu ha-navee zachoor la-tov. Hiney anochee sholayach lachem et Eliyah ha-navee lifnay bo yom Adonai ha-gadol v'ha-nora. V'heishiv lev-avot al-banim v'lev banim al-avotam.

This is the throne of Elijah the prophet, may he be remembered for good!

Lo, I will send the prophet Elijah to you before the coming of the awesome, fearful day of the Lord. He shall reconcile parents with children, and children with parents.

(From Malachi 3:23–24)

Alternative: Point to Elijah's chair and say:

This is your chair, Elijah, who returns to children the heart of a parent, and to parents the heart of a child. This is your chair, Elijah. Send your guardian powers to protect this child as she strives throughout life to keep the covenant into which we are welcoming her today. This is your chair, Elijah. Help all of us to spread the message that the time is coming for the victory over oppression, and that the time is ripe for the arrival of a newborn world of joy.

If you choose a chair or cup to symbolize Miriam, point to it and say:

This chair [or cup] is devoted to Miriam the prophetess, may her remembrance be for the good.

Then you can sing the song *Eliyahu Hanavi* (Elijah the Prophet), a traditional song that speaks of our hope for the fulfillment of messianic prophecies soon, and a song that we sing at the end of every Sabbath.

Eliyahu hanavi
Eliyahu hatishbi
Eliyahu, Eliyahu,
Eliyahu haGiladi
Bimhayrah b'yamaynu
Yavo aylaynu
Im Mashiach ben David
Im Mashiach ben David
(repeat first verse)

May the Prophet Elijah come soon, in our time, with the messiah, son of David.

To the traditional tune of *Eliyahu Hanavi*, you may choose to sing these new words about Miriam the prophetess:

Miriam hanevi'ah
oz vezimrah beyadah
Miriam tirkod itanu
lehagdil zimrat olam
Miriam tirkod
letaken et ha'olam
Bimhayrah b'yamaynu
hi tevi'enu
El mey hayeshu'a.

Miriam the prophetess, in whose hands are strength and song
Miriam will dance with us toward the greatness of the eternal song
Miriam will dance with us in repair of the world
Speedily, in our days she will bring us
To the waters of redemption.

If you are not using a chair for Elijah or Miriam, or a Miriam's cup, then begin the covenantal portion of your daughter's welcoming ceremony by choosing one or more of the following selections.

This is a *midrash*, or rabbinic interpretation of the Torah that many people choose to read at their daughter's welcoming ceremony as an introduction and transition into that section of the ritual:

When Israel Stood to Receive the Torah

FROM *SONG OF SONGS RABBAH* 1:24

When Israel stood to receive the Torah, the Holy One said to them:
I am giving you My Torah
Bring Me good guarantors that you will guard it and I shall give it
    to you.
And the people replied:
Our ancestors are our guarantors.
But the Holy One said to them:
Your ancestors are unacceptable to me
Yet bring Me good guarantors and I shall give it to you.
Israel then answered:
God, our prophets are our guarantors.
And again God said to them:
The prophets are unacceptable to me
Yet bring Me good guarantors and I shall give it to you.
The people then responded:
Behold, our children are our guarantors,
And God then gently, and with great hope and love, replied:
They are certainly good guarantors. For their sake I give the Torah
    to you.

Here are some additional readings from classical Jewish sources related to the covenant between God and the Jewish people:

All the Generations Were Present

אַתֶּם נִצָּבִים הַיּוֹם כֻּלְּכֶם לִפְנֵי יהוה אֱלֹהֵיכֶם רָאשֵׁיכֶם שִׁבְטֵיכֶם זִקְנֵיכֶם וְשֹׁטְרֵיכֶם כֹּל אִישׁ יִשְׂרָאֵל: טַפְּכֶם נְשֵׁיכֶם וְגֵרְךָ אֲשֶׁר בְּקֶרֶב מַחֲנֶיךָ מֵחֹטֵב עֵצֶיךָ עַד שֹׁאֵב מֵימֶיךָ: לְעָבְרְךָ בִּבְרִית יהוה אֱלֹהֶיךָ וּבְאָלָתוֹ אֲשֶׁר יהוה אֱלֹהֶיךָ כֹּרֵת עִמְּךָ הַיּוֹם: לְמַעַן הָקִים־אֹתְךָ הַיּוֹם לוֹ לְעָם וְהוּא יִהְיֶה־לְּךָ לֵאלֹהִים כַּאֲשֶׁר דִּבֶּר־לָךְ וְכַאֲשֶׁר נִשְׁבַּע לַאֲבֹתֶיךָ לְאַבְרָהָם לְיִצְחָק וּלְיַעֲקֹב: וְלֹא אִתְּכֶם לְבַדְּכֶם אָנֹכִי כֹּרֵת אֶת־הַבְּרִית הַזֹּאת וְאֶת־הָאָלָה הַזֹּאת: כִּי אֶת־אֲשֶׁר יֶשְׁנוֹ פֹּה עִמָּנוּ עֹמֵד הַיּוֹם לִפְנֵי יהוה אֱלֹהֵינוּ וְאֵת אֲשֶׁר אֵינֶנּוּ פֹּה עִמָּנוּ הַיּוֹם.

Atem nitzavim hayom kulchem lifnay Adonai Elohaychem rasheychem shivtaychem zikneychem v'shotreychem kol ish Yisrael. Tapchem nesheychem vgerecha asher bekerev machaneycha mechotev ey-tzeycha ad shoev maymecha. Le-ovrecha b'vrit Adonai Elohaycha oo-v'alato asher Adonai Elohaychah koret imecha hayom. Lema'an hakeem otcha hayom lo le-am v'hoo yihiyeh-lecha l'eloheem ka'asher deebare-lach, v'ka-asher nishbah l'avotecha l'Avraham l'Yitzchak oo-l'Yaakov. V'lo itchem livadchem anochee koret et ha-brit hazot v'et-ha'alah hazot.

Key et-asher yeshno po eemanoo omed hayom lifnay Adonai Elohaynoo v'et asher aynenoo po imanoo hayom.

All the generations were present at Sinai, even those yet unborn. (Deuteronomy 29:9–14)

You are standing this day, all of you, before the Lord your God; your heads, your tribes, your elders, and your officers, even all the men of Israel, your little ones, your wives, and the stranger who is in the midst of your camp, from the hewer of your wood to the drawer of your water, that you should enter into the covenant of the Lord your God—and into His oath—which the Lord your God makes with you this day that He will establish you this day unto Himself for a people, and that He will be to you a God, as He spoke to you, and as He swore to your fathers, to Abraham, to Isaac, and to Jacob.

It's not with you only that I make this covenant and this oath, but with those who stand here with us this day before the Lord our God, and also with those who are not here this day.

The Everlasting Covenant

וַהֲקִמֹתִי אֶת־בְּרִיתִי בֵּינִי וּבֵינֶךָ וּבֵין זַרְעֲךָ אַחֲרֶיךָ לְדֹרֹתָם לִבְרִית עוֹלָם לִהְיוֹת לְךָ לֵאלֹהִים וּלְזַרְעֲךָ אַחֲרֶיךָ.

Va-hakimotee et breetee baynee oo-vaynecha oo-vayn zaracha acharaycha l'dorotam l'vrit olam liheeyot lecha l'Elohim oo-lezaracha achreycha.

I will establish My covenant with you and your children as an everlasting covenant throughout the generations to be God to you and your children. (Genesis 17:7)

Alternative translation:

Then I will establish a covenant between Me and you
and your descendants who come after you;
A covenant in which I will be your God
And your children's God forever and ever.

Witnessing

FROM RUTH 4:9–11

וַיֹּאמֶר בֹּעַז לַזְּקֵנִים וְכָל־הָעָם: עֵדִים אַתֶּם הַיּוֹם ...

Va-yomer Boaz la-zekaynim v-chol ha-am. Eydim atem hayom ...

And Boaz said to the elders and the people, "You are witnesses ..."

The community responds:

וַיֹּאמְרוּ כָּל־הָעָם אֲשֶׁר־בַּשַּׁעַר וְהַזְּקֵנִים: עֵדִים. יִתֵּן יהוה אֶת־הָאִשָּׁה הַבָּאָה אֶל־בֵּיתֶךָ כְּרָחֵל וּכְלֵאָה, אֲשֶׁר בָּנוּ שְׁתֵּיהֶם אֶת־בֵּית יִשְׂרָאֵל.

Vayomroo kol ha-am asher b'sha'ar v'ha-zekanim: aydim. Yiten Adonai et ha-isha ha-ba'ah el-beytecha k'Rachel oo-ch'Leah, asher banoo shtayhem et beyt Yisrael.

And the people at the gate and the elders said, "We are witnesses. May God make the woman who is coming into your house like Rachel and Leah, who together build the house of Israel." (Genesis 17:7)

Part Two
Blessings Welcoming Her into the Covenant

This is a simple, straightforward blessing related to entry into the covenant:

בָּרוּךְ אַתָּה יהוה, אֱלֹהֵינוּ מֶלֶךְ הָעוֹלָם, אֲשֶׁר קִדְּשָׁנוּ בְּמִצְוֹתָיו וְצִוָּנוּ לְהַכְנִיסָהּ בִּבְרִית שֶׁל אַבְרָהָם וְשָׂרָה.

Baruch Atah Adonai, Eloheinu Melech ha'olam, asher kidshanu b'mitzvotav v'tsivanu l'hachnisah b'vrit shel Avraham v'Sarah.

We praise You, Adonai our God, Ruler of the universe, who sanctifies us by Your commandments and commands us to enter our daughter, _____, into the covenant of Abraham and Sarah.

This is a traditionally oriented prayer about entering your daughter into the covenant:

בָּרוּךְ אַתָּה יהוה, אֱלֹהֵינוּ מֶלֶךְ הָעוֹלָם, אֲשֶׁר קִדֵּשׁ יְדִיד מִבֶּטֶן, אֵל חַי חֶלְקֵנוּ צוּרֵנוּ צִוָּה לְהַצִּיל יְדִידוּת שְׁאֵרֵנוּ מִשַּׁחַת, לְמַעַן בְּרִיתוֹ. בָּרוּךְ אַתָּה יהוה, כּוֹרֵת הַבְּרִית.

Baruch Atah Adonai, Elohaynoo Melech ha-olam, asher kidesh yedid mibeten. El chai chelkaynoo tzooreynoo, tzivah lehatzil yedidu she-eraynoo me-shacha, lema'an britoh. Baruch Atah Adonai, koret habrit.

Blessed are You, Ruler of the universe, who has sanctified Your beloved from the womb, establishing Your holy covenant throughout the generations. May devotion to the covenant continue to sustain us as a people. Praised are You, eternal God, who has established the covenant.

אֱלוֹהַּ כָּל הַבְּרִיּוֹת, קַיֵּם אֶת הַיַּלְדָּה הַזֹּאת לְאָבִיהָ וּלְאִמָּהּ.

Elo'ah kol habriot, kayem et hayaldah hazot l'aveeha oo-la'eemah.

God of all creation, preserve this child for her parents.

אָנוּ מְצֻוִּים לְכַבֵּד אֶת הַחַיִּים כְּהַגְשָׁמַת בְּרִיתֵנוּ עִם אֱלֹהִים, כְּמוֹ שֶׁכָּתוּב: "וּבָחַרְתָּ בַּחַיִּים לְמַעַן תִּחְיֶה אַתָּה וְזַרְעֶךָ" (דברים ל, יט). לְדָתָהּ שֶׁל בַּת מְבִיאָה לָנוּ שִׂמְחָה וְתִקְוָה וְאֹמֶץ לְכוֹנֵן מֵחָדָשׁ אֶת בְּרִיתֵנוּ הַנִּמְשֶׁכֶת עִם הַחַיִּים וְעִם יוֹצְרָם.

Ano mitzoovim lechabed et hachayyim k'hagshamat britaynoo eem Elohim, kmo shekatoov: oovacharta b'chayyim lema'an tichyeh atah v'zarecha. Leydatah shel bat m'viah lanoo simchah v'tikvah v'ometz l'chonen mechadash et britaynoo ha-nimshechet eem hachayyim v'eem yotzram.

Reverence for life has been enjoined upon us as a fulfillment of our covenant with God, as it is written: And God said to Israel, "Choose life, that you and your descendants may live." (Deuteronomy 30:19) The birth of a daughter brings us joy and hope, and the courage to reaffirm our enduring covenant with life and its creator.

בְּשִׂמְחָה אֲנִי מַעֲבִירָה אֶת בִּתִּי בִּבְרִית יִשְׂרָאֵל: בְּרִית עִם אֱלֹהִים, עִם הַתּוֹרָה וְעִם הַחַיִּים.

B'simchah ani ma'avirah et biti b'vrit Yisrael: brit eem Eloheynoo, eem haTorah v'eem hachayyim.

Joyfully I bring my daughter into the covenant of Israel, a covenant with God, with Torah, and with life.

This is an innovative formula for welcoming a daughter into the covenant, but one deeply rooted in classical Jewish texts:

> We say a blessing over a cup of wine, as we do to set apart other special life-cycle events. Our daughter is symbolically welcomed into the community of Israel with a prayer that stresses her relationship with God and the ongoing covenantal relationship between God and the Jewish people.

בָּרוּךְ אַתָּה יהוה, אֱלֹהֵינוּ מֶלֶךְ הָעוֹלָם, בּוֹרֵא פְּרִי הַגָּפֶן.

בָּרוּךְ אַתָּה, מְקוֹר הַחַיִּים, אֲשֶׁר מְקַדֵּשׁ יָדִיד מִבֶּטֶן כַּכָּתוּב: בְּטֶרֶם

אֶצָּרְךָ בַבֶּטֶן יְדַעְתִּיךָ וּבְטֶרֶם תֵּצֵא מֵרֶחֶם הִקְדַּשְׁתִּיךָ (ירמיהו א, ה)

וְחוֹתֵם אֶת הַבְּרִית בִּבְשָׂרֵנוּ כַּכָּתוּב: כִּי זֹאת הַבְּרִית אֲשֶׁר אֶכְרֹת

אֶת־בֵּית יִשְׂרָאֵל נָתַתִּי אֶת־תּוֹרָתִי בְּקִרְבָּם וְעַל־לִבָּם אֶכְתְּבֶנָּה

(ירמיהו לא, לב) וּמְקַיֵּם אֶת בְּרִיתוֹ לְדוֹרוֹת כַּכָּתוּב: יהוה אֱלֹהֵינוּ

כָּרַת עִמָּנוּ בְּרִית בְּחֹרֵב: לֹא אֶת־אֲבֹתֵינוּ כָּרַת יהוה אֶת־הַבְּרִית הַזֹּאת

כִּי אִתָּנוּ אֲנַחְנוּ אֵלֶּה פֹה הַיּוֹם כֻּלָּנוּ חַיִּים (דברים ה, ב–ג) וְנֶאֱמַר:

וְזָכַרְתִּי אֲנִי אֶת־בְּרִיתִי אוֹתָךְ בִּימֵי נְעוּרָיִךְ וַהֲקִימוֹתִי לָךְ בְּרִית עוֹלָם

(יחזקאל טז, ס) בָּרוּךְ כּוֹרֵת בְּרִית.

Baruch Atah Adonai Eloheynoo Melech ha-olam, boray pri hagafen. Baruch Atah, makor hachayyim, asher mekadesh yedid mibeten ka-katoov: beterem etzorcha vabeten yadaticha ooveterem tetzeh mayrechem hi-kdashticha. V'chotaym et habrit bivsareynoo ka-katoov: ki zot ha-brit asher echrot et beit Yisrael natatee et Toratee b'kirbam v'al-libbam echtoveynah. Oomikayyam et brito l'dorot ka-katoov: Adonai Elohaynoo karet eemanoo brit b'chorev: Lo et avotaynoo karat Adonai et habrit hazot ki itano anachnoo eleh po hayom koolanoo chayyim. V'ne'emar: v'zacharti anee et britee otach bimei ne'oorayich vehakimotee lach brit olam. Baruch koret brit.

Blessed are You, Lord our God, Ruler of the universe, who creates the fruit of the vine.

(Then the parents should drink from a kiddush cup of wine or grape juice.)

Blessed are You, the Wellspring of all life, who consecrates His beloved while still in the womb, as it is written: Before I created you in the womb, I selected you; Before you were born, I consecrated you. (Jeremiah 1:5)

And who seals His covenant in our flesh, as it is written: This is the covenant I will make with the House of Israel: I will put my Torah into their innermost being and I will inscribe it upon their hearts. (Jeremiah 31:33) And who establishes His covenant for all generations, as it is written: The Lord our God made a covenant with us at Horeb. It is not with our ancestors that the Lord made this covenant, but with us, the living, every one of us who is here today. (Deuteronomy 5:2–3) And it says: I will remember the covenant that I made with you in the days of your youth, and I will establish it with you as an everlasting covenant. (Ezekiel 16:60) Blessed is he who establishes His covenant.

This is a modern-feeling welcome into the covenant for a daughter:

_____ , we welcome you into our family.
You are the latest chapter in the unfolding of our lives.
You are brand new, a symbol of today and of tomorrow.
Your life is a new and clean slate upon which people and events
    will leave their impressions.
You are a bridge over which we who welcome you can gaze from
    this day into future days,
from our generation into your generation.
You are the newest link in the endless chain of our people's
    history.
_____ , *Brucha haba-ah b'ahava.*
We welcome you into the covenant of the Jewish people with
    love.

And a final line for this part of a welcoming ceremony:

This is our child, created in love, whom we bring today into the community of Israel.

Part Three
Ritual Transitions into the Covenant

1. *Brit Nerot:* Creating Light—four ceremonies
2. *Brit Mikvah:* Immersion in the Waters of Life—two ceremonies
3. *Brit Rechitzah:* Welcoming into the Covenant with Hand- or Footwashing
4. *Brit Tallit:* Enfolding Her in the Covenant
5. *Brit Kehilla:* Entering the Covenant by Walking through the Community
6. *Brit Havdalah:* Transitioning into the Covenant through *Havdalah*
7. *Brit Melach:* Recalling the Covenant with Salt

1. *Brit Nerot:* Creating Light—four candle ceremonies

Candles have great symbolic meaning in Judaism. Each time we light candles in the context of Jewish ritual it echoes the first step of creation, when God divided light from dark. We light candles during times that are joyous and those that are solemn—to welcome holy days of celebration and to sanctify the memory of those who have died. We light two or more Shabbat candles to welcome the Sabbath and signify a transition from work into soul-restoring rest, from secular time into holy time. Likewise we use a special, multiwicked, braided ceremonial candle after the sun sets on Saturday night to mark the end of the Sabbath, the end of this interval of sacred time, and the beginning of our regular week. Lighting candles is the transition point into each of our holy days, as well. On days of national mourning, like *Tisha B'Av* and Holocaust Memorial Day, as well as on the anniversaries of the deaths of loved ones, we light long-burning candles that last from the close of the day we light it until after the completion of the following day.

A traditional custom at Jewish weddings, though not universally practiced today, is for the male guests to hold lighted candles as they escort the groom to the *bedeken*, the ritual during which he checks to see that the bride is his intended life partner before he lowers her veil over her face. Then, led by the men who hold the candles as they sing, the groom is escorted to the *chuppah*, where he awaits his bride. It is also traditional for the mother and mother-in-law of the bride to each hold a lighted candle in their outside hand as they take her arm with their other, escorting her down the aisle until she reaches the *chuppah*.

We can bring that custom forward to our daughters' welcoming ceremonies, using any of the following ceremonies. Some families, in their *brit nerot*, choose to light seven candles, each one representing one day of God's process of creation. Others choose to light six, in honor of the first six days before Shabbat, with their daughter symbolizing the covenant of the Sabbath between God and the Jewish people, and representing the completion of the creation process. Other families have each guest holding a candle, while others have each woman standing in the chain of this new baby's ancestry holding one.

A nice way to begin any of the candle-lighting ceremonies is with this Debbie Friedman song:

Light These Lights (Oh Hear My Prayer)
DEBBIE FRIEDMAN

O hear my prayer,
I sing to You.
Be gracious to the ones I love,
And bless them with goodness, and mercy and peace,
O hear my prayer to You.
Let us light these lights,
And see the way to You,
And let us say: Amen.

See page 229 in the Resources section for information on where to purchase the recorded and sheet music for these lyrics.

You may choose to then open up this part of your daughter's welcoming ceremony with remarks like "We have come together today to welcome a new baby girl into the community of the Jewish people. Boys enter the Jewish community through *brit milah*, the covenant of circumcision. Women and children as well as men, according to Deuteronomy 29:9–14, were participants in the original making of the covenant between God and Israel. One of the ways girls can be included in a covenantal ceremony today is through *brit nerot*, the covenant of candles. Just as the *ner tamid*, the eternal light over the ark in the synagogue sanctuary, reminds us of God's gift of the Torah, and the Shabbat candles remind us of God's gift of the Shabbat, so the *Brit Nerot* candles remind us of God's gift of life."

CANDLE CEREMONY 1[2]

Several honored guests are each given a candle and form two lines, facing each other. The parents or other honored guests carry the baby between the two rows. The candles may already be lit as they are given to the participants, or they may be progressively lit, one candle lighting another, as the baby is brought through. Another possibility is to light the candles one by one as the following six verses are read, with the idea that six verses correspond to the six days of creation. The candles are then placed in candlesticks that have been previously arranged on a table. It is especially significant to use cherished family candlesticks.

1.　　　　　　　　　　　　נֵר־לְרַגְלִי דְבָרֶךָ, וְאוֹר לִנְתִיבָתִי.

Ner-laragli devarecha, v'or l'netivati.

Your word is a lamp unto my feet, a light for my path. (Psalm 119:105)

2.　　　　　　　　כִּי־אַתָּה תָּאִיר נֵרִי, יהוה אֱלֹהַי יַגִּיהַּ חָשְׁכִּי.

Ki Atah ta'ir neyri, Adonai Eloheynoo yagiah choshki.

You are the One who kindles my lamp; Adonai, my God, lights up my darkness. (Psalm 18:29)

3.   קוּמִי, אוֹרִי, כִּי בָא אוֹרֵךְ, וּכְבוֹד יהוה עָלַיִךְ זָרָח.

Koomi, ori, ki vah ohrech, oo-chevod Adonai alayich zarach.

Arise, shine, for your light has dawned; God's radiance shines upon you! (Isaiah 60:1)

4.   וְעָלַיִךְ יִזְרַח יהוה, וּכְבוֹדוֹ עָלַיִךְ יֵרָאֶה.

V'alayich yizrach Adonai, oo-chevodo alayich yayra'eh.

May Adonai continue to shine upon you and God's brilliant presence surround you. (Isaiah 60:2b)

5.   שְׂאִי־סָבִיב עֵינַיִךְ וּרְאִי כֻּלָּם נִקְבְּצוּ, בָאוּ־לָךְ; בָּנַיִךְ מֵרָחוֹק יָבֹאוּ, וּבְנֹתַיִךְ עַל־צַד תֵּאָמַנָה.

See saviv aynayich oo-re-ee kulam nikbetzoo, vah-oo lach banayich, me-rachok ya-vo-oo, oo-v'notayech al-tzed te'amanah.

Lift up your eyes all about you and behold: They have all gathered around you. Your sons shall be brought from afar, your daughters like babes on your shoulders. (Isaiah 60:4)

6.   אֱלֹהִים יְחָנֵּנוּ וִיבָרְכֵנוּ, יָאֵר פָּנָיו אִתָּנוּ, סֶלָה.

Elohim yechonaynoo vi-vorchenu, ya'ir panav eetanoo, selah.

May God be gracious to us and bless us. May God's radiance shine upon us. Selah. (Psalm 67:2)

Then the parents lift up their daughter so that she is facing the lit candles, and they (or the rabbi) continue with:

Light was the first of God's creations. As light appeared, it brought with it the potential for wondrous things to follow. We, too, kindle lights—of hope, of understanding, of celebration, of countless new possibilities. This little daughter with whom we [or mother's name and father's name] have been blessed has already brought light into our [or their] lives.

May God's radiance continue to shine upon us [them]. May our [their] daughter grow to be a source of light to all those around her. May her radiance illuminate the world. May the light of Torah and *mitzvot* be reflected in her shining deeds. And may she help bring the light of redemption to the world.

CANDLE CEREMONY 2³

The mother kindles a light, takes her daughter in her arms, and says:

כִּי נֵר מִצְוָה וְתוֹרָה אוֹר.

Ki ner mitzvah v'Torah ohr.

The *mitzvah* is a lamp: Torah is a light.

בָּרוּךְ אַתָּה יהוה, הַמֵּאִיר לָעוֹלָם כֻּלּוֹ בִּכְבוֹדוֹ.

Baruch Atah Adonai, ha-me'ir la-olam kulo b'chevodo.

We praise You, oh God, whose presence gives light to all the world.

Joyfully I bring my daughter into the covenant of our people: A covenant with God, with Torah, and with our people.

בָּרוּךְ אַתָּה יהוה, אֱלֹהֵינוּ מֶלֶךְ הָעוֹלָם, אֲשֶׁר קִדְּשָׁנוּ בְּמִצְוֹתָיו וְצִוָּנוּ לְהַכְנִיסָהּ בִּבְרִית הַחַיִּים.

Baruch Atah Adonai, Eloheinu Melech ha'olam, asher kidshanu b'mitzvotav v'tsivanu l'hachnisah b'vrit hachayim.

We praise You Eternal God, Sovereign of the universe: You hallow us with Your *mitzvot*, and command us to bring our daughters into the Covenant of Life.

The father kindles a light, takes his daughter in his arms, and says:

אֲנִי יהוה, וְאֶתֶּנְךָ לִבְרִית עָם, לְאוֹר גּוֹיִם.

Ani Adonai, v'etencha l'vrit am, l'ohr goyim.

I, the Eternal One, have called you to be a covenant people, a light to the nations.

Joyfully I bring my daughter into the covenant of our people: A covenant with God, with Torah, and with the people Israel.

בָּרוּךְ אַתָּה יהוה, אֱלֹהֵינוּ מֶלֶךְ הָעוֹלָם, אֲשֶׁר קִדְּשָׁנוּ בְּמִצְוֹתָיו וְצִוָּנוּ עַל קִדּוּשׁ הַחַיִּים.

Baruch Atah Adonai, Eloheinu Melech ha'olam, Asher kidshanu b'mitzvotav v'tsivanu kidush hachayim.

We praise You, Eternal God, Sovereign of the universe: You hallow us with Your *mitzvot* and command us to sanctify our life.

Both parents say:

בָּרוּךְ אַתָּה יהוה, אֱלֹהֵינוּ מֶלֶךְ הָעוֹלָם, שֶׁהֶחֱיָנוּ וְקִיְּמָנוּ וְהִגִּיעָנוּ לַזְּמַן הַזֶּה.

Baruch Atah Adonai, Eloheinu Melech ha'olam, shehechiyanu, v'kiyemanu, v'higiyanu la'zman hazeh.

We praise You Eternal God, Sovereign of the universe, for giving us life, for sustaining us, and for enabling us to reach this season.

זֶה הַיּוֹם עָשָׂה יהוה; נָגִילָה וְנִשְׂמְחָה בוֹ.

Zeh ha-yom asah Adonai: nagilah v'nismichah vo.

This is the day the Eternal God has made, let us rejoice and be glad in it.

כִּי זֹאת הַבְּרִית אֲשֶׁר אֶכְרֹת אֶת־בֵּית יִשְׂרָאֵל אַחֲרֵי הַיָּמִים הָהֵם, נְאֻם־יהוה: נָתַתִּי אֶת־תּוֹרָתִי בְּקִרְבָּם, וְעַל־לִבָּם אֶכְתֳבֶנָּה, וְהָיִיתִי לָהֶם לֵאלֹהִים, וְהֵמָּה יִהְיוּ־לִי לְעָם.

Ki zot habrit asher echrot et beit Yisrael acharey ha-yamim ha-hem, ne'oom Adonai. Natati et Torati b'kirbam, v'al leebam echtoveynah v'hayiti lahem l'Elohim, v'haymah yihiyoo-li l'am.

This is the covenant I will make with the House of Israel in time to come, says the Eternal One: I will put My teaching within them, and engrave it on their hearts; I will be their God, and they shall be My people.

הוֹדוּ לַיהוה כִּי־טוֹב, כִּי לְעוֹלָם חַסְדּוֹ.

Hodoo l'Adonai ki tov, ki le-olam chasdo.

Give thanks to the Eternal One, who is good, whose love is ever-lasting.

CANDLE CEREMONY 3

Lighting two or more candles, the baby's parents say:

We present our child to be initiated into the house of Israel and the Covenant of Candles.

אוֹר חָדָשׁ עַל צִיּוֹן תָּאִיר.

Ohr chadash al Tziyon ta-ir.

Let a new light shine in Zion.
Today we dedicate a new life to Israel.
We share new dreams and new hopes.
We trust this infant's years will be fruitful and good,
And that the glow of love and friendship will fill her days.

We give her the gift of tradition: a heritage of strength and scholarship, of humor and quiet heroism, of love of Torah and love of humanity. This child need never wonder who she is or where she belongs. She is firmly anchored in time, and her life is forever bound up with the life of her people. May we always help her to remember this.

יִתֵּן יהוה אֶת־הָאִשָּׁה הַבָּאָה אֶל־בֵּיתֶךָ כְּרָחֵל וּכְלֵאָה אֲשֶׁר בָּנוּ שְׁתֵּיהֶם
אֶת־בֵּית יִשְׂרָאֵל. (רות ד, יא)

*Yiten Adonai et ha-isha ha-ba'ah el beytecha k'Rachel u-che-Leah,
asher banoo shtayhem et beit Yisrael.*

May the Lord make the woman who is coming into your house like Rachel and Leah, both of whom built up the house of Israel. (Ruth 4:11)

The baby's parents continue:

> Build us a Jew, who will bring honor to the names of our
>   matriarchs.
> Bestow upon her their qualities of nobility, beauty, strength, and
>   gentility.
> May she be like Ruth a fountain of our faith.
> May she be like Golda a pillar of our people.
> Instill in her the love of learning.
> Grant her the joy of marriage.
> Teach her to have compassion upon all life,
> that she be blessed with the three-fold blessing of Torah, *chuppah*,
>   and *ma'asim tovim*.

CANDLE CEREMONY 4

Those participating in the welcoming ceremony read responsively,
with the parents holding their daughter and starting:

> Light is a symbol of the Divine
> Adonai is my light and my salvation
> Light is the symbol of the Divine within us
> The human spirit is the light of the Lord
>
> Light is the symbol of the divine law
> For the *mitzvah* is a lamp and the Torah a light
> Light is a symbol of Israel's mission
> I, the Lord, have made you a people of covenant, a light to the
>   nations.

Parents read:

> Today you startle easily, _____ [child's name]. We
> light this candle of the covenant, praying that you will always be
> open to surprise. Today your eyes are filled with wonder when you
> gaze at the world. May you forever be filled with wonder at the
> everyday miracles of life.
>
> _____ , today you cry out when you feel the

pain of loneliness, of cold, of hunger. We light this candle of the covenant praying that your own pain will soon ease and yet, that you will still cry out to help correct the injustices of this world, to help clothe the naked, and to help feed the hungry, to befriend those who are alone.

Today your hand tightly grasps our finger, eager for the connection. We light this candle of the covenant praying that you will always reach out to others. In the same way, may you grasp hold of learning and grow in knowledge, wisdom, and spirit.

Today, _____, we celebrate that you bring new light and warmth to our home. We light these candles to celebrate your life and the hope that you bring to your family and to our world. We thank God for the gift of your life. We add our light to yours.

Then the parents light two or more candles.

2. *Brit Mikvah*: Immersion in the Waters of Life— two *mikvah* ceremonies

What substance is more elemental and richer in symbolism—especially for women—than water? Water is the substance from which all life is thought to have begun. Without it there is no life. Before there was life, before there were earth, plants, animals, or human beings, according to the Torah, there was water. God's first three steps of creation, according to the opening lines of Genesis, were to create the heavens as distinct from the seas, to move the waters, and, from where there was no longer water, to form land.

For Jewish women water is a particularly potent symbol. The tides of the sea are ruled by the moon, whose waxing and waning is the basis of each Jewish month, and whose cycle reminds us of our own monthly cycle that permits the creation of life, and then washes away the preparations when there is no new life to sustain, only to begin the woman's month anew by building up the physical foundation again.

That cycle is at the core of what is the essential *mitzvah,* or commandment, unique to Jewish women, the *mikvah.* A *mikvah* is a specially constructed ritual bath containing a specified amount of rain or water from another natural, moving source, into which observant married Jewish women immerse themselves each month after their menstrual period has ended, and before they again take up sexual intimacy with their husbands and the possibility of creating new life.

Jewish brides go to *mikvah* shortly before their wedding, and Chasidic men immerse in *mikvah* before the Sabbath and important Jewish holidays, particularly Yom Kippur. Why Yom Kippur? Because people immerse in *mikvah* in their effort to attain a high level of spiritual purity and awareness. *Mikvah* isn't about getting cleaned off physically—women are required to bathe beforehand and to inspect every inch of their bodies to ensure that they are clean and free from obstruction before they enter the *mikvah.* Converts to Judaism, both female and male, are required to immerse in *mikvah* as a further illustration of its role as a symbol of spiritual birth and renewal. Traditional Jewish literature refers to *mikvah* as *mayim chayim,* the waters of life. *Mikvah* is also the closest physical parallel to circumcision, as both rituals relate to sexuality and the organs God gave us so that we can give life.

While Orthodox women have always gone to *mikvah* as part of their commitment to Jewish observance, today a growing number of liberal Jewish women are reclaiming *mikvah* as their own and seeing it not as a patriarchal labeling of menstruation as a period of impurity, but as a uniquely Jewish, uniquely female way to mark the ebb and the flow of time and of life.

Many modern Jews associate a baby's immersion in water so strongly with baptism that they feel a deep aversion to the notion of making it part of a Jewish welcoming ceremony. And that is understandable, given that we are a small minority living amid an overwhelmingly Christian culture, which has used baptism as a symbol of its faith since it first became distinct from Judaism. But it's important to consider not giving up a ritual that is, in its deepest and most authentic sense, ours as Jews—particularly ours as Jewish women.

The Talmud teaches us that *mikvah* was one of the three rituals performed by the Israelites in the desert on their way to Israel that permitted their entry into the covenant. The other two were circumcision for the men and bringing sacrificial offerings to God. The medieval Jewish commentator known as the Meiri quotes an opinion saying that when Abraham was circumcised and entered the covenant, which is the basis of *brit milah* for boys, Sarah was ritually immersed in water to enter the covenant. It seems that it is time to follow Sarah's example.

Should you choose immersion as the ritual marking the covenant for your daughter, you'll need to find a good-sized portable tub or deep bowl to fill with water. You can use tap water but, since a true *mikvah* contains natural, untreated rainwater, it would be an enhancement of the ritual if you can collect rain or water from a natural, moving source like a nearby river or the ocean. Short of that, bottled spring water can also serve well.

As one of the baby's parents holds her, naked, the other parent might hold the vessel of water. Or you can rest the vessel on a table and both hold the baby as you dip her into the waters of life. She should be dipped as deeply as she can be into the vessel you're using. While Jewish law requires total submersion in *mikvah* waters for conversion, which means that parents converting their infant have to completely let go for a moment, there is no such requirement when using a mini-*mikvah* during a baby's welcoming ceremony. So even if you are using a deep vessel, you will probably want to dip the baby in up to her chest or neck, but no further. Remember to have a towel nearby to wrap the baby in as soon as she comes out of the water. You may also want to designate a friend or relative who will quickly redress the baby in warm clothes after her immersion and then hand her back to you as you continue with the ceremony.

MIKVAH CEREMONY 1

One of the baby's parents or the welcoming ceremony leader can read this *midrash* created by Rabbi Michael Strassfeld and Sharon Strassfeld:

> At first God created many worlds but destroyed them when he saw their imperfections. Finally God created a world with human beings, but though they tried, they constantly failed in their attempts to get closer to heaven. After a while they grew tired and ceased struggling. So God created death and killed every living thing and created everything anew. But God grew tired of always starting at the beginning again, seeing mankind do exactly the same thing, struggling with no memory, no inherited wisdom.
>
> God looked and saw that the world was too imperfect and God decided to create birth, the womb, generations, parents and children, progress and history. But first God created a flood to come upon the earth to make a new beginning, and He caused life to enter the ark/womb by twos—X and Y, male and female.
>
> And the ark was surrounded by water and darkness. Behold, after nine months, which was 277 days, the waters dropped and the ark sent forth life into the world, and it did not return and the umbilical cord between life and the ark was broken. Life left a state of rest—the word *Noach* in Hebrew—and became alive.
>
> God made a promise that though death should remain, life would never cease and so God took part of the line called horizon, which marks the sacred place where the earth meets heaven. And God bent it and placed it in the sky and called it rainbow. And God said: "This rainbow shall be a sign of the everlasting renewal of life and whenever you see a straight line swelling, like a pregnant woman, like a dough filled with yeast, or like this rainbow, you shall know that I will keep my covenant."
>
> And so, when people see these things, they will know that life is ever renewing and they will feel enclosed and secure once more in the womb of God, the Mother of all Creation, and say:

קָדוֹשׁ קָדוֹשׁ קָדוֹשׁ יהוה צְבָאוֹת מְלֹא כָל הָאָרֶץ כְּבוֹדוֹ.

Kadosh kadosh kadosh Adonai tzva'ot m'lo chol ha-aretz kvodo.

Holy Wholly Holy is the Creator of Hosts,
the whole earth is pregnant, full of God's glory.

Parents, ritual leader, and others may read one or more of these further selections relating to water and *mikvah:*

How precious is Your constant love, O God.
We take shelter under Your wings.
We feast in the abundance of Your house.
You give us to drink from Your stream of delights.
With You is the fountain of life.
In Your light we are bathed in light.
(Psalm 36:8–10)

How fair are your tents, O Jacob,
Your dwellings, O Israel!
Like palm-groves that stretch out,
Like gardens beside a river,
Like aloes planted by the Lord,
Like cedars beside the water;
Water shall flow from his branches,
And his seed shall be in many waters.
(Numbers 24:5–7)

Blessed is the person who trusts in the Lord,
And whose trust the Lord is.
For he shall be as a tree planted by the waters,
And that spreads out its roots by the river,
And shall not see when heat comes,
But its foliage shall be luxuriant;
And shall not be anxious in the year of drought,
Neither shall cease from yielding fruit.
(Jeremiah 17:7–8)

Parents pour the *mikvah* water from a cup or bottle into the vessel and say:

> Behold, God is my salvation;
> I will trust, and will not be afraid;
> For God the Lord is my strength and song;
> And Adonai is become my salvation.
> Therefore with joy shall you draw water
> Out of the wells of salvation.
> And in that day shall you say:
> Give thanks unto the Lord, proclaim Adonai's name,
> Declare Adonai's doings among the peoples,
> Make mention that Adonai's name is exalted.
> Sing unto the Lord; for Adonai hath done gloriously;
> This is made known in all the earth.
> Cry aloud and shout, thou inhabitants of Zion,
> For great is the Holy One of Israel in the midst of you.
> (Isaiah 12:2–6)

Parents recite this blessing before immersing their daughter:

בָּרוּךְ אַתָּה יהוה, אֱלֹהֵינוּ מֶלֶךְ הָעוֹלָם, אֲשֶׁר קִדְּשָׁנוּ בְּמִצְוֹתָיו וְצִוָּנוּ עַל הַמִּקְוֶה.

Baruch Atah Adonai, Eloheynoo Melech ha-olam, asher kidshanoo b'mitzvotav vitzivanoo al ha-mikvah.

Blessed are You Lord our God, Creator of the universe, who has sanctified us through Your commandments, and commanded us about immersion.

Everyone responds:

> The Lord is the *mikvah*/hope of Israel!
> All who forsake You shall be put to shame,
> Those in the land who turn from You
> Shall be doomed men
> For they have forsaken the Lord,
> The Fount of living waters.
> (Jeremiah 17:13)

The parents then continue:

בָּרוּךְ אַתָּה יהוה, אֱלֹהֵינוּ מֶלֶךְ הָעוֹלָם, אֲשֶׁר קִדְּשָׁנוּ בְּמִצְוֹתָיו וְצִוָּנוּ
לְהַכְנִיסָהּ בִּבְרִיתָהּ שֶׁל שָׂרָה אִמֵּנוּ.

Baruch Atah Adonai, Eloheynoo Melech ha-olam, asher kidshanoo
b'mitzvotav vitzivanoo lehachnisa b'vritah shel Sarah imaynoo.

Blessed are You, Lord our God, Creator of the universe, who has
sanctified us through Your commandments and commanded us
to enter our daughters into the covenant of Sarah our mother.

The baby girl is then dipped into the *mikvah* water. Guests respond:

כְּשֵׁם שֶׁנִּכְנְסָה לַבְּרִית, כֵּן תִּכָּנֵס לְתוֹרָה וּלְחֻפָּה וּלְמַעֲשִׂים טוֹבִים.

K'shem she-nichnesah la-brit, ken tikaness l'Torah u-lechuppah u-
lema'asim tovim.

Even as this child has entered into the covenant, so may she enter
into the Torah, the marriage canopy, and good deeds.

Parents continue:

בָּרוּךְ אַתָּה יהוה, אֱלֹהֵינוּ מֶלֶךְ הָעוֹלָם, אֲשֶׁר קִדֵּשׁ יְדִיד מִבֶּטֶן וְכוֹנַנְתָּ
בְּרִית זוֹ עִם עַמְּךָ יִשְׂרָאֵל כַּכָּתוּב: "וְזָרַקְתִּי עֲלֵיכֶם מַיִם טְהוֹרִים
וּטְהַרְתֶּם... וְנָתַתִּי לָכֶם לֵב חָדָשׁ וְרוּחַ חֲדָשָׁה אֶתֵּן בְּקִרְבְּכֶם". שֶׁכָּל
טְבִילָה תִּהְיֶה זֵכֶר לְיוֹם זֶה וְסִימָן לְצֶאֱצָאֶיהָ הָעֲתִידִים לָבוֹא. בִּשְׂכַר
זֹאת אֵל חַי, צוּרֵנוּ צַוֵּה לְהַצִּיל יְדִידוּת שְׁאֵרֵנוּ מִשַּׁחַת. לְמַעַן בְּרִית
מִקְוָה אֲשֶׁר טָבַלְנוּ טַפֵּנוּ. בָּרוּךְ אַתָּה יהוה, כּוֹרֵת הַבְּרִית.

Baruch Atah Adonai, Eloheynoo Melech ha-olam, asher kidesh yedid
mibeten v'chonanta brit zo im amecha Yisrael kakatoov "v'zarakti
alechem mayim tahorim oo-tehartem ... v'natati lachem lev
chadash v'ruach chadash etayn b'kirbachem." She-kol tevilah
yehiyeh zecher l'yom zeh v'siman le-tse-e-tsa-eha ha-atidim lavoh.
Bischar zot El chai tzoraynoo tzaveh lehatzil yedidoot she'ayraynoo
mishachat. Lema'an brit mikvah asher tavalnoo tapaynoo. Baruch
Atah Adonai koret habrit.

Blessed are You Lord our God, Creator of the universe, who did sanctify the well-beloved from the womb, and established this covenant with Your people Israel, as it is written: "And I will sprinkle clean water upon you and you shall be clean…A new heart also will I give you, and a new spirit will I put within you…" (Ezekiel 36:25–26).

That every immersion shall be a remembrance of this day, and a sign of future generations. On this account, O living God our rock, give command to deliver from destruction your beloved people, for the sake of the covenant of *mikvah* for which we have immersed our children. Blessed are You, Lord our God, who establishes the covenant.

MIKVAH CEREMONY 2

As the baby is immersed in water already poured into a *mikvah* vessel, her parents say:

O God and God of our ancestors, may the life of this child, _____ , be one of happiness, goodness, and wisdom. Grant that she may seek peace and justice, and pursue an end to strife among her fellow men and women. May she spread light on all who know her. Strengthen us to guide our daughter in the path of our Torah and its beliefs, and towards independence. Help us to lead her in the footsteps of the great leaders of Israel, men and women whose deeds continue to shine across the ages of our people.

May the Lord bless you and keep you.
May the Lord make His face shine upon you and be gracious to you.
May the Lord turn His face to you and give you peace.

Alternative:

May the Creator of all life bless you and keep you.
May the Creator make Her face shine upon you and be gracious to
    you.
May the Creator turn Her face to you and give you peace.

3. *Brit Rechitzah*: Welcoming into the Covenant with Hand- or Footwashing

Genesis tells us about the story of Abraham and his circumcision. Soon after Abraham and his son Ishmael were circumcised, and as Abraham was recovering, three messengers appeared before him.

Abraham greeted them eagerly, and as a sign of hospitality offered them water and washed their feet. In a desert culture where water is the most precious commodity of life, using water for washing shows trust that the Eternal will always provide abundance. Because Abraham so eagerly welcomed his guests, God promised to sustain Abraham's descendants by providing for them in their desert wanderings.

Just as Abraham provided water to his visitors, God provided the Israelites with special waters of sustenance as they made their journey through the desert from Egypt to Sinai, and then to the Promised Land. These waters from the Well of Miriam—which followed the prophetess wherever she went in the desert, according to *midrash*—satisfied every thirst, both physical and spiritual. They existed because of Miriam and then, when she died, they disappeared.

Washing hands is also a symbol of ritual purification before every meal for observant Jews, who wash their hands before eating, each time thanking God in a formal blessing for commanding them to do so.

Using water as a symbol of God's promise to the Jewish people, some families elect to gently wash their new daughter's hands or feet in a basin of water during the covenantal part of her welcoming ceremony. Living water collected from stream, ocean, or rain is optimal for use in this ceremony. Barring access to that, bottled spring water may be used.

The water can be poured into the basin as the opening part of this ritual. A special cup, particularly if the family has one specially designated for ritual handwashing, may be used to pour the water in. If one isn't already in the family and this is the ritual being used to welcome your daughter, then it is a lovely occasion for which to buy a cup that will become her own as she grows up. You can note this gift to her as you begin her *brit rechitzah*.

A parent or the ritual leader should say:

> When Abraham and Sarah welcomed honored guests, they offered water to drink and washed the visitors' feet. In the same way we welcome our daughter into this world and into the covenant, with food and drink and by washing her feet. We welcome you, _____, into the holy covenant by washing your feet.
>
> Our prayer for you, _____, is that in all your future journeys you find guidance and sustenance in God's care and in *mayim chayim*, the living waters that Judaism offers to all who draw from the well of our tradition.

בָּרוּךְ אַתָּה יהוה, אֱלֹהֵינוּ מֶלֶךְ הָעוֹלָם, זוֹכֵר הַבְּרִית.

Baruch Atah Adonai, Eloheinu Melech ha'olam, zocher ha-brit.

Blessed are You, Adonai our God, Ruler of the universe, who is mindful of the covenant.

בָּרוּךְ אַתָּה יהוה, אֱלֹהֵינוּ מֶלֶךְ הָעוֹלָם, זוֹכֵר הַבְּרִית בִּרְחִיצַת רַגְלָיִם.

Baruch Atah Adonai, Eloheinu Melech ha'olam, zocher ha-brit b'rechitzat raglayim.

Blessed are You, Adonai our God, Ruler of the universe, who is mindful of the covenant through the washing of the feet.

Wash the baby's feet in a basin of spring or other natural water.

Alternative blessing while washing the baby's feet or hands:

בָּרוּךְ אַתָּה יהוה, מְקוֹר מַיִם חַיִּים הַמְחַיֶּה נֶפֶשׁ כָּל חָי.

Baruch Atah Adonai, Mekor mayim chayim, ham'chayeh nefesh kol chai.

Blessed are You, Source of living water, who revives the souls of all that live.

For concluding a *mikvah* or footwashing ritual:

Blessing of Peace

MARCIA FALK, FROM *THE BOOK OF BLESSINGS*

נִשְׁאַל מֵעֵין הַשָּׁלוֹם:

יִזַּל כַּטַּל,

יֵעָרֹף כַּמָּטָר הַשָּׁלוֹם,

וְתִמָּלֵא הָאָרֶץ שָׁלוֹם

כַּמַּיִם לַיָּם מְכַסִּים.

נְבָרֵךְ אֶת עֵין הַחַיִּים

וְכֹה נִתְבָּרֵךְ.

Nish'al mey'eyn hashalom:
Yizal katal,
ya'arof kamatar hashalom,
v'timla ha'aretz shalom
kamayim layam m'khasim.

N'vareykh et eyn hahayim
v'khoh nitbareykh.

Eternal wellspring of peace—
may we be drenched with the longing for peace
that we may give ourselves over
as the earth to the rain, to the dew,
until peace overflows our lives
as living waters overflow the seas.

As we bless the source of life
so we are blessed.

4. *Brit Tallit*: Enfolding Her in the Covenant

A *tallit*, the large, fringed shawl that Jewish men and a growing number of women wear in prayer, is many things. It is, at its simplest level, a traditional prayer shawl whose fringes, called *tzitzit*, are reminders of God's commanded *mitzvot*, or obligations. We wrap the *tzitzit* around our fingers to literally touch it to the letters of the Torah if we are honored with an *aliyah*, called to bless the Torah during synagogue services. In traditional congregations we wrap them around our fingers and hold them high, toward the ark, during certain moments of the synagogue service.

A *tallit* is also often used as a wedding canopy, or *chuppah*, suspended from a pole at each corner. It is a special article of religious expression for Jews, passed down lovingly from one generation to the next. And it is a sign of maturity: A young man, in Orthodox circles, first wears a *tallit* when he marries. In non-Orthodox circles, young men and women often receive *tallitot* (plural for *tallit*) when they become bar and bat mitzvah. A growing number of liberal Jewish women have begun wearing *tallitot* and exploring the emotional resonance that it can add to their prayer experience as it brings with it associations of comfort, covering, protection, warmth, and shelter.

Those who are deeply comfortable wearing large *tallitot* enfold their heads, necks, and shoulders during the standing, silent portion of the synagogue service known as the *Amidah*. Wrapped in their *tallitot*, they are separated from the congregation even as they stand in its midst, and feel they are standing alone. They are alone with their prayers, alone with the meditations of their hearts, alone with their effort to find a sense of close connection to the Creator.

With the advent of do-it-yourself-Judaism in the late 1960s, leaders of the *havurah* movement and others began to expand on what a *tallit* could look like. In the past it had been a garment woven of wool, with black or dark blue stripes running down the sides. Now there were new notions of what a *tallit* could be, and today they can be found with many different appearances, from those that are modeled on the traditional look of a *tallit* to some that are very feminine, like hand-painted silk and more the size of a neck scarf than the traditional shawl. What they all share, however, is the essence of the *tallit*—the ritually tied *tzitzit* hanging from each corner.

You can incorporate a *tallit* into the covenantal part of your daughter's welcoming ritual. Her father's *tallit* may be used or, if her mother regularly wears one, it would be significant to use that, representing the transmission of a relatively new Jewish ritual practice from mother to daughter. If the couple used a *tallit* as their wedding canopy, then that would be the most meaningful one of all in which to enfold their new child. Using a *tallit* during your daughter's welcoming ceremony symbolizes the way you hope she will be surrounded by and enfolded within the covenant, her community, and Jewish tradition.

If you like the idea of integrating a *tallit* into your daughter's welcoming ceremony but don't want to make it the focus, you may have your daughter brought into the room already wrapped in a prayer shawl. If the *tallit* is to be a focus of her welcome into the covenant, the baby should be wrapped in it as an integral part of the ceremony in front of your assembled guests. The *tallit* may either be spread out on a sofa or coffee table, or, more dramatically, be unfurled and suspended by two honored guests over the heads of the parents and their new child as they stand together, before laying it down.

This *tallit* ceremony is adapted from the Conservative movement's rabbis' manual:

The baby is placed at the center of a large *tallit*. Each of the four corners of the *tallit* is held by a parent or honored guest—this is a great place in the ceremony to involve even young brothers and sisters of the baby (an adult can recite the verse of Psalms for the child), aunts, uncles, grandparents, and close friends.

As each corner is folded over or around the baby, participants recite the following verses from Psalms:

מַה־יָּקָר חַסְדְּךָ אֱלֹהִים, וּבְנֵי אָדָם בְּצֵל כְּנָפֶיךָ יֶחֱסָיוּן.

Mah-yakar hasdecha Elohim, oovnay adam batzel k'nafecha yechesayoon.

How precious is Your constant love, O God; You shelter us under Your wings. (Psalm 36:8)

בָּרְכִי נַפְשִׁי אֶת־יהוה, יהוה אֱלֹהַי גָּדַלְתָּ מְּאֹד, הוֹד וְהָדָר לָבָשְׁתָּ. עֹטֶה־אוֹר כַּשַּׂלְמָה, נוֹטֶה שָׁמַיִם כַּיְרִיעָה. תְּשַׁלַּח רוּחֲךָ יִבָּרֵאוּן, וּתְחַדֵּשׁ פְּנֵי אֲדָמָה.

Borchi nafshi et-Adonai, Adonai Elohai gadalta me'od, hod v'hadar levashta. Oteh-ohr kesalmah, noteh shamayim k'yiriah. Tishalach ruchachah yibareyoon, ootichadesh pnai adamah.

Let all my being praise Adonai, who is clothed in splendor and majesty. Wrapped in light like a garment, You unfold the heavens like a curtain. You send forth Your spirit and there is creation; You renew the face of the earth. (Psalm 104:1–2, 30)

יֹשֵׁב בְּסֵתֶר עֶלְיוֹן, בְּצֵל שַׁדַּי יִתְלוֹנָן. אֹמַר לַיהוה מַחְסִי וּמְצוּדָתִי, אֱלֹהַי אֶבְטַח־בּוֹ ... בְּאֶבְרָתוֹ יָסֶךְ לָךְ, וְתַחַת־כְּנָפָיו תֶּחְסֶה, צִנָּה וְסֹחֵרָה אֲמִתּוֹ.

Yoshev b'seter eylyon, betzel shaddai yitlonan. Omar l'Adonai, machsee oo-metzudati, Elohai evtach-bo ... b'evrato yasech lach, vtachat-knafav techseh, tzinah v'socherah amitoh.

For you who dwell in the shelter of the Most High
And abide in the protection of Shaddai—
I say of Adonai, my refuge and stronghold,
My God in whom I trust ...
God will shelter you,
You will find refuge,
For God's fidelity is an encircling shield.
(After Psalm 91:1–2, 4)

יהוה יִשְׁמָרְךָ מִכָּל־רָע, יִשְׁמֹר אֶת־נַפְשֶׁךָ. יהוה יִשְׁמָר־צֵאתְךָ וּבוֹאֶךָ, מֵעַתָּה וְעַד־עוֹלָם.

Adonai yishmorcha mikol-ra, yishmor et-nafshecha. Adonai yishmor tzaytcha oo-voecha, mayatah v'ad-olam.

Adonai is your protection,
a guardian at your right hand.
Adonai will guard you from all harm;
and guard your life.

Adonai guards your going and coming,
now and forever.
(Psalm 121:5, 7–8)

The parents or the rabbi continue:

Our God and God of our ancestors, we thank You for the gift of our
daughter/this child. May she grow to maturity embraced by God's
love and the love of all who know her. May the *Shechinah*, God's
sheltering presence, be with her always. May the words of Torah surround her. Clothed in majesty and honor, may she always look to
the future with joy.

Continue to the naming part of your daughter's welcoming ceremony.

An alternative blessing after the baby is wrapped:

בָּרוּךְ אַתָּה יהוה, אֱלֹהֵינוּ מֶלֶךְ הָעוֹלָם, אֲשֶׁר קִדְּשָׁנוּ בְּמִצְוֹתָיו וְצִוָּנוּ
לְהַכְנִיסָהּ בִּבְרִיתוֹ שֶׁל עַם יִשְׂרָאֵל.

*Baruch Atah Adonai, Eloheynoo Melech ha-olam, asher kidshanoo
b'mitzvotav vitzivanoo lehachnisa b'vrito shel am Yisrael.*

Praised be You, Adonai our God, Ruler of the universe, who has
made us holy with Your commandments and has commanded us
to make this child enter into the covenant of Torah.

As we wrap you in this *tallit,* _____ , so may your
life be wrapped in justice and righteousness. As we embrace you
today, so may you embrace your tradition and your people.

5. *Brit Kehillah:* Entering the Covenant by Walking through the Community

This ceremony comes at the suggestion of Rabbi Nina Beth Cardin,
who has been a pivotal figure in the creation of new Jewish rituals for
women over the past twenty-five years. She suggests wrapping your
new daughter in a *tallit* and then passing her through your gathered

relatives and friends—who are standing in two parallel lines—as a sign of the *brit*. Your daughter might be passed from person to person down one line and up the other, or, if you are concerned about her exposure to germs or want the assembled guests to be holding candles, then she can be carried between the two lines by her parents.

Several elements of tradition inspired Cardin to develop this concept, including one of the ways in which God demonstrated the covenant with Abraham in the Torah. The Creator instructed Abraham to take animals and cut them in half, and then caused a fire to go between their halves as a symbol of God's promise. Walking through the two halves of the community also reminds us of the way God miraculously parted the Red Sea, permitting the Israelites to escape the Egyptian enslavers and continue on to the land that they were promised by the Creator. The idea of walking between two halves of the community is also reminiscent of a bride walking between the wedding guests on either side of her as she makes her way toward the *chuppah*. "To walk through two halves, one on either side, is like crossing a threshold to wholeness. It is something which cleanses and changes you. It is a transition," says Cardin.

This is a briefer covenantal ritual than some of the others offered earlier, one opened by a short explanation and getting the guests properly arranged with their candles lit. The walk between them should be slow and deliberate, permitting guests to have a good look at the baby as you walk her down the aisle. It can be closed with you leading everyone in a song or *niggun*, a wordless tune.

6. *Brit Havdalah:* Transitioning into the Covenant through *Havdalah*—two *havdalah* ceremonies

Shabbat has always been one of the greatest treasures belonging to the Jewish people. This day of rest, this day separated from the work of the rest of the week, this day of restoration and of focus on family and God, is also said in Jewish tradition to be one of the signs of the covenant God gave to the Jewish people.

Havdalah, which is the Hebrew word for separation, is the traditional ritual held Saturday evening after three stars have been seen in the sky, and it marks the transition from the peaceful rest and holiness of the Sabbath into the regular work week.

Some families elect to use this moment of liminality and transition to welcome their daughter into the Jewish people. Saturday night is also a nice time for a party.

HAVDALAH CEREMONY 1

In the following example, Florence Hutner and her husband, David Holmes, integrated the *brit bat* of their daughter, Miriam Eleanor, directly into the *havdalah* service.

We have chosen to welcome _____ into this covenant at the close of the Sabbath, during the ceremony of *havdalah*. *Havdalah*, which means separation, marks and sanctifies the formal end of the holy time that is Shabbat and the transition into the routine of the rest of the week. This *brit bat* formalizes and celebrates our daughter's transition from not being into being, our transformation into parents, and _____'s inclusion among the Jewish people. As the ritual of *havdalah* makes holy the moment of leaving the specialness of Shabbat and returning to the ordinariness of the work week, so this *brit bat* sanctifies _____'s arrival into this world and her membership in the community of Israel.

Havdalah softens the departure from the Sabbath sensuously, comforting us with lingering echoes of Shabbat. We chant prayers and blessings, taste a cup of wine, savor the aroma of sweet spices, and gaze at the flame of the special braided candle as it is lit, then quenched. Tonight, each of these actions is enhanced by the knowledge that _____ is learning day by day to use her senses to explore more of the world around her: In the womb, she heard my voice. After birth, she knew me first only by smell and taste, gradually she became better able to focus and recognize people and objects by sight. Now she also reaches out to touch things.

To counter the darkness that follows Shabbat, we now kindle the *havdalah* candle whose strands are woven together to create a fuller flame, just as the many people and traditions that come together in _____ enrich her life.

We recite this blessing over a full cup of wine, a symbol of joy.

בָּרוּךְ אַתָּה יהוה, אֱלֹהֵינוּ מֶלֶךְ הָעוֹלָם, בּוֹרֵא פְּרִי הַגָּפֶן.

Baruch Atah Adonai, Eloheinu Melech ha'olam, borei p'ri hagafen.

Blessed are You, God, Ruler of the universe, who creates the fruit of the vine.

Drink from the kiddush cup.

These spices carry the sweet scent of the day of rest and remind us that the Sabbath will return again next week.

בָּרוּךְ אַתָּה יהוה, אֱלֹהֵינוּ מֶלֶךְ הָעוֹלָם, בּוֹרֵא מִינֵי בְשָׂמִים.

Baruch Atah Adonai, Eloheinu Melech ha'olam, borei minei v'samim.

Blessed are You, God, Ruler of the universe, who creates spices.

The spice box is passed around for everyone to smell.

According to legend, as night descended at the end of the world's first Shabbat, Adam and Eve feared and wept. The God showed them how to make fire, and, by its light and warmth, to dispel the darkness.

בָּרוּךְ אַתָּה יהוה, אֱלֹהֵינוּ מֶלֶךְ הָעוֹלָם, בּוֹרֵא מְאוֹרֵי הָאֵשׁ.

Baruch Atah Adonai, Eloheinu Melech ha'olam, borei me'orei ha'eish.

Blessed are You, God, Ruler of the universe, who creates the lights of fire.

Raise up the *havdalah* candle.

Just as Shabbat is separate from the rest of the week, so is _____ a very special person and so may she distinguish herself among Israel and the nations.

בָּרוּךְ אַתָּה יהוה, אֱלֹהֵינוּ מֶלֶךְ הָעוֹלָם, הַמַּבְדִּיל בֵּין קֹדֶשׁ לְחֹל, בֵּין אוֹר לְחֹשֶׁךְ, בֵּין יוֹם הַשְּׁבִיעִי לְשֵׁשֶׁת יְמֵי הַמַּעֲשֶׂה. בָּרוּךְ אַתָּה יהוה, הַמַּבְדִּיל בֵּין קֹדֶשׁ לְחֹל.

Baruch Atah Adonai, Eloheinu Melech ha'olam, hamavdil bein kodesh l'chol, bein or l'choshech, bein yom hash'vi'i l'shaishet yemei hama'aseh. Baruch Atah Adonai, hamavdil bein kodesh l'chol.

Blessed are You, God, Ruler of the universe, who separates the holy from the profane, light from darkness, and the seventh day of rest from the six days of labor. Blessed are You, God, Ruler of the universe, who separates the holy from the ordinary.

To conclude the *havdalah* ritual, we now quench the candle.

Dip the candle flame into the wine or grape juice. Then continue:

We have just made the transition from Shabbat to the new week. We will now formally celebrate _____'s embarking on life as part not only of her immediate family but also of her extended family, the people of Israel. To symbolize her joining the community of Israel, we touch her hand to the Torah, the fundamental teachings that sustain Israel as the Jewish people keep and observe those teachings.

We have many reasons to thank and praise God on this occasion.

בָּרוּךְ אַתָּה יהוה, אֱלֹהֵינוּ מֶלֶךְ הָעוֹלָם, אֲשֶׁר קִדְּשָׁנוּ בְּמִצְוֹתָיו וְצִוָּנוּ עַל קִדּוּשׁ הַחַיִּים.

Baruch Atah Adonai, Eloheinu Melech ha'olam, asher kidshanu b'mitzvotav v'tzivanu al kidush hachayim.

Blessed are You, God, Ruler of the universe, who commands us to sanctify life.

בָּרוּךְ אַתָּה יהוה, אֱלֹהֵינוּ מֶלֶךְ הָעוֹלָם, זוֹכֵר הַבְּרִית וְנֶאֱמָן בִּבְרִיתוֹ וְקַיָּם בְּמַאֲמָרוֹ.

Baruch Atah Adonai, Eloheinu Melech ha'olam, zocher ha-brit v'ne'eman b'vrito v'kayam bima'amaro.

Blessed are You, God, Ruler of the universe, who remembers the covenant and who is steadfastly faithful in Your covenant, keeping Your promise.

בָּרוּךְ אַתָּה יהוה, אֱלֹהֵינוּ מֶלֶךְ הָעוֹלָם, אֲשֶׁר קִדְּשָׁנוּ בְּמִצְוֹתָיו וְצִוָּנוּ לְהַכְנִיסָהּ בִּבְרִיתוֹ שֶׁל עַם יִשְׂרָאֵל.

Baruch Atah Adonai, Eloheinu Melech ha'olam, asher kidshanu b'mitzvotav v'tzivanu l'hachnisa biv'rito shel am Yisrael.

Blessed are You, God, Ruler of the universe, who has made us holy through Your commandments and commanded us to bring our daughters into the covenant of the people of Israel.

HAVDALAH CEREMONY 2

The second example of a *havdalah brit* ceremony is from David Grupper and Hedda Kafka when they welcomed their daughter, Naava Tzipora. They focused on the transitions made explicit by *havdalah* and by welcoming a new life into their family, and they used the kiddush cup from which they had both drunk under their wedding canopy.

They began this part of their daughter's welcoming ceremony by saying:

> For thousands of years the Sabbath has been a sign of covenantal commitment that has inspired generations of our people with the drive to creativity and the values of human dignity. Creativity and human dignity are not achieved in the moments of high anxiety, but in the quiet, the relaxation, the peace and the love that are fostered by the Sabbath. The time during which we permit ourselves the luxury of leaving our daily labors and concerns is vital to our own well-being and to the well-being of our family.
>
> We hope that our daughter may learn this most important concept of Shabbat and understand how to relax from her toils to appreciate and enjoy the beauty of life around her. It is appropriate, therefore, that on this Saturday night, remembering the Sabbath that is ending, that we bring our daughter before this community so that she may be linked to the covenant of the people of Israel.

בָּרוּךְ אַתָּה יהוה, אֱלֹהֵינוּ מֶלֶךְ הָעוֹלָם, אֲשֶׁר קִדְּשָׁנוּ בְּמִצְוֹתָיו וְצִוָּנוּ לְהַכְנִיס אֶת בִּתֵּנוּ בִּבְרִית עַם יִשְׂרָאֵל.

Baruch Atah Adonai, Eloheynoo Melech ha-olam, asher kidshanoo b'mitzvotav vitzivanoo lehachnis et bitaynoo b'vrit am Yisrael.

Blessed are You, our God, who sanctified us with Your commandments and has commanded us to initiate our daughter into the covenant of the people of Israel.

Father:

In every transition, blessed is the beginning ...
As we separate from a Shabbat of peace to begin a new week;
As we separate ourselves from the last year to begin a new one;
As we separate from our original families to begin a new one;
As we remember dear departed loved ones while we sanctify new
    life;
We somberly yet joyfully recite this *havdalah* service.

Mother, lighting *havdalah* candle:

As I kindle this light, I joyfully bring my daughter into the covenant of Israel, a covenant with God, community, with ancestry, with Torah, and with life.

בָּרוּךְ אַתָּה יהוה, אֱלֹהֵינוּ מֶלֶךְ הָעוֹלָם, אֲשֶׁר קִדְּשָׁנוּ בְּמִצְוֹתָיו וְצִוָּנוּ עַל קִדּוּשׁ הַחַיִּים.

Baruch Atah Adonai, Eloheynoo Melech ha-olam, asher kidshanoo b'mitzvotav vitzivanoo al kidush hachayyim.

Blessed are You, Lord our God, Ruler of the universe, by whose *mitzvot* we are hallowed, and who commands us to sanctify life.

Father, pouring wine:

With this cup we sanctified our marriage. Today we share this cup of sweetness with our daughter.

The traditional *havdalah* ceremony is then recited. It is available in any prayer book.

One further reading appropriate for a Shabbat or *havdalah* ceremony was written by Hanna Tiferet Siegel:

Welcome Woman-Child

HANNA TIFERET SIEGEL

Welcome Woman-Child
Newborn guardian
of the sacred gift
of cycles and seasons.
Within and all around you,
Be witness to the rhythms of
surrender and renewal
faith and love
knowledge and intuition
as you awaken
to the indwelling presence of—*Shekhina.*

We welcome you
into the world
into your family
into your people.

May you know from your early days
how we dance through the spiral of
dark and light
slavery and freedom
wandering and revelation
planting and harvest
new moons and full moons
returning always to the luminous now
within the timeless refuge of Shabbat.

7. *Brit Melach*: **Recalling the Covenant with Salt[4]**

While blood is mentioned often in Torah as a sign of the covenant, it is not the only type of covenantal representation in the text. There is also specifically mentioned another type of covenant—the *brit melach*, or salt covenant, which is related to those belonging to the priestly tribe and their families, including their sons and their daughters. The creator of this contemporary salt ritual suggests that the *brit melach* be held on the baby's eighth day just as a *brit milah* is, and writes that "We face a new cycle (of history) with a sense of security, saying that although it is in God's hands, we have faith that yes, our people will choose the covenant, will choose to serve, and will choose to survive. With the priestly clan gone, we are now 'a nation of priests.' We are all part of the salt covenant."

The *brit melach* focuses not only on salt, but also on the five senses and the soul given to the baby by God, using representations of the elements that were part of priests' induction into Temple service in Jerusalem. The core theme of the *brit melach* is service to God. What follows is the central, covenantal section of the ritual.

The leader says:

> Before us sit the parents of this daughter of Israel, in the seat of the prophets. Which prophets attend the entering of a new daughter into the covenant of Israel? Avigayle, the peacemaker; Devorah, the judge; Huldah, who knew the Torah that had been hidden, and who returned it to Israel; and Miriam, who foretold redemption.
>
> May your daughter be blessed with their wisdom.

The baby's mother recites:

הִנְנִי מוּכָנָה וּמְזֻמֶּנֶת לְהַכְנִיס בִּבְרִית יִשְׂרָאֵל אֶת בִּתִּי.

Hinneni moochana oo-mezoomenet lehachnis b'vrit Yisrael et biti.

Behold, I am prepared and ready to bring my daughter into the covenant of Israel.

The baby's father recites:

הִנְנִי מוּכָן וּמְזֻמָּן לְהַכְנִיס בִּבְרִית יִשְׂרָאֵל אֶת בִּתִּי.

Hinneni moochan oo-mezooman lehachnis b'vrit Yisrael et biti.

Behold, I am prepared and ready to bring my daughter into the covenant of Israel.

Both say:

בָּרוּךְ אַתָּה יהוה, אֱלֹהֵינוּ מֶלֶךְ הָעוֹלָם, אֲשֶׁר קִדְּשָׁנוּ בְּמִצְוֹתָיו וְצִוָּנוּ לְהַכְנִיסָהּ בִּבְרִיתוֹ שֶׁל אַבְרָהָם אָבִינוּ, וְשָׂרָה אִמֵּנוּ.

Baruch Atah Adonai, Eloheynoo Melech ha-olam, asher kidshanoo b'mitzvotav vitzivanoo lehachnisah b'vritoh shel Avraham avinoo, v'Sarah imeynoo.

Blessed are You God, Ruler of the universe, who has sanctified us with commandments and has commanded us to bring our children into the covenant of Abraham our forefather and Sarah our foremother.

Leader says:

Salt, meal, and incense are the induction of priests into service (in the holy temple in Jerusalem). We thus bring our daughters into a life of service to God.

A drop of salt water is placed on the baby's tongue.

May her tongue always speak Torah.

כִּי־אֱמֶת יֶהְגֶּה חִכִּי וְתוֹעֲבַת שְׂפָתַי רֶשַׁע.

Ki-emet yehigeh chikey v'toavat safatai reshah.

My palate will utter truth, wickedness is an abomination to my lips. (Proverbs 8:7)

A drop of salt and a few grains of meal are placed on the palms of the baby's hands.

May her hands serve God faithfully, and be always engaged in *tikkun olam,* repair of the world.

בְּאֹרַח־צְדָקָה אֲהַלֵּךְ בְּתוֹךְ נְתִיבוֹת מִשְׁפָּט.

B'orach-tzedakah ahalaych b'toch netivot mishpat.

I lead in the path of righteousness, amid the pathways of justice. (Proverbs 8:20)

A drop of salt water is placed on the baby's closed eyelids and on her ears.

May her eyes see the light of Torah, and may she be blessed to study Torah all her days; may her ears hear the truth of Torah.

אוֹר־צַדִּיקִים יִשְׂמָח וְנֵר רְשָׁעִים יִדְעָךְ.

Ohr-tzadikim yismach v'ner resha-im yidach.

The light of the righteous will rejoice, but the lamp of the wicked will flicker out. (Proverbs 13:9)

A few grains of salt are placed on the baby's feet.

May she walk before God, and be pure.

הוֹלֵךְ אֶת־חֲכָמִים יֶחְכָּם וְרֹעֶה כְסִילִים יֵרוֹעַ.

Holech et-chachamim yechkam v'roeh k'silim yayrooah.

One who walks with the wise will grow wise, but the companion of fools will be broken. (Proverbs 13:20)

Rose petals, as a stand-in for the priestly incense, are waved below the baby's nose.

May the *ruach* (spirit) of God be within her, and may her *ruach* be filled with the sweet scent of holiness.

בָּרוּךְ אַתָּה יהוה, אֱלֹהֵינוּ מֶלֶךְ הָעוֹלָם, בּוֹרֵא מִינֵי בְשָׂמִים.

Baruch Atah Adonai, Eloheynoo Melech ha-olam, borey minay v'samim.

Blessed are You, God, Ruler of the universe, who creates species of spices.

Parents recite the *shehechiyanu*:

בָּרוּךְ אַתָּה יהוה, אֱלֹהֵינוּ מֶלֶךְ הָעוֹלָם, שֶׁהֶחֱיָנוּ וְקִיְּמָנוּ וְהִגִּיעָנוּ לַזְּמַן הַזֶּה.

Baruch Atah Adonai, Eloheynoo Melech ha-olam, shechechiyanoo v'kiyimanoo v'higiyanoo la-zman ha-zeh.

Blessed are You, our God, Ruler of the universe, who has kept us alive, sustained us, and brought us to this season.

All respond:

Amen!

All proclaim loudly:

כְּשֵׁם שֶׁנִּכְנֶסֶת לַבְּרִית, כֵּן תִּכָּנֵס לְתוֹרָה וּלְחֻפָּה וּלְמַעֲשִׂים טוֹבִים.

K'shem shenichneset labrit, ken tikanes l'Torah oo-l'chuppah oo-l'ma'asim tovim.

Just as she has entered the covenant, so may she enter into the study of Torah, the marriage canopy, and the performance of good deeds.

A cup of wine is filled and the leader recites:

בָּרוּךְ אַתָּה יהוה, אֱלֹהֵינוּ מֶלֶךְ הָעוֹלָם, בּוֹרֵא פְּרִי הַגָּפֶן.

Baruch Atah Adonai, Eloheynoo Melech ha-olam, borey pri hagafen.

Blessed are You, God, Ruler of the universe, who creates the fruit of the vine.

All respond:

Amen!

בָּרוּךְ אַתָּה יהוה, אֱלֹהֵינוּ מֶלֶךְ הָעוֹלָם, אֲשֶׁר קִדֵּשׁ יְדִידָה מִבֶּטֶן, וְצִיֵּן
אוֹתָהּ לַעֲבוֹדָה. עַל כֵּן בִּשְׂכַר זֹאת, אֵל חַי, חֶלְקֵנוּ צוּרֵנוּ, צַוֵּה לְהַצִּיל
יְדִידוּת שְׁאֵרֵנוּ מִשַּׁחַת לְמַעַן בְּרִיתוֹ אֲשֶׁר שָׂם בְּתוֹכֵנוּ. אַתָּה חוֹנֵן
לְאָדָם דַּעַת, וּמְלַמֵּד לֶאֱנוֹשׁ בִּינָה. חָנֵּנוּ מֵאִתְּךָ דֵּעָה בִּינָה וְהַשְׂכֵּל.
בָּרוּךְ אַתָּה יהוה, חוֹנֵן הַדַּעַת כְּדֵי שֶׁנַּעֲבֹד אוֹתָךְ.

Baruch Atah Adonai, Eloheynoo Melech ha-olam, asher keydesh
yedidah mibeten, v'tziyeyn otah la-avodah. Al ken bischar zot, El chai,
chelkaynoo tzooreynoo, tzaveh l'hatzil yedidoot she-ehreynoo
mishachat lema'an brito asher sam betochaynoo. Atah chonen
l'adam da'at, oo-melamed leh-ehnosh binah. Choneynoo meyitcha
dey-ah bina v'haskel. Baruch Atah Adonai, chonen hada-at k'day she-
na'avood otcha.

Blessed are You, God, Ruler of the universe, who has sanctified the
beloved one from the womb and marked her for service. Therefore, as a reward for this, Living God, our Portion, our Rock, may
You issue the command to rescue the beloved soul within our
flesh from destruction for the sake of Your covenant that You have
placed within us. For humans You create the sprout of intelligence, and teach humankind understanding. From You we ask for
intelligence, wisdom, and understanding. Blessed are You, God,
who causes our intelligence in order that we can serve You.

Naming Your Daughter

It used to be that a baby's name was announced without fanfare or
fuss. Until recently, in fact, a baby's name would be announced at a
boy's *brit milah* or in synagogue when a girl's father was called to the
Torah on the Shabbat following her birth. The name would be recited within the format of a traditional prayer, and that was that. Today
the names we choose get much more public attention during our
daughters' welcoming ceremonies and at our sons' *brit milah* rituals.

Why do we treat names differently today than we did in years past? We are more conscious and aware of the multiple meanings of names, as we are about most religious rituals. When we name our child after a family member, we speak at some length about the characteristics possessed by the person for whom we are naming our child and about his or her life history. It is a way of extending the chain between the generations, *midor l'dor.*

Perhaps it is because we are a generation cut off from our Jewish past in many ways—historically from family and from a way of life that all but perished in the Holocaust, and spiritually from a religious path that may not have been taught to us as children while our parents worked to emphasize the American part of being American Jews. There are many broken links separating us from our own Jewish past, and we have had to reclaim Jewish living for ourselves, in many cases to find it as adults, to learn it intellectually and to integrate it into our hearts and souls and daily lives. Having children and dedicating ourselves to raising them as Jews can be a critical step in our own Jewish identity formation, and naming our children is a deeply important way of creating links to our birthright.

Whether we choose to give our child one name in Hebrew with which she will go out into the world, or two separate names, one English (public and secular) and the other Hebrew (private and religious), is telling. It says a great deal about our own sense of Jewish identity and how we view religiousness or spirituality within the context of our whole life. The Jewish names we pick for our child, too, say a great deal—whether they are Hebrew or Yiddish, traditional or contemporary, biblical or avant-garde.

If we are of Ashkenazic (Eastern and Central European) descent, the custom is to name our children in memory of people who have died, whose positive character traits we hope our children will grow to possess. If we are of Sephardic (Spanish, Middle Eastern, and North African) descent, the custom is to name our children after the living, usually our sons after their grandfathers and our daughters after their grandmothers.

We may use the names of our forebears directly. But often today the names of our grandparents just don't sound modern enough to suit contemporary sensibilities, so sometimes we adapt the names of the ancestors we wish to recall and honor by coming up with a name for our baby that begins with the same letter. It can work in English and in Hebrew. Our son Aryeh, for example, is named after my late and beloved uncle Artie. Our daughter Aliza, whose name in Hebrew begins with the letter *aleph*, is named for my husband's late mother, Esther, whose name in Hebrew began with the same letter.

When unable to come up with a name they like that way, some people take the personality quality they liked best about the person they're remembering and find the Hebrew word that corresponds to it to use as the name. For example, my sister and her husband, wanting to name their second son after our maternal grandfather George and paternal grandmother Bertha, named the baby Adin Boaz, using the Hebrew words for gentleness and strength in order to recall those qualities in our grandparents.

Adopted girls are often named Sarah, after the first woman to become a Jew, or Ruth, who is famous in the Bible for choosing to join her mother-in-law Naomi and the Jewish people in a great act of love, courage, and fidelity.

Whatever name we select, the process of announcing it has taken on a very self-conscious aspect in the last two decades. Naming our children has become a historical genealogical reckoning, a way of explaining who we are, of rooting ourselves in an often-neglected past, and, by extension, a way of bringing forth our own Jewish history. It is a way of reminding ourselves who we are and from where we have come. It is a way of restoring our past as a foundation for the future we hold in our arms, as we name our baby daughters. And of course, naming them is also a way of seeing into the future, telescoping our hopes for them and our own line.

One of the nicest ways to bring the past into the present at a *simchat bat* is to include in the program guide color or black-and-white photocopied pictures of the person or people for whom this new girl is being named.

A custom frequently used in welcoming ceremonies for girls is to create an acrostic by selecting a line of biblical text that begins with the same letter as each of the letters in your daughter's name, and assembling the lines in the same order as the letters of your daughter's name. When the first letter of each line is read top to bottom, they form her name. See page 165 for acrostic assistance.

There's another way to use the acrostic idea as well. Hilary Blue named her daughter Jessica Ann and gave her the Hebrew name Shira, which means song. Shira comes from a family with impressive musical lineage, which her parents described as they explained her name during her welcoming ceremony. They also went to a deeper, almost mystical level as they took each letter of Shira's Hebrew name and explained the quality it is associated with: *Shalom*, or inner peace and contentment for the letter *shin*; beauty and straightforwardness for the letter *yud*, as in *yaffa* and *yashar*; a high standard of living for the word *ramah*, height, which is associated with the letter *resh*; and wisdom and understanding in connection with the word *hacham*.

The Blues also recalled outstanding women in Jewish history whose names each begin with one letter from Shira's. The *shin*, for example, stands for Shifra, one of the two midwives in Egypt who disobeyed Pharaoh's cruel instruction to kill all newborn Israelite boys and, in the process, showed great compassion. The *yud* is the initial letter in the names Yael and Yehudith, two women who took decisive action against the enemies of their people in times of war when others around them were full of despair. It is also the first letter in the name of Yocheved, mother of Judaism's great leaders Moses, Miriam, and Aaron. The Blues used that reference to talk about their hopes for their daughter to become a mother herself. The *resh* stands for Ruth, the symbol of love and devotion, whose loyalty to her mother-in-law Naomi and her adopted people are traits to be admired. The *hay* is the initial letter of the name Hadassah, who in Persia was known as Queen Esther and whose beauty, bravery, and wisdom have made her a heroine to us today.

If you decide not to include an acrostic in your daughter's welcoming ceremony but are giving her a biblical name, you can include a passage from Torah in which the name is mentioned, or speak about the biblical foremother and the characteristics she possessed that you hope your daughter will inherit.

If your daughter is born on or near a Jewish holiday, you can speak about the Jewish women associated with those holy days as well and their positive character traits. My daughter, Aliza, for instance, was born between Purim and Passover, holidays associated with several strong women. I spoke about the way Queen Esther used her intelligence, intuition, and wholly female charm to save the Jews, and about how the wisdom of Miriam, Moses' sister, spurred her to action when she arranged for their mother to be the wet-nurse to Moses after Pharaoh's daughter had pulled him from the Nile. I spoke of Miriam as a primary actor in the drama of deliverance from Egypt.

In Judaism, a person's uniqueness is made concrete through the act of naming. Jewish tradition also tells us that parents are endowed with the holy spirit when it comes to naming their baby. As one mother said, "All of the gates of consciousness are open, and what flows is often beyond us."[5]

Below are poems and selections of text related to naming, followed by five examples of different blessings that can be used to ritually name your daughter. Traditionally, Jews are identified in religious rituals by their Hebrew name followed by their father's name, as in Sarah, daughter of Isaac. Today we generally add the mother's name to the identification, for example Sarah, daughter of Isaac and Ruth. In the naming blessings that follow, insert the baby's name, followed by her father's name and then her mother's.

Readings Related to Naming

Adapted from 1 Samuel 25:25

Like her name, so is she.

There Are Three Names

ADAPTED FROM *MIDRASH TANHUMA, PARASHAT VAYIKAHAL*

There are three names by which a person is called:
One which her father and mother call her,
And one which people call her,
And one which she earns for herself.
The best one of these is the one that she earns for herself.

Hallowing Our Namings

MARCIA FALK, FROM *THE BOOK OF BLESSINGS*

נָשִׁיר לְנִשְׁמַת כָּל שֵׁם
וּלְשֵׁם כָּל נְשָׁמָה,
נָשִׁיר לְנִשְׁמַת כָּל שֵׁם
וְלִקְדֻשַׁת כָּל נְשָׁמָה.

Nashir l'nishmat kol sheym
ulsheym kol n'shamah,
nashir l'nishmat kol sheym
v'likdushat kol n'shamah.

Let us sing the soul in every name
and the name of every soul,
let us sing the soul in every name,
the sacred name of every soul.

Each Person Has a Name

ZELDA

Each person has a name,
given her by God and
given her by father and mother.

Each person has a name given
her by her stature and her
way of smiling, and given
her by her clothes.

Each person has a name given
her by the mountains and
given her by her walls.

Each person has a name given
her by the planets and given
her by her neighbors.

Each person has a name given
her by her sins and given
her by her longing.

Each person has a name given
her by her enemies and given
her by her love.

Each person has a name given
her by her feast days and
given her by her craft.

Each person has a name given
her by the seasons of the year and given
her by her blindness.
Each person has a name given
her by the sea and given
her by her death.

Naming Blessings

There are several options when it comes to the actual formula of the
prayer for naming. Depending on your orientation to tradition, you
may elect to use the parallel prayer to that used for boys in *brit milah*
(the first example) or you may choose from contemporary adapta-
tions of this and of the traditional Sephardic *zeved habat* naming

prayer. In each of these blessings, the baby and parents are called by their Hebrew names or, if the parents don't have Hebrew names, by their first names. Last names are not used. The traditional order is for the father's name to come before the mother's.

NAMING EXAMPLE 1

We now enter the part of today's ceremony in which we name this baby. Until this moment, we have not spoken _____ 's Hebrew name, and so she has been "the baby." During the time of the naming she is Sarah, Rebecca, Rachel and Leah, her mother, her grandmothers, her great-grandmothers, and the Messiah.

   After the naming, she becomes herself—a Jew linked through ritual to covenant and the Messiah, and transformed through ritual into _____, the daughter of her particular parents within the context of the Jewish people. She is transformed, named, given tribe and history, roots, purpose, baggage, and wings. And as she is transformed so are we, the community gathered for the ritual who have relived again the biblical stories of our ancestors and the messianic promise of our redemption, in the process of welcoming another Jew into our covenantal community.

אֱלֹהֵינוּ וֵאלֹהֵי אֲבוֹתֵינוּ וְאִמּוֹתֵינוּ קַיֵּם אֶת הַיַּלְדָּה הַזֹּאת לְאָבִיהָ

וּלְאִמָּהּ, וְיִקָּרֵא שְׁמָהּ בְּיִשְׂרָאֵל: [הַשֵּׁם שֶׁנָּתַן] בַּת [שֵׁם הָאָב]

וְ[שֵׁם הָאֵם] יִשְׂמַח הָאָב בְּיוֹצֵאת חֲלָצָיו, וְתָגֵל אִמָּהּ בִּפְרִי רַחְמָהּ.

כַּכָּתוּב: "יִשְׂמַח אָבִיךָ וְאִמֶּךָ וְתָגֵל יוֹלַדְתֶּךָ" (מִשְׁלֵי כג, כה) וְנֶאֱמַר:

"וָאֶעֱבֹר עָלַיִךְ וָאֶרְאֵךְ מִתְבּוֹסֶסֶת בְּדָמָיִךְ וָאֹמַר לָךְ בְּדָמַיִךְ חֲיִי וָאֹמַר

לָךְ בְּדָמַיִךְ חֲיִי" (יְחֶזְקֵאל טז, ו) וְנֶאֱמַר: "זָכַר לְעוֹלָם בְּרִיתוֹ דָּבָר

צִוָּה לְאֶלֶף דּוֹר. אֲשֶׁר כָּרַת אֶת־אַבְרָהָם וּשְׁבוּעָתוֹ לְיִצְחָק: וַיַּעֲמִידֶהָ

לְיַעֲקֹב לְחֹק לְיִשְׂרָאֵל בְּרִית עוֹלָם" (תְּהִלִּים קה, ח–י) וְנֶאֱמַר: "וַיָּמָל

אַבְרָהָם אֶת־יִצְחָק בְּנוֹ בֶּן־שְׁמֹנַת יָמִים כַּאֲשֶׁר צִוָּה אֹתוֹ אֱלֹהִים"

(בְּרֵאשִׁית כא, ד).

הוֹדוּ לַיהוה כִּי טוֹב, כִּי לְעוֹלָם חַסְדּוֹ. זוֹ הַקְּטַנָּה [שֵׁם הַיַּלְדָּה] גְּדוֹלָה

תִּהְיֶה. כְּשֵׁם שֶׁנִּכְנְסָה לַבְּרִית כֵּן תִּכָּנֵס לְתוֹרָה וּלְחֻפָּה וּלְמַעֲשִׂים
טוֹבִים.

אָמֵן.

Elohaynoo v'Elohay avotaynoo v'imotaynoo kayem et hayaldah
hazot l'aviyha oo-l'imah, v'yikareh shemah b'Yisrael:
_____ (shem bat) bat _____
(shem ha-av) v'_____ (shem ha-em). Yismach ha-
av b'yotzet chalatzav, v'tagel ima b'fri rachmah. Kakatoov: yismach
avichah v'imecha v'tagel yoledtecha. V'ne'emar: "va'evor alayich
v'ehraych mitbossesset b'damayich va-omar lach b'damayich chayi
va-omar lach b'damayich chayi." V'ne'emar: "zachar le-olam brito
davar tzivah l'elef dor. Asher karat et-Avraham oo-shvooato
l'Yitzchak: va-ya'amideha l'Yaakov l'chok l'Yisrael brit olam."
V'ne'emar: "Veyamol Avraham et-Yitzchak beno ben-shmonat
yamim ka'asher tzivah otoh Elohim."

Hodoo la-Adonai ki tov, ki le-olam chasdoh. Zo haketanah
_____ (shem bat) g'dolah tihiyeh. K'sheym she-
nichnesa labrit ken tikanes l'Torah oo-l'chuppah oo-lma'asim tovim.
Amen.

Our God and God of our ancestors, preserve this child for her
father and mother, and let her name be called in Israel
_____ , the daughter of _____
and _____ . Let them rejoice in their offspring, as
it is written: "Let your father and mother rejoice, and let her that
bore you be glad." (Proverbs 23:25) And it is said: "When I passed
by you, and saw you wallowing in your blood, I said to you: 'Live in
spite of your blood.'" (Ezekiel 16:6) And it is said: "God has remembered the covenant forever, the word which God commanded to a
thousand generations, the covenant with Abraham, Isaac, and
Jacob." (Psalm 105:8–10) And it is said: "Abraham circumcised his
son Isaac when he was eight days old, as God commanded him."
(Genesis 21:4) Give thanks to God, for God is good and God's kindness lasts forever. May this child _____ grow into
adulthood as a blessing to her family, the Jewish people, and

humankind. As she has entered the covenant, so may she attain the blessings of Torah, marriage, and a life of good deeds. Amen.

Then discuss the significance of your daughter's name.

NAMING EXAMPLE 2

מִי שֶׁבֵּרַךְ אִמּוֹתֵינוּ שָׂרָה רִבְקָה רָחֵל וְלֵאָה וּמִרְיָם הַנְּבִיאָה וַאֲבִיגַיִל וְאֶסְתֵּר הַמַּלְכָּה בַּת אֲבִיחַיִל. הוּא יְבָרֵךְ אֶת הַנַּעֲרָה הַנְּעִימָה הַזֹּאת וְיִקָּרֵא שְׁמָהּ בְּיִשְׂרָאֵל _____ בְּמַזָּל טוֹב וּבִשְׁעַת בְּרָכָה. וִיגַדְּלָהּ בִּבְרִיאוּת שָׁלוֹם וּמְנוּחָה לְתוֹרָה וּלְחֻפָּה וּלְמַעֲשִׂים טוֹבִים. וִיזַכֶּה אֶת אָבִיהָ וְאֶת אִמָּהּ לִרְאוֹת בְּשִׂמְחָתָהּ בְּבָנִים וּבָנוֹת עֹשֶׁר וְכָבוֹד דְּשֵׁנִים וְרַעֲנַנִּים יְנוּבוּן בְּשֵׂיבָה וְכֵן יְהִי רָצוֹן וְנֹאמַר אָמֵן.

Mi she-beyrach imoteynoo Sarah, Rivkah, Rachel v'Leah oo-Miriam ha-neviyah v'Avigayil v'Esther ha-malkah bat Avichayil hoo yivarech et ha-na'arah ha'ne'imah hazot v'yikareh shemah b'Yisrael _____. B'mazal tov oo-vsha'aht bracha. V'yigadlah b'vrioot shalom oo-menoocha l'Torah oo-l'chuppah oo-l'ma'asim tovim. V'yizakeh et avi-ha, v'et eemah lirot b'simchata bvanim oo-vanot osher v'chavod d'shenim v'ra'ananim yinoovoon b'sayva v'chen yihi ratzon v'nomar amen.

May God who blessed our mothers Sarah, Rivkah, Rachel and Leah, Miriam the prophet, Avigail, and Queen Esther, bless this lovely girl _____, daughter of _____ and _____ at this favorable and blessed hour.

May she grow in health, peace, and tranquillity and be raised to a life of Torah, the wedding canopy, and good deeds. May her parents merit to see her joyful, blessed with children, prosperity, and honor, bringing fulfillment and refreshment to their old age. May this be God's will. Amen.

Discuss the significance of the baby's name.

NAMING EXAMPLE 3

A Torah ritual in synagogue[6]: A parent or honored guest cradling the baby should draw the baby to the Torah handle until the two gently make contact.

מִי שֶׁבֵּרַךְ אֲבוֹתֵינוּ אַבְרָהָם יִצְחָק וְיַעֲקֹב, שָׂרָה רִבְקָה רָחֵל וְלֵאָה, הוּא

יְבָרֵךְ אֶת הַיּוֹלֶדֶת _____ בַּת _____

וְאֶת בִּתָּהּ הַנּוֹלְדָה לָהּ בְּמַזָּל טוֹב. וְיִקָּרֵא שְׁמָהּ בְּיִשְׂרָאֵל

_____ בַּת _____ . יְהִי רָצוֹן שֶׁיִּזְכּוּ

הוֹרֶיהָ לְגַדְּלָהּ לְתוֹרָה וּלְחֻפָּה וּלְמַעֲשִׂים טוֹבִים, וְנֹאמַר אָמֵן.

Mi she-beyrach avoteynoo Avraham, Yitzchak v'Yaakov, Sarah, Rivkah, Rachel v'Leah, who yivarech et-ha'yoledet
_____ *bat* _____ *v'et-bitah ha-noldah lah b'mazal tov. V'yikareh shemah b'Yisrael*
_____ *bat* _____ . *Yehi ratzon sheyizkoo horeha legadlah l'Torah oo-l'chuppah oo-l'ma'asim tovim, v'nomar amen.*

May God who blessed our ancestors Abraham, Isaac, and Jacob, Sarah, Rebecca, Rachel and Leah, bless _____
and _____ and their newborn daughter.

Let her be known among the people Israel as
_____ , daughter of _____ and
_____ . As this little child has touched the Torah, so may the Torah touch her life, filling her mind with wisdom and her heart with understanding.

May _____ and _____ , who have brought her here today, always strive to bring her close to the ways of God and our people. May they teach her Torah every day through their words and their deeds. May the parents be privileged to raise their child to womanhood and may
_____ enjoy the blessings of Torah, *chuppah*, and a life of *ma'asim tovim*, good deeds. And let us say: Amen.

NAMING EXAMPLE 4[7]

Our God and Creator, we have come into Your presence with grateful hearts, to reflect on our responsibilities as parents. Give us the wisdom to teach our daughter to be faithful to the heritage of the Household of Israel, that she may grow up with the knowledge that You are always near to her, guiding and sustaining her. Keep open her eyes and spirit, that she may ever be conscious of the beauty and wonder of Your world. And let her learn to love the goodness that is in man or woman, that she may ever nourish the goodness that has been implanted within her. Though none can escape sorrow and pain, we humbly ask for her the courage to face evil, the faith to transcend it, and the strength to subdue it. Grant her health of mind and body that she may enjoy fullness of years and live to do your will in faithfulness.

בָּרוּךְ אַתָּה יהוה, אֱלֹהֵינוּ מֶלֶךְ הָעוֹלָם, גּוֹמֵל חֲסָדִים טוֹבִים.

Baruch Atah Adonai, Eloheynoo melech ha-olam, gomel chasadim tovim.

We praise You, Eternal God, Sovereign of the universe. Your love and kindness extend to all the world.

Ceremony leader or honored guest says to the parents:

Friends, may you dedicate yourselves to give your holiest gifts— love and respect—to this new person, whom you have brought to be named, and may you ever give freely of yourselves so that in time's fullness your love will bestow upon this child the gift of freedom. May joy ever accompany such giving and receiving.

Then s/he says to the child:

Now, in the presence of loved ones, we give to you the name _____ , daughter of _____ and _____ . Let it become a name honored and respected for wisdom and good deeds. _____ , we commit ourselves to the unfolding of your promise; may you walk the path of goodness, beauty, and truth. Do justly and love mercy, and be humble before the mystery of life and the grandeur of the universe into which you have been born.

May God's blessing rest on you now and always:

יְבָרֶכְךָ יהוה וְיִשְׁמְרֶךָ. יָאֵר יהוה פָּנָיו אֵלֶיךָ וִיחֻנֶּךָּ. יִשָּׂא יהוה פָּנָיו אֵלֶיךָ וְיָשֵׂם לְךָ שָׁלוֹם.

Yivarechecha Adonai v'yishmerecha.
Yaeir Adonai panav eilecha vichunecka.
Yisa Adonai panav eilecha v'yasim lacha shalom.

May God bless you and keep you. May God look kindly upon you and be gracious to you. May God reach out to you in tenderness, and give you peace.

NAMING EXAMPLE 5

אֱלֹהֵינוּ וֵאלֹהֵי אִמּוֹתֵינוּ קַיֵּם אֶת הַיַּלְדָּה הַזֹּאת לְאִמָּהּ וּלְאָבִיהָ וְיִקְרָא שְׁמָהּ בְּיִשְׂרָאֵל, _____ . יִשְׂמַח הָאָב בְּיוֹצֵא חֲלָצָיו וְתָגֵל הָאֵם בִּפְרִי הַבֶּטֶן. כַּכָּתוּב: יִשְׂמַח אָבִיךָ וְאִמֶּךָ וְתָגֵל יוֹלַדְתֶּךָ תָּמְכָה וְהַחֲלִיקָה בְּעֵץ חַיִּים, קָרְבָה לְתוֹרָתֶךָ, לַמְּדָה מִצְוֹתֶיךָ, וְהוֹרָה דַּרְכְּךָ הַט לִבָּהּ לְאַהֲבָה וּלְיִרְאָה אֶת שְׁמֶךָ. הוֹדוּ לַיהוה כִּי טוֹב, כִּי לְעוֹלָם חַסְדּוֹ. זֹאת הַקְּטַנָּה _____ גְּדוֹלָה תִּהְיֶה. כְּשֵׁם שֶׁנִּכְנְסָה לַבְּרִית, כֵּן תִּכָּנֵס לְתוֹרָה וּלְחֻפָּה וּלְמַעֲשִׂים טוֹבִים.

Eloheynoo v'Elohey imotaynoo kayem et hayaldah ha-zot l'imah oo-l'aviha vayikareh shemah b'Yisrael, _____ .
Yismach ha-av b'yotzeh halatzav v'tagel ha-em b'fri habeten.
Kakatoov: yismach avicha v'imecha v'tagel yoladetech tomcha v'hachazika ba-etz chayyim, korvah l'Toratecha, lamdah mitzvotecha, v'horah darkecha hat libah l'ahavah oo-lyira'ah et shemecha. Hodoo l'Adonai ki tov, ki le-olam hasdo. Zot ha-ketanah _____ , gedolah tehiyeh. K'shem she-nichnesa labrit, ken tikanes l'Torah, oo-l'chuppah, oo-l'ma'asim tovim.

Our God, and God of our mothers and fathers, preserve this child to her mother and father, and let her name be called in Israel _____, daughter of _____ and _____. Let her father rejoice in his offspring and her mother be glad with the fruit of her body; as it is written, "Let your father and mother rejoice and let her that bore you be glad." (Proverbs 23:25)

Support her and strengthen her with the Tree of Life, bring her close to your Torah, teach her your commandments, show her your ways, incline her heart to be in love and to be in awe of Your name. O give thanks to Adonai for God is good, for God's loving-kindness endures forever. This little child _____, daughter of _____ and _____, may she become great. Even as she enters into the covenant, so may she enter God's teachings, a lifelong love, and worthy deeds.

יְבָרֶכְךָ יהוה וְיִשְׁמְרֶךָ. יָאֵר יהוה פָּנָיו אֵלֶיךָ וִיחֻנֶּךָ. יִשָּׂא יהוה פָּנָיו אֵלֶיךָ וְיָשֵׂם לְךָ שָׁלוֹם.

Y'va-rech-cha A-don-ai v'yeesh-m'recha,
ya-erh Adonai pa-nayv eh-ley-cha v'choo-necha.
yee-sa A-do-nai pa-nayv eh-leh-cha v'yee-sem l'cha shalom.

May God bless and protect you,
May God's presence shine for you and be favorable to you.
May God's face turn to you and give you peace.

Giving Her Gifts and Good Wishes

A sweet practice developing into custom at many welcoming ceremonies is that of giving the new little girl a special gift, one associated with Judaism or with Jewish women and one that also speaks about her family's hopes for her future. Another way for guests to offer the baby gifts is through their blessings and prayers, with which they can come to the front of the room and offer her at this point in the ceremony. You might want to ask those you invite to your daughter's welcoming ceremony, or perhaps just a handful of the most important people in your lives, to prepare something in advance.

Carol Rose and her husband created a ceremony for their daughter in which a chain of ten women, which she called "a *minyan* of love," passed the baby girl from hand to hand, each holding the new daughter at her breast as she offered a blessing. At the end of the chain, seated in a place of honor, was the baby's godmother, who carried her to a specially designated seat in honor of Miriam the prophetess.

Popular choices for gifts for the baby include a kiddush cup, a *Chumash* (a copy of the Five Books of Moses), or a *tzedakah* (charity) box. Giving the baby a Shabbat candlestick or a pair of candlesticks is also meaningful, as lighting the candles is one of the three obligations specifically given to women in traditional Judaism, with the others being separating challah and going to the *mikvah*. A child often begins lighting a single Shabbat candle when she turns three, and she will begin lighting a pair when she gets married. There's a lovely custom of a mother adding a candle to light with the birth or adoption of each child, and she can use the new candlestick with her daughter in mind until the baby is old enough to do it herself.

When there are older siblings, it's nice for them to give their new sister a gift. In the days and weeks following the birth, shopping together with mommy or daddy, without the baby, for a *tzedakah* box or kiddush cup is a meaningful way for parents to spend time alone with the big brother or sister. One mother I know took her seven-year-old son to a paint-your-own-pottery place, where he crafted a special, colorful kiddush cup for his new sister, which he presented to her at her *simchat bat*. If the baby is being given a *tzedakah* box, her parents might want to put in the first money in her honor as part of the ceremony and ask people to consider adding their own coin or two during the reception.

The older siblings' public presentation of a gift, unwrapped, to their sister at her welcoming ceremony gives them an integral role in the ritual. If they're old enough, roughly age five or over, they can also speak briefly on how happy they are to have the baby join their family, or how they hope she'll use the gift they've given her. Children younger than that, and even some older than that, will likely clam up in shyness when they realize that they're supposed to speak in front of all those people in the room, and so the program can note the place where the gift will be given, and the big brother or sister can simply hand it over to the parent holding the new baby.

Another idea for gift-giving to the new baby is for her grandmothers, her aunts, or her mother's closest friends to give her things that will be put away for her until she marries or sets out on her own as an adult, in an updated version of an old-fashioned dowry chest. Items might include a handmade quilt or special Jewish books, a treasured piece of jewelry, and perhaps the specially embroidered pillowcase on which your daughter rested during her welcoming ceremony. Grandmothers or other talented loved ones might crochet afghans, challah covers, or even a *kippah* to be put away for your daughter's future.

Another gift for your daughter might be a special blank book, with the cover tooled or stamped with her name, birth date, and the date of her welcoming ceremony. Guests at her *simchat bat* could write down their hopes and good wishes for her and then it could be taken out again at her bat mitzvah, for the same additions, and finally, presented to her as an adult, shortly before she gets married or soon after she has her first child.

Prayer When Giving the Gift of a *Chumash*

בָּרוּךְ אַתָּה יהוה, אֱלֹהֵינוּ מֶלֶךְ הָעוֹלָם, אֲשֶׁר קִדְּשָׁנוּ בְּמִצְוֹתָיו וְצִוָּנוּ לְגַדֵּל בָּנִים וּבָנוֹת לַתּוֹרָה.

Ba-ruch a-ta Adonai, Eh-lo-hei-nu meh-lech ha-o-lam, a-sher ki-d'sha-nu b'mitz-vo-tav v'tzi-va-nu l'ga-deil ba-nim u-va-not la-torah.

We praise You eternal God, Sovereign of the universe: You hallow us with Your mitzvot and command us to bring up our children to love Torah.

Psalms and Acrostics

Psalms are among the Torah's most powerful poetry and a favorite source of readings at times of both great sorrow and great joy. An interesting custom for *simchat bat* ceremonies is to take each letter of the baby girl's first and middle names, find a verse from Psalms or other Jewish text that starts with the same letter, and assemble them in the form of an acrostic reading as the child's name going from north to south, but also as Jewish poetry, reading across from right to left.

Here is one example, for the name Aliza:

אָנֹכִי יהוה אֱלֹהֶיךָ, אֲשֶׁר הוֹצֵאתִיךָ מֵאֶרֶץ מִצְרַיִם, מִבֵּית עֲבָדִים.

לַיְּהוּדִים הָיְתָה אוֹרָה וְשִׂמְחָה וְשָׂשֹׂן וִיקָר.

יִרְאַת יהוה מְקוֹר חַיִּים, לָסוּר מִמֹּקְשֵׁי מָוֶת.

זָכוֹר אֶת־יוֹם הַשַּׁבָּת לְקַדְּשׁוֹ.

הַמִקְנֵא אַתָּה לִי, וּמִי יִתֵּן כָּל־עַם יהוה נְבִיאִים, כִּי יִתֵּן יהוה אֶת־רוּחוֹ עֲלֵיהֶם.

Anochi Adonai Elohecha, asher hotzeyticha me'eretz Mitzrayim,
m'bayt avadim.
L'Yehudim hay'tah orah v'simchah v'sason v'yikar.
Yirat Adonai mekor chayyim, lasoor limokshey mavet.
Zachor et yom ha-Shababt l'kadshoh.
Hamikaneh atah lee, oo-mee yiten kol am Adonai nivi'im, key yiten
Adonai et-roochoh alayhem.

What follows are some favorite verses to consider incorporating into your daughter's welcoming ceremony, either as stand-alone readings from Psalms, or to assemble into an acrostic using the first letter from each to correspond to a letter in your daughter's name:

From Psalm 127

הִנֵּה נַחֲלַת יהוה בָּנִים, שָׂכָר פְּרִי הַבָּטֶן. כְּחִצִּים בְּיַד־גִּבּוֹר, כֵּן בְּנֵי הַנְּעוּרִים. אַשְׁרֵי הַגֶּבֶר אֲשֶׁר מִלֵּא אֶת־אַשְׁפָּתוֹ מֵהֶם.

Hiney nachalat Adonai banim, sachar pri ha-baten. K'chitzim b'yad gibor, ken bnay ha-ne'urim. Ashray ha-gever asher mileh et ashpatoh mehem.

The heritage of *Hashem* is children; a reward is the fruit of the womb. Like arrows in the hand of a warrior, so are the children of youth. Praiseworthy is the man who fills his quiver with them.

לְמַעַן אַחַי וְרֵעָי, אֲדַבְּרָה נָּא שָׁלוֹם בָּךְ. לְמַעַן בֵּית יהוה אֱלֹהֵינוּ, אֲבַקְשָׁה טוֹב לָךְ.

Le-ma'an achai v'ray-ai adabrah nah shalom bach. Le-ma'an beit Adonai Eloheynoo, avakshah tov lach.

On behalf of my family and friends, I pronounce peace for you. For the sake of the house of the Lord, our God, I will seek your good. (Psalms 122:7–9)

Acrostics can be simply be included in your program or read out loud as well by a parent or with each verse assigned as a way of honoring special guests.

An acrostic can be in Hebrew or in English. Below are examples of lines that can be used in a Hebrew acrostic, followed by an example of an English-language acrostic. It is most meaningful to go through a Bible and pick out lines and verses, in Hebrew or in English, that resonate deeply for you. Here are some convenient examples.[8]

Aleph

אָנֹכִי יהוה אֱלֹהֶיךָ, אֲשֶׁר הוֹצֵאתִיךָ מֵאֶרֶץ מִצְרַיִם, מִבֵּית עֲבָדִים.

Anochey Adonai Elohecha, asher hotzeytecha me'eretz Mitzrayim, m'bayt avadim.

I Adonai am your God who brought you out of the land of Egypt, out of the house of bondage. (Exodus 20:2)

Bet

בְּרוּכִים אַתֶּם לַיהוה, עֹשֵׂה שָׁמַיִם וָאָרֶץ.

Broochim atem l'Adonai, oseh shamayim va-aretz.

May you be blessed by Adonai, maker of heaven and earth. (Psalm 115:15)

Gimel

גַּל־עֵינַי וְאַבִּיטָה נִפְלָאוֹת מִתּוֹרָתֶךָ.

Gal-aynai v'abitah niflaot mi-Toratecha.

Open my eyes that I may perceive the wonders of Your teachings. (Psalm 119:18)

Dalet

דּוֹר לְדוֹר יְשַׁבַּח מַעֲשֶׂיךָ, וּגְבוּרֹתֶיךָ יַגִּידוּ.

Dor l'dor yishabach ma-asecha, v'gvoorotecha yagidoo.

One generation shall laud Your works to another and declare Your mighty acts. (Psalm 145:4)

Hay

הַמְקַנֵּא אַתָּה לִי, וּמִי יִתֵּן כָּל־עַם יהוה נְבִיאִים, כִּי יִתֵּן יהוה אֶת־רוּחוֹ עֲלֵיהֶם.

Hamikaneh atah lee, oo-mee yiten kol am Adonai nivi'im, key yiten Adonai et-roochoh alayhem.

Are you wrought up on my account? Would that all Adonai's people were prophets, that God put the divine spirit upon them! (Numbers 11:29)

Vav

וְאָהַבְתָּ לְרֵעֲךָ כָּמוֹךָ, אֲנִי יהוה.

V'ahavatah l'rayacha k'mocha, ani Adonai.

Love your neighbor as yourself; I am Adonai. (Leviticus 19:18)

Zayin

זָכוֹר אֶת־יוֹם הַשַּׁבָּת לְקַדְּשׁוֹ.

Zachor et yom ha-Shababt l'kadshoh.

Remember Shabbat and keep it holy. (Exodus 20:8)

Chet

חָנֵּנוּ מֵאִתְּךָ דֵּעָה, בִּינָה, וְהַשְׂכֵּל.

Chonaynoo m'eetecha dayah, binah, v'haskel.

Grant us knowledge, discernment, and wisdom. (*Amidah*)

Tet

טוֹב טַעַם וָדַעַת לַמְּדֵנִי, כִּי בְמִצְוֹתֶיךָ הֶאֱמָנְתִּי.

Toov ta'am v'da'at lamdaynee, key b'mitzvotecha he-emantee.

Teach me good sense and knowledge, for I have put my trust in Your *mitzvot*. (Psalm 119:66)

Yud

יִרְאַת יהוה מְקוֹר חַיִּים, לָסוּר מִמֹּקְשֵׁי מָוֶת.

Yirat Adonai mekor chayyim, lasoor mimokshey mavet.

Reverence for Adonai is the source of life, enabling one to avoid dangerous snares. (Proverbs 14:27)

Kaf

כִּי־פָתֹחַ תִּפְתַּח אֶת־יָדְךָ לוֹ, וְהַעֲבֵט תַּעֲבִיטֶנּוּ דֵּי מַחְסֹרוֹ אֲשֶׁר יֶחְסַר
לוֹ.

Key fato-ach tiftach et yadcha loh, v'ha-evet ta-ahvitaynoo day machsoroh asher yechsahr loh.

Rather, you must open your hand and lend to the poor enough of whatever is needed. (Deuteronomy 15:8)

Lamed

לַיְּהוּדִים הָיְתָה אוֹרָה וְשִׂמְחָה וְשָׂשֹׂן וִיקָר.

La-Yehudim hay'tah orah v'simchah v'sason v'yikar.

The Jews enjoyed light and gladness, happiness and honor. (Esther 8:16)

Mem

מַה־נָּאווּ עַל־הֶהָרִים רַגְלֵי מְבַשֵּׂר מַשְׁמִיעַ שָׁלוֹם, מְבַשֵּׂר טוֹב, מַשְׁמִיעַ
יְשׁוּעָה, אֹמֵר לְצִיּוֹן מָלַךְ אֱלֹהָיִךְ.

Mah navoo al he-harim raglay mivasehr mashmiyah shalom, mivasehr tov, mashmiyah yishooah, omer l'Tzion malach Elohayich.

How welcome on the mountains are the footsteps of the herald, announcing happiness, heralding good fortune, announcing victory, telling Zion "Your God rules." (Isaiah 52:7)

Nun

נֵר יהוה נִשְׁמַת אָדָם, חֹפֵשׂ כָּל־חַדְרֵי בָטֶן.

Ner Adonai nishmat adam, chofes kol-chadray vaten.

The human spirit is the light of God, a light penetrating one's most intimate being. (Proverbs 20:27)

Samech

סוֹמֵךְ יהוה לְכָל־הַנֹּפְלִים, וְזוֹקֵף לְכָל־הַכְּפוּפִים.

Somech Adonai l'chol hanoflim, v'zokef l'chol ha'k'foofim.

Adonai supports all who stumble, and makes all who are bent stand straight. (Psalm 145:14)

Ayin

עָזִי וְזִמְרָת יָהּ וַיְהִי לִי לִישׁוּעָה.

Ozi v'zimrat Yah v'yihiy lee l'shoo-ah.

Yah is my strength and my might: God is my deliverance ... (Exodus 15:2)

Pay

פְּנֵה אֵלַי וְחָנֵּנִי, כְּמִשְׁפָּט לְאֹהֲבֵי שְׁמֶךָ.

Paneh eylee v'choneynee, k'mishpat l'ohavey shemecha.

Turn to me and be gracious to me, as is Your rule with those who love Your name. (Psalm 119:132)

Tzadi

צַדִּיק כַּתָּמָר יִפְרָח, כְּאֶרֶז בַּלְּבָנוֹן יִשְׂגֶּה.

Tzadik k'tamar yifrach, k'erez b'Levanon yisgeh.

The righteous shall flourish like palm trees; they shall thrive like a cedar in Lebanon. (Psalm 92:13)

Kuf

קָדוֹשׁ קָדוֹשׁ קָדוֹשׁ, יהוה צְבָאוֹת, מְלֹא כָל־הָאָרֶץ כְּבוֹדוֹ.

Kadosh kadosh kadosh, Adonai tzva'ot, m'lo chol-ha-aretz kvodo.

... Holy, holy, holy is Adonai *tzevao't*; the earth is filled with God's glory. (Isaiah 6:3)

Resh

רַחוּם וְחַנּוּן יהוה, אֶרֶךְ אַפַּיִם וְרַב חָסֶד.

Rachoom v'chanoon Adonai, erech apayim v'rav chesed.

Adonai is compassionate and gracious, slow to anger, abounding in lovingkindness. (Psalm 103:8)

Shin

שְׁמַע בְּנִי מוּסַר אָבִיךָ, וְאַל תִּטֹּשׁ תּוֹרַת אִמֶּךָ.

Sh'ma bni musar avicha, v'al titosh Torat imecha.

My child, heed the discipline of your father and do not forsake the instruction of your mother. (Proverbs 1:8)

Sin

שְׂאוּ שְׁעָרִים רָאשֵׁיכֶם, וְהִנָּשְׂאוּ פִּתְחֵי עוֹלָם, וְיָבוֹא מֶלֶךְ הַכָּבוֹד.

Se-ooh sha'arim rasheychem, v'hinasoo pitchay olam, v'yavoh melech hakavod.

Lift up your heads, O gates! And be lifted up, O ancient doors, that the monarch of glory may come in. (Psalm 24:7)

Tav

תּוֹרַת יהוה תְּמִימָה, מְשִׁיבַת נָפֶשׁ.

Torat Adonai temimah, m'shivat nafesh.

The precepts of Adonai are just, gladdening the heart. (Psalm 19:7)

Here is an English-language acrostic composed for Rebecca Lynne Lenkiewicz by her grandfather, Raymond Schneider, for the occasion of her *simchat bat:*

> **R**ebecca—how long we have waited
> **E**very—day it drew closer, then—
> **B**irth—a miracle-perfect baby
> **E**lation—just before Shabbat, we welcomed you into the world
> **C**lose—the waiting room wasn't good enough, we needed
> **C**ontact—with the new generation
> **A**donai—Adonai, we give thanks.

> **L**ove—you will never lack for it
> **Y**our—aunts and uncles are your biggest fans
> **N**ever—forget, always call your grandparents
> **N**achas—what you bring to your great-grandmothers
> **E**cstasy—the way you make your parents feel.

Prayers, Poems, and Other Readings
for Relatives and Honored Guests

Ask loved ones to read from these selections or to pick their own appropriate poems or passages of prose as a lovely addition to your welcoming ceremony and as a gift to your daughter.

Other widely available poems and readings to consider integrating into your ceremony include Shel Silverstein's "Listen to the Musn'ts" and a selection from Dr. Seuss' "Off to Great Places." If you are lucky enough to count a good guitar or piano player among your family and friends, think about having someone—or everyone gathered—sing the Bob Dylan song "Forever Young." You might also consider adapting the words to the lovely John Lennon song "Beautiful Boy" to the occasion, making it about your beautiful girl.

May You Live to See Your World Fulfilled
AUTHOR UNKNOWN

May you live to see your world fulfilled
May your destiny be for worlds still to come
And may you trust in generations past and yet to be.
May your heart be filled with intuition
And your words be filled with insight
May songs of praise ever be upon your tongue
May your vision be on a straight path before you.
May your eyes sparkle with the light of Torah,
And your ears hear the music of its words.
May the space between each letter of the scrolls
Bring warmth and comfort to your soul.
And may your conversation,
Even of the commonplace,
Be a blessing to all who listen to your words
And see the Torah glowing on your face.

May You Always Have Enough
RABBI HARRY H. EPSTEIN

May you always have—
Enough happiness to keep you sweet,
Enough trials to keep you strong,
Enough hope to keep you happy,
Enough failure to keep you humble,
Enough success to keep you eager,
Enough friends to give you comfort,
Enough wealth to meet your needs,
Enough enthusiasm to look forward,
Enough faith to banish depression,
Enough determination to make each day better than yesterday,
And let us all say: Amen.

A Modern Blessing to Be Offered by a Relative or Dear Friend

_____ , as you are wrapped in your parents' arms, so may your life be wrapped in justice and righteousness. As we embrace you today, so may you embrace your tradition and your people. As your eyes are filled with wonder when you gaze at the world, so too may you be filled with wonder at the everyday miracles of life. As you startle to the world around you, so may you remain ever open both to the happiness and to the pain of those you encounter in the world. As you cry for food and comfort now, so may you one day cry out to correct the injustices of the world, to help clothe the naked and feed the hungry. As your hand tightly grasps your parent's finger, so may you grasp hold of learning and grow in knowledge and wisdom.

Poem of Thanksgiving

ADAPTED BY RABBI MAGGIE WENIG FROM A POEM BY
RABBI JUDY SHANKS

With all my heart, with all my soul, with all my might
I thank you, God, for the gift of this wonderful child.
I thank you for a healthy pregnancy, a safe delivery and a speedy
    recovery.
With all my heart, with all my soul, with all my might
I pray for the continued health of this child.
I pray for her to be strong in mind and body,
To grow steadily and sturdily in a home filled with joy.
I pray for her to become a person who greets the world
With passion, courage, humility, honor and patience.
With all my heart, with all my soul, with all my might
I pray for God to watch over me and my family.
I pray for the ability to love and nurture this child
To provide for her and to educate her
To understand her and to allow her the freedom to grow.

For Aunts and Uncles

We pray that our niece, _____, shall grow in vigor of mind to become an intelligent and caring human being. Grant our niece length of days and vigor of body and mind. We ask Your blessing on her that she may find health, happiness, and contentment. May we be privileged to add love to her growing years as she becomes a blessing to her family, her community, and all humanity.

For Godparents

For the gift of childhood, whose innocence and laughter keep the world young, we as godparents rejoice and give thanks. May we ever be a good influence on this new life and may she learn from us as we learn from her. We pray that she will grow up to be a valiant young woman who will be a blessing to us all, and we pledge to her our love and support in all of her endeavors.

There Rises a Light

TRADITIONAL

From every human being there rises a light that reaches straight to heaven, and when two souls that are designed to be together find each other, their streams of light flow together and a single, brighter light goes forth from their united being.

For a Friend:
To a Friend's Child

ALIKI BARNSTONE

You sit in the middle of the bed
smaller than a pillow.
Your eyes are two blue planets.
I'm too tired and loaded
to party in the next room
or understand the conversation.

In the soft landscape of the room
you crawl to every corner of our plateau
and I reach for you
with my giant's arms.
You know better than to fall
but please, stay with me.
I remember these nights
when I was small, when
somewhere in the unexplored city
a train rumbles and calls
like the people in the next room.
Outside the window
lights move as a shining mobile.
You climb across my legs
kneel on my breasts,
and pull my monstrous ears,
my hard china teeth.
At last you lie across my hips
and rock.
Who is mother?
Who is child?
Our bodies rise and fall
like boats tapping a calm sea.
Your baby smell could almost make me sleep.

We Are . . .

YSAYE MARIA BARNWELL

For each child that's born
a morning star rises and sings to the universe
who we are

We are our grandfather's prayers
We are our grandmother's dreamings
We are the breath of the ancestors
We are the spirit of God.

We are
Mothers of courage
Fathers of time
Daughters of dust
The sons of great visions
Brothers of love
Lovers of life
Builders of nations
Seekers of truth
Keepers of faith
Makers of peace
Wisdom of ages ...

Your Children Are Not Your Children

FROM *THE PROPHET* BY KAHLIL GIBRAN

Your children are not your children.
They are the sons and daughters of Life's longing for itself.
They come through you but not from you,
And though they are with you, yet they belong not to you.

You may give them your love but not your thoughts,
For they have their own thoughts.
You may house their bodies but not their souls,
For their souls dwell in the house of tomorrow, which you cannot
    visit, not even in your dreams.

You may strive to be like them, but seek not to make them like
    you.
For life goes not backward nor tarries with yesterday.
You are the bows from which your children as living arrows are
    sent forth.
The archer sees the mark upon the path of the infinite, and He
    bends you with His might that His arrows may go swift and far.

Let your bending in the archer's hand be for gladness;
For even as He loves the arrow that flies, so He loves also the bow
    that is stable.

God Will Be with You

AUTHOR UNKNOWN

God will be with you as you grow physically from a child to a woman, for God is the Power that makes for growth.

God will be with you as you grow emotionally, from an infant who thinks primarily of her own pleasure, to a truly human being who somehow comes to care about the needs of others, for God is the Power that makes for love.

God will be with you as your own mind grows in wisdom, as you come to understand more about yourself and your world, for God is the power that makes for the clear use of reason.

God will be with you when, after days of anxiety and confusion, the dawn breaks and suddenly you see where you are going, for God is the Power that makes for a better tomorrow.

Give of Yourself

ANNE FRANK

Give of yourself, give as much as you can! And you can always, always give something, even if it is only kindness! If everyone were to do this, and not be as mean, with a kindly word, then there would be much more justice and love in the world. Give and you shall receive, much more than you would have thought possible. Give, give again and again, don't lose courage, keep it up and go on giving! No one has ever become poor from giving!

A Bag of Tools

R. L. SHARPE

Isn't it strange that princes and kings,
And clowns that caper in sawdust rings,
And common people like you and me,
Are builders for eternity?

Each is given a bag of tools,
A shapeless mass, a book of rules,
And each must make —
Ere life is flown—
A stumbling block or a stepping stone.

This is lovely for any family's welcoming ceremony, but particularly apt where there has been an adoption:

The Rainbow
AUTHOR UNKNOWN

The rainbow, subtle shades
of color caught in sunlight
after a late afternoon rain
…the promise of freshness.

The child is a rainbow,
a living blend of families,
dreams, values, backgrounds
…the promise of new life.

The parent has a rainbow role,
catching the sunlight and joy and mystery,
absorbing the unanticipated showers and changes
…the promise of daily growth.

May You Be
LEONARD NIMOY

May you be guided by the heavenly light,
May your dreams become solid and sound,
May your goals be well chosen and surely formed,
May your deeds be touched by decency and grace,
And above all, may you find the time to be kind.

This is perfect for an older sibling to say to his or her new sister:

Welcome to the World!
RABBI SANDY EISENBERG SASSO

Welcome to the world! You are so small and you cry so much.
People make such a big fuss. I don't know why.
I think I will take care of you and play with you sometimes
    because I am big.
I hope you like me. I hope you learn to say my name.
Sometimes you will pull my hair but I will not mind, unless you
    pull it very hard.
Sometimes I will fight with you because you want my toys. I hope
    you will not mind.
Sometimes I will be angry at Mommy and Daddy because they
    spend too much time with you.
I hope you will forgive me.
Thank You, God, for little fingers and toes just like mine.
Thank You, God, for arms that are large enough to hold one more.
Thank You, God, for a love that is big enough to include my sister
    and ME!

From Psalm 127

Children are the Lord's heritage;
The fruit of the womb is a reward.
As arrows in the hand of a mighty man,
So are the children of one's youth.
Happy is the one whose quiver is full of them.

What Is Truly Precious
RABBI ABRAHAM ISAAC KOOK

Radiant is the world soul,
Full of splendor and beauty,
Full of life,
Of souls hidden,
Of treasures of the Holy Spirit,

Of fountains of strength,
Of greatness and beauty.
Proudly I ascend
Toward the heights of the world soul
That gives life to the universe.
How majestic the vision,
Come enjoy,
Come, find peace,
Embrace delight,
Taste and see that God is good.
Why spend your substance on what does not nourish
And your labor on what cannot satisfy?
Listen to me, and you will enjoy what is good,
And find delight in what is truly precious.

The following readings are all perfect for grandparents, though they may also be said by other loved ones.

Grateful for New Beginnings

RABBI SANDY EISENBERG SASSO

God and God of all generations, we are grateful for new beginnings, for the bond of life that links one generation to another. We are thankful for the blessings of family that bring meaning and happiness to our lives, and we rejoice with our children at the birth of their child, our granddaughter. May we all grow together as a family in health and in strength, in harmony and in love.

This modern blessing can be offered by a relative or dear friend, but it is also a good choice for a non-Jewish grandparent:

A Modern Blessing

Let _____ be a person whose heart will be clear, whose goals will be high, a person who will master herself before she seeks to master others, one who will learn to laugh, yet never forget how to weep, one who will reach into the future, yet never forget the past. After all these things are hers, this we pray, enough sense of humor that she may always be serious but never take herself too seriously. Give her humility so that she may always remember the simplicity of true greatness, the open mind of true wisdom, the meekness of true strength. Then we, her family and friends, will dare to whisper that we, too, have been enriched.

Raise This Child to a Long Life

אֱלֹהֵינוּ וֵאלֹהֵי אֲבוֹתֵינוּ וְאִמּוֹתֵינוּ, גַּדֵּל אֶת הַיַּלְדָּה הַזֹּאת לְחַיִּים אֲרֻכִּים, חַיִּים שֶׁל שָׁלוֹם, חַיִּים שֶׁל טוֹבָה, חַיִּים שֶׁל בְּרָכָה, חַיִּים שֶׁל פַּרְנָסָה, חַיִּים שֶׁל חִלּוּץ עֲצָמוֹת, חַיִּים שֶׁיֵּשׁ בָּהֶם יִרְאַת שָׁמַיִם וְיִרְאַת חֵטְא, חַיִּים שֶׁאֵין בָּהֶם בּוּשָׁה וּכְלִמָּה, חַיִּים שֶׁל עֹשֶׁר וְכָבוֹד, חַיִּים שֶׁתְּהֵא בָנוּ אַהֲבַת תּוֹרָה וְיִרְאַת שָׁמַיִם, חַיִּים שֶׁיִּמָּלְאוּ מִשְׁאֲלוֹת לִבֵּנוּ לְטוֹבָה, אָמֵן סֶלָה. מִי שֶׁעָשָׂה נִסִּים לַאֲבוֹתֵינוּ וְאִמּוֹתֵינוּ וְגָאַל אוֹתָם מֵעַבְדוּת לְחֵרוּת, הוּא יִגְאַל אוֹתָנוּ בְּקָרוֹב וִיקַבֵּץ נִדָּחֵינוּ מֵאַרְבַּע כַּנְפוֹת הָאָרֶץ, חֲבֵרִים כָּל יִשְׂרָאֵל, וְנֹאמַר אָמֵן.

Elohaynoo v'Elohai avotaynoo v'imateynoo, gadel et ha-yaldah hazot l'chayyim arookim, chayyim shel shalom, chayyim shel tovah, chayyim shel bracha, chayyim shel parnassah, chayyim shel chalutz atzamot, chayyim she-yesh bahem yirat shamayim v'yirat chet, chayyim she-ain b'hem busha uchelimah, chayyim shel osher v'chavod, chayyim shetehay banu ahavat Torah v'yirat shamayim, chayyim sh'yimaloo m'sha'alot libenoo l'tovah, amen selah. Mi sh'aseh nisim l'avoteynoo v'imotaynoo v'ga'al otam m'avdoot l'eheroot, who yigal otanoo b'karov vikabetz nadacheynoo m'arbah kanfot ha-aretz, chaverim kol Yisrael, v'nomar amen.

Our God and God of our fathers and mothers, raise this child to a long life, a life of peace and well-being, a life of blessing and sustenance, a life of health, a life of devotion and fear of transgression, a life without shame or disgrace, a life of riches and honor, a life shaped by our love of Torah and devotion to God, a life in which the requests of our heart be fulfilled for the good. Amen.

May God who made miracles for our ancestors and redeemed them from slavery to freedom, redeem us soon and gather our dispersed ones from the four corners of the earth, so that all of Israel will be knit to one another in friendship. Amen.

A new life, a new child to love, the opening of a new chapter in the chronicle of our family's existence has begun with _____'s arrival. May she grow up in health and in happiness, to become a blessing to her family, friends, and neighbors. And may I, her grandparent, be granted the joy of seeing her develop all of her faculties and the gratification of helping her to fulfill the best that is in her. Then my humble prayer will have found its answer: That the days and the years to come will be for us times of peace and of wondrous fulfillment.

From Proverbs 17:6

The crown of the aged are children's children
And the glory of children are their parents.

Blessings of Gratitude

As the welcoming ceremony transitions toward its conclusion, the baby's parents recite blessings of gratitude for having reached this moment. You can say as many blessings as your feelings—and time—allow, but it is appropriate to begin with one or both of the following two: *shehechiyanu* and *hatov v'hameitiv*. This chapter lists several other blessings as well, which can be recited by the parents, a rabbi or other designated leader of the *simchat bat*, or relatives.

Traditional authorities differ over which prayer (if any!) is to be said upon the arrival of a daughter, but the *shehechiyanu* is generally said in gratitude for something good happening to an individual, and *hatov v'hameitiv* is said when something wonderful has happened for the benefit of the entire community. There is also a religious principle dictating that the same blessing should not be said twice over the same thing, so if you said the *shehechiyanu* when you first held your daughter, then you may want to recite *hatov v'hameitiv* during her welcoming ceremony. After all, her arrival is without doubt a benefit to the entire community.

The last set of blessings in this section is modeled after the *sheva brachot*, the seven blessings said at the end of the meal celebrating a Jewish wedding. A beautiful way to conclude your daughter's *simchat bat* is with seven blessings amended creatively to suit this occasion. They provide an opportunity to create a line of continuity between the life-cycle events of your marriage and her birth, and also to foreshadow the blessings that you hope your daughter will one day have the opportunity to hear as she stands side by side under the wedding canopy with her own *bashert*, the life partner who Jewish tradition says has already been destined for her. The *sheva brachot* are also a lovely way to mark the new, momentous occasion in the life of a couple who have now become parents as well as partners. As is customary at a wedding, each blessing can be assigned to a different honored guest.

Shehechiyanu

בָּרוּךְ אַתָּה יהוה, אֱלֹהֵינוּ מֶלֶךְ הָעוֹלָם, שֶׁהֶחֱיָנוּ וְקִיְּמָנוּ וְהִגִּיעָנוּ לַזְּמַן הַזֶּה.

Baruch Atah Adonai, Eloheynoo Melech ha-olam, shehechiyanoo v'kiyamanoo v'higiyanoo la-zman ha-zeh.

Blessed are You, Lord our God, Source of the universe, who has kept us in life, sustained us, and brought us to this special time.

Hatov v'hameitiv

בָּרוּךְ אַתָּה יהוה, אֱלֹהֵינוּ מֶלֶךְ הָעוֹלָם, הַטּוֹב וְהַמֵּטִיב.

Baruch Atah Adonai, Eloheynoo Melech ha-olam, ha-tov v'hameitiv.

Blessed are You, Lord our God, King of the universe, who is good and beneficent.

This blessing is to say when holding your newborn child for the first time. It can also be utilized during her welcoming ceremony.[9]

וַיִּבְרָא אֱלֹהִים אֶת־הָאָדָם בְּצַלְמוֹ בְּצֶלֶם אֱלֹהִים בָּרָא אֹתוֹ זָכָר וּנְקֵבָה בָּרָא אֹתָם: וַיְבָרֶךְ אֹתָם אֱלֹהִים וַיֹּאמֶר לָהֶם אֱלֹהִים פְּרוּ וּרְבוּ וּמִלְאוּ אֶת־הָאָרֶץ:

בָּרוּךְ אַתָּה יהוה, אֱלֹהֵינוּ מֶלֶךְ הָעוֹלָם, מְשַׂמֵּחַ הָאֵם בִּפְרִי בִטְנָהּ וּמֵגִיל הָאָב בְּיוֹצֵא חֲלָצָיו:

V'yivrah Elohim et-ha'adam b'tzalmo b'tzelem Elohim barah otoh zachar oo-nekevah barah otam. Vayvarech otam Elohim vayomer lahem proo oo-rvoo oo-miloo et ha-aretz. Baruch Atah Adonai Eloheynoo melech ha-olam m'sameyach ha-em b'fri bitnah oo-megil ha-av b'yotzeh chalatzav.

God created the human in the divine image; in that image God created the human—male and female, God created them. God blessed them and said to them "Be fruitful and multiply, and fill up the earth!"

Blessed are You, the Incomparable our God, the Sovereign of all worlds, who lets the mother rejoice in the fruit of her womb, and the father with his offspring.

Another blessing:

בָּרוּךְ אַתָּה יהוה, אֱלֹהֵינוּ מֶלֶךְ הָעוֹלָם, מְשַׂמֵּחַ הוֹרִים בְּיַלְדֵיהֶם.

Baruch Atah Adonai, Eloheynoo Melech ha-olam misameach horim beyaldeyhem.

Blessed are You, O God, who makes parents rejoice with their children.

Prayer When the Daughter Is the Firstborn

Our God and God of our ancestors, our Rock and our Redeemer, with gratitude for the gift of life we pray that our firstborn grow to accept joyfully her share in the tradition of our people. Bless her, *Adonai,* with health and full years, with happiness and moral strength. Bless us with understanding and wisdom, so that we may truly share in the creation of a life guided by Torah. May our firstborn daughter find favor before You, *Adonai,* and in the sight of all people. And let us say: Amen.

Prayer by Grandparents

God and God of all generations, we are grateful for new beginnings, for the bond of life that links one generation to another. We are thankful for the blessings of family that bring meaning and happiness to our lives, and we rejoice with our children at the birth of their child, our granddaughter. May we all grow together as a family in health and in strength, in harmony and in love.

Traditional Priestly Blessing

If you have a kohen, *or member of the priestly class, among your family members or dear friends, this may be recited by him. If not, any rabbi or parent may offer this lovely blessing to your daughter.*

יְבָרֶכְךָ יהוה וְיִשְׁמְרֶךָ, יָאֵר יהוה פָּנָיו אֵלֶיךָ וִיחֻנֶּךָ, יִשָּׂא יהוה פָּנָיו אֵלֶיךָ וְיָשֵׂם לְךָ שָׁלוֹם.

Y'va-rech-cha A-don-ai v'yeesh-m'recha,
ya-er Adonai pa-nayv eh-ley-cha vi-choo-ne-ka.
yee-sa A-do-nai pa-nayv eh-leh-cha v'ya-sem l'cha shalom.

May God bless and protect you,
May God's presence shine for you and be favorable to you.
May God's face turn to you and give you peace.

Traditional Blessing over a Daughter

יְשִׂימֵךְ אֱלֹהִים כְּשָׂרָה רִבְקָה רָחֵל וְלֵאָה. יְבָרֶכְךְ יהוה וְיִשְׁמְרֶךָ. יָאֵר
יהוה פָּנָיו אֵלֶיךָ וִיחֻנֶּךָ. יִשָּׂא יהוה פָּנָיו אֵלֶיךָ, וְיָשֵׂם לְךָ שָׁלוֹם.

*Yisimech Elohim k'Sarah, Rivkah, Rachel v'Leah. Yivarechecha Adonai
v'yishmarecha. Ya'er Adonai panav alayich v'yichooneyich. Yisah
Adonai panav alayich, v'yasemsam lach shalom.*

May God make you like Sara, Rebecca, Rachel and Leah.
May God bless you and guard you.
May God cause a light to shine on you and be gracious to you.
May God lift up his face to you and grant you peace.

How Shall I Bless Her?

AUTHOR UNKNOWN

"How shall I bless her, how shall this daughter be blessed?" asked
    the angel.
With a smile full of light,
Wide eyed to see,
Each flower and bird and creature that lives,
And a heart that can feel for all that she sees.

"How shall I bless her, how shall this daughter be blessed?" asked
    the angel.
With feet that can dance on and on without end,
And a soul to remember all the melodies she hears,
With hands to collect pretty shells by the sea,
And an ear that's attuned to all things great and small.

"How shall I bless her, how shall this daughter be blessed?" asked
    the angel.
We have blessed her with all in our power to give;
Songs and smiles and feet that can dance,
A gentle hand,
A heart that beats true,
And a soul that is filled with unbounding love.

Sheva Brachot, Seven Blessings

The first blessing is made over a kiddush cup filled with wine or grape juice, a symbol of joy.

1.   בָּרוּךְ אַתָּה יהוה, אֱלֹהֵינוּ מֶלֶךְ הָעוֹלָם, בּוֹרֵא פְּרִי הַגָּפֶן.

Baruch Atah Adonai, Eloheynoo Melech ha-olam, borey pri hagafen.

Blessed are You, Lord our God, Source of the universe, who created the fruit of the vine

2.   בָּרוּךְ אַתָּה יהוה, אֱלֹהֵינוּ מֶלֶךְ הָעוֹלָם, יוֹצֵר הָאָדָם.

Baruch Atah Adonai, Eloheynoo Melech ha-olam, yotzer ha-adam.

Blessed are You, Lord our God, source of the universe, Creator of humanity.

3.   בָּרוּךְ אַתָּה יהוה, אֱלֹהֵינוּ מֶלֶךְ הָעוֹלָם, אֲשֶׁר יָצַר אֶת הָאָדָם בְּצַלְמוֹ בְּצֶלֶם דְּמוּת תַּבְנִיתוֹ וְהִתְקִין לוֹ מִמֶּנּוּ בִּנְיַן עֲדֵי עַד. בָּרוּךְ אַתָּה יהוה, יוֹצֵר הָאָדָם.

Baruch Atah Adonai, Eloheynoo Melech ha-olam, asher yatzar et ha-adam b'tzalmo b'tzelem dimoot tavneytoh v'hitkin lo mimaynoo binyan adi ad. Baruch Atah Adonai yotzer ha-adam.

Praised are You, Lord our God, Source of the universe, who created humans in Your image and Your likeness. And out of their very selves You prepared for them a perpetual spiritual being. Praised are You, our Lord, Creator of humanity.

4.   בָּרוּךְ אַתָּה יהוה, אֱלֹהֵינוּ מֶלֶךְ הָעוֹלָם, אֲשֶׁר קִדְּשָׁנוּ בְּמִצְוֹתָיו וְצִוָּנוּ עַל קִדּוּשׁ הַחַיִּים.

Baruch Atah Adonai, Eloheynoo Melech ha-olam, asher kidshanoo b'mitzvotav vitzivanoo al kidush ha-chayyim.

Blessed are You, Lord our God, Source of the universe, who commands us to sanctify life.

5. בָּרוּךְ אַתָּה יהוה, אֱלֹהֵינוּ מֶלֶךְ הָעוֹלָם, זוֹכֵר הַבְּרִית וְנֶאֱמָן בִּבְרִיתוֹ
וְקַיָּם בְּמַאֲמָרוֹ.

*Baruch Atah Adonai, Eloheynoo Melech ha-olam, zocher habrit
v'ne'eman b'vrito v'kayam b'ma'amroh.*

Blessed are You, Lord our God, Source of the universe, who
remembers the covenant and who is steadfastly faithful in Your
covenant, keeping Your promise

6. שׂוֹשׂ תָּשִׂישׂ וְתָגֵל הָעֲקָרָה בְּקִבּוּץ בָּנֶיהָ לְתוֹכָהּ בְּשִׂמְחָה. בָּרוּךְ אַתָּה
יהוה, מְשַׂמֵּחַ צִיּוֹן בְּבָנֶיהָ.

*Sos ta-sis v'tagel ha-akarah b'kibutz baneha letocha b'simcha.
Baruch Atah Adonai misameach Tzion b'vaneha.*

Rejoice, shall the barren one rejoice and delight in the regathering
of her children amidst her in gladness. Blessed are You, Lord our
God, who gladdens Zion with her children.

7. בָּרוּךְ אַתָּה יהוה, אֱלֹהֵינוּ מֶלֶךְ הָעוֹלָם, מְשַׂמֵּחַ הוֹרִים עִם יַלְדֵיהֶם.

*Baruch Atah Adonai, Eloheynoo Melech ha-olam, mi-sameach horim
im yaldayhem.*

Blessed are You, Lord our God, Source of the universe, who causes
parents to rejoice with their children.

An alternative Seven Blessings, *or* sheva brachot:

1. בָּרוּךְ אַתָּה יהוה, אֱלֹהֵינוּ מֶלֶךְ הָעוֹלָם, עוֹשֶׂה מַעֲשֵׂה בְּרֵאשִׁית.

*Baruch Atah Adonai, Eloheynoo Melech ha-olam, oseh ma'aseh
breishit.*

Praised are You, Adonai our God, Lord of the cosmos, creator of the
mystery of creation.

2.   בָּרוּךְ אַתָּה יהוה, אֱלֹהֵינוּ מֶלֶךְ הָעוֹלָם, שֶׁהַכֹּל בָּרָא לִכְבוֹדוֹ.

Baruch Atah Adonai, Eloheynoo Melech ha-olam, she-hakol bara lichvodoh.

Praised are You, Adonai our God, Lord of the cosmos, Creator of everything for Your glory.

3.   בָּרוּךְ אַתָּה יהוה, אֱלֹהֵינוּ מֶלֶךְ הָעוֹלָם, יוֹצֵר הָאָדָם.

Baruch Atah Adonai, Eloheynoo Melech ha-olam, yotzer ha-adam.

Praised are You, Adonai our God, Lord of the cosmos, Creator of humanity.

4.   בָּרוּךְ אַתָּה יהוה, אֱלֹהֵינוּ מֶלֶךְ הָעוֹלָם, אֲשֶׁר יָצַר אֶת הָאָדָם בְּצַלְמוֹ בְּצֶלֶם דְּמוּת תַּבְנִיתוֹ וְהִתְקִין לוֹ מִמֶּנּוּ בִּנְיַן עֲדֵי עַד. בָּרוּךְ אַתָּה יהוה, יוֹצֵר הָאָדָם.

Baruch Atah Adonai, Eloheynoo Melech ha-olam, asher yatzar et ha-adam b'tzalmoh b'tzelem d'moot tavnito v'hitkin lo mimaynoo binyan adi ad. Baruch Atah Adonai, yotzer ha-adam.

Praised are You, Adonai our God, Lord of the cosmos, who created human beings in Your image and Your likeness, and out of their very selves You prepared for them a perpetual spiritual being. Praised are You, Lord, Creator of humanity.

5.   בָּרוּךְ אַתָּה יהוה, אֱלֹהֵינוּ מֶלֶךְ הָעוֹלָם, שֶׁכָּכָה לוֹ בְּעוֹלָמוֹ.

Baruch Atah Adonai, Eloheynoo Melech ha-olam, shekachah lo b'olamoh.

Praised are You, Adonai our God, Lord of the cosmos, who has such as these Your creatures in the world.

6.   בָּרוּךְ אַתָּה יהוה, אֱלֹהֵינוּ מֶלֶךְ הָעוֹלָם, זוֹכֵר הַבְּרִית וְנֶאֱמָן בִּבְרִיתוֹ וְקַיָּם בְּמַאֲמָרוֹ.

Baruch Atah Adonai, Eloheynoo Melech ha-olam, zocher habrit v'ne'eman b'vrito vikayam b'ma'amaro.

Praised are You, Adonai our God, Lord of the cosmos, rememberer of the covenant and steadfastly faithful in Your covenant, keeping Your promise.

7. בָּרוּךְ אַתָּה יהוה, אֱלֹהֵינוּ מֶלֶךְ הָעוֹלָם, שֶׁהֶחֱיָנוּ וְקִיְּמָנוּ וְהִגִּיעָנוּ לַזְּמַן הַזֶּה.

Baruch Atah Adonai, Eloheynoo Melech ha-olam, shehechiyanoo v'kiyamanoo v'higiyanoo la-zman ha-zeh.

Praised are You, Adonai our God, Lord of the cosmos, who has sustained us in life and being and brought us to this very moment.

Another alternative set of Seven Blessings:

1. May the One who blessed Eve with the choice to eat from the tree of knowledge and the courage to pave the way for humanity bless this child with wisdom and with strength.

2. May the One who blessed Sarah with faith to believe in the impossible bless this child with the *Shechina,* a divine presence in her life.

3. May the One who blessed Miriam with a voice to speak out even when her views were unpopular give this child the strength to be a spokeswoman for her beliefs.

4. May the One who blessed Shifra and Puah with the courage to save an entire generation bless this child with the knowledge to know that life is sacred.

5. May the One who blessed Deborah with the wisdom and power to be a judge bless this child with self-esteem so that she may be a leader and a sage.

6. May the One who blessed Tzipporah with the knowledge that God speaks through those we love bless this child with a community of loving and nurturing people.

7. May the One who blessed Ruth with loyalty to another woman bless this child with love and concern for the future of women.

Concluding in Song and Prayer

The way you end your daughter's welcoming ceremony is as important as the way you begin it. A prayer or reading that ties together the themes that have run through your daughter's ceremony brings closure to the entire event. Joining together in song also brings everyone together again joyfully in the spirit of community, after their focus has been on the baby and you. Before the final song, one of the baby's parents may want to direct those in attendance to the food set up for their enjoyment after the conclusion of the welcoming ceremony, and thank everyone for joining them and making it such a special, loving day.

Parents' Prayer

RABBI SANDY EISENBERG SASSO

This contemporary prayer sounds nice when read by two people, alternating stanzas:

What I/we wish for _____, I/we wish for all children. I/we wish for you to be a person of character, strong but not tough, gentle but not weak.

I/we wish for you to be righteous but not self-righteous, honest but not unforgiving.

Whenever you journey, may your steps be firm and may you walk in just paths and not be afraid.

Whenever you speak, may your words be words of wisdom and friendship.

May your hands build, and your heart preserve what is good and beautiful in our world.

May the voices of the generations of our people move through you, and may the God of our ancestors be your God as well.

May you know that there is a people, a rich heritage to which you belong, and from that sacred place you are connected to all who dwell on earth.

May the stories of our people be upon your heart, and the grace of the Torah rhythm dance in your soul.

What Is This Covenant?
ADAPTED FROM RABBI KINNERET SHIRON

As she entered the covenant, so she will enter into the realm of the Torah and nuptials and good deeds.

What is the covenant of the Torah? It is the covenant of a person with her family.

What is the covenant of good deeds? It is the covenant of a person with her people and her community.

Nor are these covenants separate, each unto itself, but on the contrary, they are bound together and intertwined as the Shabbat challah and the *havdalah* candle, whose lights join all the lights into one large flame. So too, Torah and *chuppah* and good deeds combine to a complete life for a daughter of Israel.

The *Sh'ma*

The parents or the assembled guests, collectively, may recite this proclamation of faith, which is central to Judaism. What follows are the traditional *Sh'ma* and a contemporary, alternative rendering.

Traditional *Sh'ma*

שְׁמַע יִשְׂרָאֵל יהוה אֱלֹהֵינוּ יהוה אֶחָד.

Sh'ma Yisrael, Adonai Eloheinu, Adonai Echad.

Hear! O Israel, the Lord our God, the Lord is One.

Sh'ma: **Communal Declaration of Faith**

MARCIA FALK, FROM *THE BOOK OF BLESSINGS*

שְׁמַע, יִשְׂרָאֵל —
לָאֱלֹהוּת אַלְפֵי פָנִים,
מְלֹא עוֹלָם שְׁכִינָתָהּ,
רִבּוּי פָּנֶיהָ אֶחָד.

נֶאֱהַב אֶת־הַחַיִּים
וְאֶת עֵין הַחַיִּים
בְּכָל־לְבָבֵנוּ וּבְכָל־נַפְשֵׁנוּ
וּבְכָל־מְאֹדֵנוּ.
יִהְיוּ הַדְּבָרִים הָאֵלֶּה
בִּלְבָבֵנוּ וּבְקִרְבֵּנוּ:
שְׁמִירַת אֶרֶץ וְיוֹשְׁבֶיהָ,
רְדִיפַת צֶדֶק וְשָׁלוֹם,
אַהֲבַת חֶסֶד וְרַחֲמִים.
נְשַׁנְּנֵם
לִבְנוֹתֵינוּ וּלְבָנֵינוּ
וּנְדַבֵּר בָּם
בְּשִׁבְתֵּנוּ בְּבֵיתֵנוּ,
בְּלֶכְתֵּנוּ בַדֶּרֶךְ,
בְּשָׁכְבֵנוּ וּבְקוּמֵנוּ.
וְיִהְיוּ מַעֲשֵׂינוּ
נֶאֱמָנִים לִדְבָרֵינוּ,
לְמַעַן יֵדְעוּ דוֹר אַחֲרוֹן,
בָּנוֹת וּבָנִים יִוָּלֵדוּ:
חֶסֶד וֶאֱמֶת נִפְגָּשׁוּ,
צֶדֶק וְשָׁלוֹם נָשָׁקוּ.

Sh'ma, yisra'eyl—
la'elohut alfey panim,
m'lo olam sh'khinatah,
ribuy paneha ehad.

Nohav et-hahayim
v'eyt eyn hahayim
b'khol-l'vaveynu uvkhol-nafsheynu
uvkhol-m'odeynu.
Yihyu had'varim ha'eyleh
bilvaveynu uvkirbeynu:
sh'mirat eretz v'yoshveha,
r'difat tzedek v'shalom,
ahavat hesed v'rahamim.
N'shan'nam
livnoteynu ulvaneynu
undabeyr bam
b'shivteynu b'veyteynu,
b'lekheynu baderekh
b'shokbeynu uvkumeynu.

V'yihyu ma'aseynu
ne'emanim lidvareynu,
l'ma'an yeyd'u dor aharon,
banot uvanim yivaleydu:
Hesed ve'emet nifgashu,
tzedek v'shalom nashaku.

Hear, O Israel—
The divine abounds everywhere
and dwells in everything;
the many are One.

Loving life
and its mysterious source
with all our heart
and all our spirit,
all our senses and strength,
we take upon ourselves
and into ourselves
these promises:
to care for the earth
and those who live upon it,

to pursue justice and peace,
to love kindness and compassion.
We will teach this to our children
throughout the passage of the day—
as we dwell in our homes
and as we go on our journeys,
from the time we rise
until we fall asleep.

And may our actions
be faithful to our words
that our children's children
may live to know:
Truth and kindness
have embraced,
peace and justice have kissed
and are one.

L'chi Lach

DEBBIE FRIEDMAN

L'chi lach to a land that I will show you
Lech l'cha to a place you do not know
L'chi lach, on your journey I will bless you.
And you shall be a blessing, you shall be a blessing
You shall be a blessing, *L'chi lach.*

L'chi lach, and I shall make your name great
Lech l'cha, and all shall praise your name
L'chi lach, to the place that I will show you
L'simchat chochma, l'simchat chayim
L'simchat chayim, L'chi lach.
And you shall be a blessing, you shall be a blessing
You shall be a blessing, *L'chi lach.*

Sachaki—Laugh

SAUL TCHERNICHOVSKY

שַׂחֲקִי, שַׂחֲקִי עַל הַחֲלוֹמוֹת.
זוּ אֲנִי הַחוֹלֵם שָׂח.
שַׂחֲקִי כִּי בָּאָדָם אַאֲמִין,
כִּי עוֹדֶנִּי מַאֲמִין בָּךְ.

כִּי עוֹד נַפְשִׁי דְרוֹר שׁוֹאֶפֶת.
לֹא מְכַרְתִּיהָ לְעֵגֶל פָּז.
כִּי עוֹד אַאֲמִין גַּם בָּאָדָם,
גַּם בְּרוּחוֹ, רוּחַ עַז.

Sachaki, Sachaki, al ha-chalomot—
Zu ani ha-cholem sach:
Sachaki ki be'adam a'amin,
Ki odeni ma'amin bach.

Ki od nafshi dror sho'efet
Lo m'chartiha le'egel paz.
Ki od a'amin gam be'adam,
Gam be'rucho, ruach az.

Laugh, laugh at me for my dreams—this I say, the dreamer. Laugh at me because I still believe in humanity, because I still believe in you. Because my soul still yearns for freedom. I have not sold it for a golden calf. Because I still believe in humanity and in its powerful spirit.

L'Dor vaDor

This rousing tune is traditional.

לְדוֹר וָדוֹר נַגִּיד גָּדְלֶךָ וּלְנֵצַח נְצָחִים קְדֻשָּׁתְךָ נַקְדִּישׁ וְשִׁבְחֲךָ אֱלֹהֵינוּ
מִפִּינוּ לֹא יָמוּשׁ לְעוֹלָם וָעֶד.

L'dor vador, l'dor vador, l'dor vador nagid godlecha
u-le'netzach netza-chim, ke-du-shatcha nak-dish
v-shive-cha Eloheynu mi-pinu lo ya-mush l'olam va'ed.

In every generation we will declare Your greatness.
We will sanctify Your holiness forever.
Your praise, God, will never cease to flow from our lips.

Everybody sings together this simple song that is traditional at bar and bat mitzvahs and other Jewish occasions of joyous good fortune:

סִמָּן טוֹב וּמַזָּל טוֹב יְהֵא לָנוּ וּלְכָל־יִשְׂרָאֵל.

Siman tov u'mazal tov, yehe lanu ulechol Yisrael.

May there be good fortune for us, and for all of Israel!

Blessings over the Wine and Bread

Before coming to this final part of your daughter's welcoming cere-mony, be sure to have a kiddush cup filled with wine or grape juice handy, and a challah at the ready. You may choose to provide plastic cups containing sips of wine or grape juice for everyone to share, but pouring and distributing them would be time-consuming. One special cup and one challah held aloft by a parent or an honored guest who recites the prayers over wine and bread generally suffices. These ritual blessings provide a Jewish transition from the body of your daughter's welcoming ceremony into the festive meal that fol-lows. It is also customary at any significant gathering of Jews for kid-dush and *ha-motzi* to be recited before they eat together.

Blessing over Wine or Grape Juice—Traditional
FROM THE BIRNBAUM *SIDDUR*

בָּרוּךְ אַתָּה יהוה, אֱלֹהֵינוּ מֶלֶךְ הָעוֹלָם, בּוֹרֵא פְּרִי הַגָּפֶן.

Baruch Atah Adonai, Eloheynoo Melech ha-olam, borey pri hagafen.

Blessed are You, Lord our God, King of the universe, who created the fruit of the vine.

Blessing over Wine or Grape Juice—Contemporary
FROM *KOL HANESHAMAH: SHIRIM U'VRACHOT*,
THE RECONSTRUCTIONIST PRESS

בָּרוּךְ אַתָּה יהוה, אֱלֹהֵינוּ מֶלֶךְ הָעוֹלָם, בּוֹרֵא פְּרִי הַגָּפֶן.

Baruch Atah Adonai, Eloheynoo Melech ha-olam, borey pri hagafen.

Blessed are You, the Boundless One our God, Sovereign of all worlds, who creates the fruit of the vine.

Blessing over Wine or Grape Juice—Alternative
MARCIA FALK, FROM *THE BOOK OF BLESSINGS*

נְבָרֵךְ אֶת עֵין הַחַיִּים
מַצְמִיחַת פְּרִי הַגָּפֶן.

*N'vareykh et eyn hahayim
matzmihat p'ri hagefen.*

Let us bless the source of life
that ripens fruit on the vine.

After blessing the challah, it is nice to mark this sweet occasion by dipping it into honey before eating it.

Blessing over Bread—Traditional
FROM THE BIRNBAUM *SIDDUR*

בָּרוּךְ אַתָּה יהוה, אֱלֹהֵינוּ מֶלֶךְ הָעוֹלָם, הַמּוֹצִיא לֶחֶם מִן הָאָרֶץ:

Baruch Atah Adonai, Eloheynoo Melech ha-olam, ha-motzi lechem min ha-aretz.

Blessed are You, Lord our God, King of the universe, who has brought forth bread from the earth.

Blessing over Bread—Contemporary

FROM *KOL HANESHAMAH: SHIRIM U'VRACHOT*,
THE RECONSTRUCTIONIST PRESS

בָּרוּךְ אַתָּה יהוה, אֱלֹהֵינוּ מֶלֶךְ הָעוֹלָם, הַמּוֹצִיא לֶחֶם מִן הָאָרֶץ:

Baruch Atah Adonai, Eloheynoo Melech ha-olam, ha-motzi lechem min ha-aretz.

Blessed are You, Bountiful, the sovereign of all worlds, who brings forth bread from the earth.

Blessing over Bread—Alternative

MARCIA FALK, FROM *THE BOOK OF BLESSINGS*

נְבָרֵךְ אֶת עֵין הַחַיִּים
הַמּוֹצִיאָה לֶחֶם מִן הָאָרֶץ.

N'vareykh et eyn hahayim
hamotzi'ah lehem min ha'aretz.

Let us bless the source of life
that brings forth bread from the earth.

CHAPTER TEN

Complete
Sample Ceremonies

*E*ach of these ceremonies provides an example of a welcoming ritual with a different orientation toward Judaism. The first, the *zeved habat*, is the traditional Sephardic approach. The second offers an example of what one religiously observant mother created within the constraints of her understanding of Jewish law to welcome her new daughter with insight and gratitude. The third is a traditionally oriented ceremony that is based on a contemporary concept of *simchat bat* but views the baby girl's inclusion in the covenant as implicit, and so does not include a ritual marking her entry into it. The fourth example takes a different view and utilizes a miniature *mikvah* to welcome the baby into the covenant. The final example is the least traditional and provides a welcoming ceremony that focuses most on humanistic values.

You may choose to use one of these ceremonies exactly as shown here or use them as a guide to orient you as you compose your own, built from the elements included earlier in this book and those discovered by you in other sources. Reviewing all of the sample ceremonies provided here will give you a sense of the range of possibilities for your own daughter's welcoming ceremony.

Traditional Sephardic *Zeved Habat*

This ceremony, *seder zeved habat*, or celebration of the gift of a daughter,[1] is the welcoming ceremony routinely used at Congregation Shearith Israel, the Upper West Side congregation in New York that is known as the Spanish and Portuguese Synagogue and is the most prominent Sephardic congregation in the country.

When the mother is present, this ceremony follows her recitation of the *gomel*, the prayer of thanksgiving for having come through a dangerous passage. If the mother is not present, the final part of this *zeved habat*, Psalm 128, should be omitted.

The rabbi or other ceremony leader recites this from the Song of Songs:

יוֹנָתִי בְּחַגְוֵי הַסֶּלַע בְּסֵתֶר הַמַּדְרֵגָה. הַרְאִינִי אֶת מַרְאַיִךְ. הַשְׁמִיעִינִי
אֶת־קוֹלֵךְ. כִּי־קוֹלֵךְ עָרֵב וּמַרְאֵיךְ נָאוֶה:

Yonati b'chagvay ha-selah b'setehr ha-madregah. Har-ini et marayich. Hashmi'ini et-kolech. Ki-kolech arev oo-maraych naveh.

O my dove in the rocky clefts,
In the covert of terrace high,
Let me see thy countenance,
Let me hear thy voice,

For sweet is thy voice
And thy countenance comely.

If the child is the firstborn, add:

אַחַת הִיא יוֹנָתִי תַמָּתִי. אַחַת הִיא לְאִמָּהּ. בָּרָה הִיא לְיוֹלַדְתָּהּ. רָאוּהָ
בָנוֹת וַיְאַשְּׁרוּהָ. מְלָכוֹת וּפִילַגְשִׁים וַיְהַלְלוּהָ:

Achat he yonati tamati. Achat he l'imah. Barah he l'yoladetah. Ra-ooha banot vay-ashrooha. Melakhot oo-filagshim vay-halleluha.

One alone is my dove, my perfect one,
The darling of her mother,
The choice one of her who bore her,
Daughters saw her, they acclaimed her,
Queens and consorts, they sang her praises.

Then the rabbi offers this prayer:

מִי שֶׁבֵּרַךְ שָׂרָה וְרִבְקָה רָחֵל וְלֵאָה. וּמִרְיָם הַנְּבִיאָה וַאֲבִיגַיִל. וְאֶסְתֵּר
הַמַּלְכָּה בַּת אֲבִיחַיִל. הוּא יְבָרֵךְ אֶת הַיַּלְדָּה הַנְּעִימָה (הַזֹּאת). וְיִקָּרֵא
שְׁמָהּ _____ בְּמַזָּל טוֹב וּבְשַׁעַת בְּרָכָה. וִיגַדְּלֶהָ
בִּבְרִיאוּת שָׁלוֹם וּמְנוּחָה. וִיזַכֶּה אֶת־אָבִיהָ וְאֶת־אִמָּהּ לִרְאוֹת בְּשִׂמְחָתָהּ
וּבְחֻפָּתָהּ. בְּבָנִים זְכָרִים עֹשֶׁר וְכָבוֹד. דְּשֵׁנִים וְרַעֲנַנִּים יְנוּבוּן בְּשֵׂיבָה.
וְכֵן יְהִי רָצוֹן וְנֹאמַר אָמֵן:

Mi-sheberach Sarah v'Rivkah, Rachel v'Leah oo-Miriam ha-neviah v'Avigayil. V'-Esther ha-malka bat Avihayil. Who yivarech et ha-yaldah ha'na'imah hazot. V'yikareh shem-ah _____ b'mazal tov oo-v'sha'aht bracha. V'yigadlah b'vrioot shalom oo-menoocha. V'yizakeh et avi-ha, v'et eem-ah lirot b'simchata oo-v'chuppatah. B'vanim z'charim osher v'chavod. D'shaynim v'ra'ananim yinoovoon b'sayva. V'chen yihi ratzon v'nomar amen.

May He who blessed our mothers Sarah, Rebecca, Rachel and Leah, Miriam the prophetess, Avigail, and Esther the queen, bless also this darling babe. In happy augury may her name be called _____, daughter of _____ (father's name).

May He bless her to grow up in weal, health, and happiness. May He give to her parents the joy of seeing her happily married, a radiant mother of children, rich in honor and joy to a ripe old age. May this be the will of God and let us say: Amen.

Psalm 128

שִׁיר הַמַּעֲלוֹת; אַשְׁרֵי כָּל־יְרֵא יהוה, הַהֹלֵךְ בִּדְרָכָיו. יְגִיעַ כַּפֶּיךָ כִּי
תֹאכֵל, אַשְׁרֶיךָ וְטוֹב לָךְ. אֶשְׁתְּךָ כְּגֶפֶן פֹּרִיָּה בְּיַרְכְּתֵי בֵיתֶךָ; בָּנֶיךָ
כִּשְׁתִלֵי זֵיתִים סָבִיב לְשֻׁלְחָנֶךָ. הִנֵּה כִי־כֵן יְבֹרַךְ גָּבֶר יְרֵא יהוה. יְבָרֶכְךָ
יהוה מִצִּיּוֹן, וּרְאֵה בְּטוּב יְרוּשָׁלָיִם כֹּל יְמֵי חַיֶּיךָ. וּרְאֵה בָנִים לְבָנֶיךָ,
שָׁלוֹם עַל־יִשְׂרָאֵל.

Shir ha-ma'alot: Ashrey kol yireh Adonai, ha-holech b'drachayv.
Yigiah kapeycha ki tochayl, ashreycha v'tov lach. Ishticha k'gefen
poriah b'yarketey beitecha baneicha chshtiley zeitim saviv le-shu-
lchonecha. Hiney chi chen yivorech gever yireh Adonai. Yivarechecha
Adonai mitzion, oo-ra'eh b'tuv Yerushalayim kol yimei chayyecha.
Oo-ra'eh vanim livanecha, shalom al Yisrael.

A song of ascents. Praiseworthy is each person who fears *Hashem,*
who walks in His paths. When you eat the labor of your hands you
are praiseworthy, and it is well with you. Your wife shall be like a
fruitful vine in the inner chambers of your home; your children
shall be like olive shoots surrounding your table. Behold! For so is
blessed the man who fears *Hashem.* May *Hashem* bless you from
Zion, and may you gaze upon the goodness of Jerusalem, all the
days of your life. And may you see children born to your children,
peace upon Israel.

A Contemporary Orthodox Ceremony

The parents of Shoshana Meira Lambert-Caplan wanted to welcome
her in a special, religiously significant way, and searched for a way to do
so within the boundaries of Orthodox Jewish law. They held a festive
religious meal with close friends who had a daughter at about the same

time. They rented a synagogue basement, invited their friends, and brought in trays of bagels and lox and a sheet cake that said *"Bruchot Haba'ot,"* welcome to the girls who had come into their lives.

Newborn Shoshana's mother, Rivkah Lambert, wrote out insightful, inspiring comments based on the Torah and on traditional Jewish prayers and beliefs. She read them out loud in honor of her daughter's birth, recognizing in them the power of the Almighty and the miracle of creation.[2]

This kind of creation from nothing, like the way a new baby is created within a woman's body, out of nothing, is one aspect of what we mean when we talk about women's Torah.

While I was pregnant with Shoshana, many of the blessings that are part of our morning prayers took on additional meaning for me. I saw new relevance for the blessings in terms of what G-d provides to the infant before birth, after her birth, and as she grows. This new way of thinking about the morning blessings differs from any of the traditional interpretations I have ever heard. I share them with you with a full acknowledgment that this way of understanding them is mine alone and not meant to represent traditional commentary. This type of enhanced interpretation, coming directly out of my own experience, is also a form of women's Torah, a Torah that is lived as much as it is learned.

Each morning we bless G-d *"rokah ha'aretz al hamayim,"* Who spreads out the earth upon the waters. At conception, the cells that will become the child are barely distinguishable from the rest of the uterine environment. As the baby grows and forms, her body becomes increasingly separate and distinct from the surrounding environment, just as, in the beginning, G-d made separate the earth from the water.

Each morning we bless G-d *"she'asa li kol tzorki,"* Who has provided me my every need. G-d designed the uterine environment to be completely self-contained. All the baby's needs are met within it. The miracle of this becomes clear as soon as the baby is born and parents have to buy all sorts of gear to duplicate all the functions that the mother's body had provided for the child!

Each morning we bless G-d *"matir asurim"* and *"zokaif kifufim,"* Who releases the bound and straightens the bent. Before birth, the child is cramped into the limited space within the mother's body. At birth, the infant is released and can stretch the whole length of her body and straighten out for the first time.

Each morning we bless G-d *"malbish arumim,"* Who clothes the naked. All babies come into this world naked and among the first things we do for a newborn, in her first hour of life, is to clothe her just as G-d clothed Adam and Chava (the Hebrew name for Eve) as an act of kindness.

Each morning we bless G-d *"pokeach ivrim,"* Who gives sight to the blind. Before birth a child cannot see. At birth, G-d grants her the ability to open her eyes and use her sense of sight.

Each morning we bless G-d *"asher natan binah l'havchin bein yom uvein lalah,"* Who gave the heart understanding to distinguish between day and night. On the simplest level, before a child is born, she cannot distinguish between day and night, as any exhausted parent of a newborn will confirm! After birth, G-d gives her the ability to learn the different rhythms of daytime and nighttime and to adjust herself to them. In addition, to a newborn, the entire physical world seems an extension of herself. As the baby grows, G-d grants her the ability to begin to distinguish between her physical self and the world around her.

Each morning we bless G-d *"ozair Yisrael b'gevurah,"* Who girds Israel with strength. A new baby does not have the strength even to hold her head up straight. Over time, G-d provides her with increasing strength physically, emotionally and spiritually.

Each morning we bless G-d *"hamaychin mitzadey gaver,"* Who firms our footsteps. Babies are born with legs that cannot support them. As toddlers, G-d grants them the ability to stand and then to walk, wobbly at first and then, over time, their footsteps are firmed.

I wish for Shoshana what I wish for my first daughter, Ariella, and for myself and for all Jewish women—that the feminine aspects of G-d, Torah and Judaism are revealed and made accessible to us speedily in our days.

A Traditionally Oriented Contemporary Ceremony

The baby is carried in by her grandmother. Then the assembled guests sing:

בְּרוּכָה הַבָּאָה בְּשֵׁם יהוה,

Brucha haba-ah b'shem Adonai!

Welcome, in the name of the Lord!

To be read by her grandmother or godmother:

From *Shir HaShirim*—The Song of Songs

מִי־זֹאת הַנִּשְׁקָפָה כְּמוֹ שָׁחַר, יָפָה כַלְּבָנָה, בָּרָה כַּחַמָּה...?

Mi-zot ha-nishkafah k'mo-shachar, yafah chalevana, barah kachamah?

Who is she who shines through like the dawn,
Beautiful as the moon, radiant as the sun?

From *Shir HaShirim*—The Song of Songs

אַחַת הִיא יוֹנָתִי תַמָּתִי. אַחַת הִיא לְאִמָּהּ. בָּרָה הִיא לְיוֹלַדְתָּהּ. רָאוּהָ בָנוֹת וַיְאַשְּׁרוּהָ.

Achat he yonati tamati. Achat he l'imah. Barah he l'yoladetah. Ra-ooha banot vay-ashrooha.

Only one is my dove, my perfect one; she is unique to her mother, the delight of her who bore her, maidens see and praise her.

This material is from *Celebrating Your New Jewish Daughter: Creating Jewish Ways to Welcome Baby Girls into the Covenant—New and Traditional Ceremonies* by Debra Nussbaum Cohen, © 2001, published by Jewish Lights Publishing, P.O. Box 237, Woodstock, VT 05091. (802) 457-4000; www.jewishlights.com.

This can be read by a parent, rabbi or other ceremony leader:

When Israel Stood to Receive the Torah

FROM *SONG OF SONGS RABBAH* 1:24

When Israel stood to receive the Torah, the Holy One said to them:
I am giving you My Torah
Bring me good guarantors that you will guard it and I shall give it
    to you.
And the people replied:
Our ancestors are our guarantors.
But the Holy One said to them:
Your ancestors are unacceptable to me
Yet bring me good guarantors and I shall give it to you
Israel then answered:
God, our prophets are our guarantors.
And again God said to them:
The prophets are unacceptable to me
Yet bring me good guarantors and I shall give it to you.
The people then responded:
Behold, our children are our guarantors,
And God then gently, and with great hope and love, replied:
They are certainly good guarantors. For their sake I give the Torah
    to you.
All the generations were present at Sinai, even those yet unborn.
(Deuteronomy 29:9–14)

וַהֲקִמֹתִי אֶת־בְּרִיתִי בֵּינִי וּבֵינֶךָ וּבֵין זַרְעֲךָ אַחֲרֶיךָ לְדֹרֹתָם לִבְרִית
עוֹלָם לִהְיוֹת לְךָ לֵאלֹהִים וּלְזַרְעֲךָ אַחֲרֶיךָ.

*Va-hakamotee et breetee bayni oo-vaynecha oo-vayn zaracha
acharecha l'dorotam l'vrit olam liheeyot lecha l'Elohim oo-lezaracha
achareycha.*

Then I will establish a covenant between Me and you
and your descendants who come after you;
A covenant in which I will be your God
And your children's God forever and ever.

A parent may read:

בָּרוּךְ אַתָּה יהוה, אֱלֹהֵינוּ מֶלֶךְ הָעוֹלָם, אֲשֶׁר קִדַּשׁ יְדִיד מִבֶּטֶן, אֵל חַי
חֶלְקֵנוּ צוּרֵנוּ צִוָּה לְהַצִּיל יְדִידוּת שְׁאֵרֵנוּ מִשַּׁחַת, לְמַעַן בְּרִיתוֹ. בָּרוּךְ
אַתָּה יהוה, כּוֹרֵת הַבְּרִית.

*Baruch Atah Adonai, Elohaynoo Melech ha-olam, asher kidash yedid
mibeten. El chai chelkeynoo tzooreynoo, tzivah lehatzil yedidut she-
eraynoo me-shachat, lema'an britoh. Baruch Atah Adonai, koret
habrit.*

Blessed are You, Ruler of the universe, who has sanctified Your
beloved from the womb, establishing Your holy covenant
throughout the generations. May devotion to the covenant continue to sustain us as a people. Praised are You, eternal God, who
has established the covenant.

Next comes the naming. A parent, the rabbi, or other ceremony
leader says:

מִי שֶׁבֵּרַךְ שָׂרָה וְרִבְקָה רָחֵל וְלֵאָה. וּמִרְיָם הַנְּבִיאָה וַאֲבִיגָיִל. וְאֶסְתֵּר
הַמַּלְכָּה בַּת אֲבִיחַיִל. הוּא יְבָרֵךְ אֶת הַיַּלְדָּה הַנְּעִימָה (הַזֹּאת). וְיִקָּרֵא
שְׁמָהּ _____ בְּמַזָּל טוֹב וּבִשְׁעַת בְּרָכָה. וְיִגְדְּלֶהָ בִּבְרִיאוּת שָׁלוֹם
וּמְנוּחָה. וְיִזְכֶּה אֶת־אָבִיהָ וְאֶת־אִמָּהּ לִרְאוֹת בְּשִׂמְחָתָהּ וּבְחֻפָּתָהּ.
בְּבָנִים זְכָרִים עֹשֶׁר וְכָבוֹד. דְּשֵׁנִים וְרַעֲנַנִּים יְנוּבוּן בְּשֵׂיבָה. וְכֵן יְהִי
רָצוֹן וְנֹאמַר אָמֵן:

*Mi-sheberach Sarah v'Rivkah, Rachel v'Leah oo-Miriam ha-neviah
v'Avigayil oo-Esther ha-malka bat Avihayil. Who yivarech et ha-
yaldah ha'na'imah hazot. V'yikarah shem-ah _____
b'mazal tov oo-v'sha'aht bracha. V'yigadlah b'vrioot shalom oo-
menoocha. V'yizakeh et avi-ha, v'et eem-ah lirot b'simchata oo-
v'chuppatah. B'vanim z'charim osher v'kavod. D'shenim v'ra'ananim
yinoovoon b'sayva. V'chen yihi ratzon v'nomar amen.*

May God who blessed our mothers Sarah, Rebecca, Rachel and
Leah, Miriam the prophetess, Avigail, and Esther the queen, bless
also this darling babe. In happy augury may her name be called

_____ , daughter of _____
(father's name) and _____ (mother's name).

May God bless her to grow up in wealth, health, and happiness.
May God give to her parents the joy of seeing her happily married,
a radiant mother of children, rich in honor and joy to a ripe old
age. May this be the will of God and let us say: Amen.

A grandparent says:

God and God of all generations, we are grateful for new beginnings,
for the bond of life that links one generation to another. We are
thankful for the blessings of family that bring meaning and happiness to our lives, and we rejoice with our children at the birth of
their child, our granddaughter. May we all grow together as a family in health and in strength, in harmony and in love.

This is also good for a grandparent to recite:

The crown of the aged are children's children
And the glory of children are their parents (Proverbs 17:6)

Parents say together:

בָּרוּךְ אַתָּה יהוה, אֱלֹהֵינוּ מֶלֶךְ הָעוֹלָם, הַטּוֹב וְהַמֵּטִיב.

Baruch Atah Adonai, Eloheinu Melech ha-olam, ha-tov v'hameitiv.

Blessed are You, Lord our God, King of the universe, who is good
and beneficent.

בָּרוּךְ אַתָּה יהוה, אֱלֹהֵינוּ מֶלֶךְ הָעוֹלָם, מְשַׂמֵּחַ הוֹרִים בְּיַלְדֵיהֶם.

Baruch Atah Adonai, misameach horim beyaldeyhem.

Blessed are You, O God, who makes parents rejoice with their
children.

Then the father continues with the blessings over the wine and
bread.

A Modern *Mikvah* Ceremony

The baby, wrapped in her mother's or father's *tallit*, is carried in by her godmother or a female relative. After she is handed to her mother, everyone assembled sings:

B'ruchot Haba'ot
DEBBIE FRIEDMAN

בְּרוּכוֹת הַבָּאוֹת תַּחַת כַּנְפֵי הַשְּׁכִינָה

בְּרוּכִים הַבָּאִים תַּחַת כַּנְפֵי הַשְּׁכִינָה.

B'ruchot haba'ot, tachat kanfe hash'china
B'ruchim haba'im, tachat kanfe hash'china

May you be blessed beneath the wings of *sh'china*
Be blessed with love, be blessed with peace

The baby's mother then recites:

Blessing of Creation
MARCIA FALK, FROM *THE BOOK OF BLESSINGS*

נְבָרֵךְ אֶת עֵין הַחַיִּים,

מְקוֹר הַחֹשֶׁךְ וְהָאוֹר,

מְקוֹר הַשְּׁלֵמוּת וְהַתֹּהוּ,

מְקוֹר הַטּוֹב וְהָרֵע,

מְקוֹר כָּל יְצִירָה.

N'vareykh et eyn hahayim,
m'kor hahoshekh v'ha'or,
m'kor hash'leymut v'hatohu,
m'kor hatov v'hara,
m'kor kol y'tzirah.

> Let us bless the source of life,
> source of darkness and light,
> heart of harmony and chaos,
> creativity and creation.

The baby's father or mother should welcome those who have come and introduce the ceremony by briefly speaking about what will happen. They should speak about the baby's birth date, if it coincides with any significant date or holiday on the Jewish calendar, and what this baby's arrival means to their family.

Then, three women—the mother and the grandmothers, or, if both are not available, two other significant women in the family's life—will occupy the three chairs set up side by side at the front of the room. The mother will sit with her new daughter in her arms in the center chair. Her mother will sit to their right, the mother of the baby's father in the chair to their left.

The father points to the center chair where his wife and their daughter sit and says:

> This is your chair, Elijah, who returns to children the heart of a parent, and to parents the heart of a child. This is your chair, Elijah. Send your guardian powers to protect this child as she strives throughout life to keep the covenant into which we are welcoming her today. This is your chair, Elijah. Help all of us to spread the message that the time is coming for the victory over oppression, and that the time is ripe for the arrival of a newborn world of joy.

For the covenant an honored guest may read:

> How precious is Your constant love, O God.
> We take shelter under Your wings.
> We feast in the abundance of Your house.
> You give us to drink from Your stream of delights.
> With You is the fountain of life.
> In Your light we are bathed in light.
> (Psalm 36:8–10)

Another honored guest may read:

> How fair are your tents, O Jacob,
> Your dwellings, O Israel!
> Like palm-groves that stretch out,
> Like gardens beside a river,
> Like aloes planted by the Lord,
> Like cedars beside the water;
> Water shall flow from his branches,
> And his seed shall be in many waters.
> (Numbers 24:5–7)

Another honored guest may read:

> Blessed is the person who trusts in the Lord,
> And whose trust the Lord is.
> For he shall be as a tree planted by the waters,
> And that spreads out its roots by the river,
> And shall not see when heat comes,
> But its foliage shall be luxuriant;
> And shall not be anxious in the year of drought,
> Neither shall cease from yielding fruit.
> (Jeremiah 17:7–8)

Now the parents pour water collected from a natural source, or from a bottle of spring water, into a vessel representing the *mikvah* and say:

> Behold, God is my salvation;
> I will trust, and will not be afraid;
> For God the Lord is my strength and song;
> And Adonai is become my salvation.
> Therefore with joy shall you draw water
> Out of the wells of salvation.
> And in that day shall you say:
> Give thanks unto the Lord, proclaim Adonai's name,
> Declare Adonai's doings among the peoples,

Make mention that Adonai's name is exalted.
Sing unto the Lord; for Adonai hath done gloriously;
This is made known in all the earth.
Cry aloud and shout, thou inhabitants of Zion,
For great is the Holy One of Israel in the midst of you.
(Isaiah 12:2–6)

Parents recite the following blessing before they immerse their daughter:

בָּרוּךְ אַתָּה יהוה, אֱלֹהֵינוּ מֶלֶךְ הָעוֹלָם, אֲשֶׁר קִדְּשָׁנוּ בְּמִצְוֹתָיו וְצִוָּנוּ
עַל הַמִּקְוֶה.

*Baruch Atah Adonai, Eloheynoo Melech ha-olam, asher kidshanoo
b'mitzvotav vitzivanoo al ha-mikvah.*

Blessed are You, Lord our God, Creator of the universe, who has
sanctified us through His commandments, and commanded us
about immersion.

Now the baby is immersed in the waters of the *mikvah*. Everyone responds:

The Lord is the *mikvah*/hope of Israel!
All who forsake you shall be put to shame,
Those in the land who turn from You
Shall be doomed men
For they have forsaken the Lord,
The Fount of living waters.
(Jeremiah 17:13)

The parents then continue:

בָּרוּךְ אַתָּה יהוה, אֱלֹהֵינוּ מֶלֶךְ הָעוֹלָם, אֲשֶׁר קִדְּשָׁנוּ בְּמִצְוֹתָיו וְצִוָּנוּ
לְהַכְנִיסָהּ בִּבְרִיתָהּ שֶׁל שָׂרָה אִמֵּנוּ.

*Baruch Atah Adonai, Eloheynoo Melech ha-olam, asher kidshanoo
b'mitzvotav vitzivanoo lehachnisa b'vritah shel Sarah imeynoo.*

Blessed are You, Lord our God, Creator of the universe, who has
sanctified us through His commandments and commanded us to
enter our daughters into the covenant of Sarah our mother.

Guests respond:

כְּשֵׁם שֶׁנִּכְנְסָה לַבְּרִית, כֵּן תִּכָּנֵס לְתוֹרָה וּלְחֻפָּה וּלְמַעֲשִׂים טוֹבִים.

*K'shem she-nichnesah labrit ken tikaness l'Torah u-lechuppah ule-
ma'asim tovim.*

Even as this child has entered into the covenant, so may she enter
into the Torah, the marriage canopy, and good deeds.

Parents continue:

בָּרוּךְ אַתָּה יהוה, אֱלֹהֵינוּ מֶלֶךְ הָעוֹלָם, אֲשֶׁר קִדַּשׁ יְדִיד מִבֶּטֶן וְכוֹנַנְתָּ
בְּרִית זוֹ עִם עַמְּךָ יִשְׂרָאֵל כַּכָּתוּב: "וְזָרַקְתִּי עֲלֵיכֶם מַיִם טְהוֹרִים
וּטְהַרְתֶּם ... וְנָתַתִּי לָכֶם לֵב חָדָשׁ וְרוּחַ חֲדָשָׁה אֶתֵּן בְּקִרְבְּכֶם". שֶׁכָּל
טְבִילָה תִּהְיֶה זֵכֶר לְיוֹם זֶה וְסִימָן לְצֶאֱצָאֶיהָ הָעֲתִידִים לָבוֹא. בִּשְׂכַר
זֹאת אֵל חַי, צַוֵּרנוּ צַוֵּה לְהַצִּיל יְדִידוּת שְׁאֵרֵנוּ מִשַּׁחַת. לְמַעַן בְּרִית
מִקְוֶה אֲשֶׁר טָבַלְנוּ טַפֵּנוּ. בָּרוּךְ אַתָּה יהוה, כּוֹרֵת הַבְּרִית.

*Baruch Atah Adonai, Eloheynoo Melech ha-olam, asher kidash yedid
mibeten v'chonantah brit zeh im amecha Yisrael kakatoov "v'zarakti
aleychem mayim tahorim oo-tehartem ... v'natati lachem lev
chadash v'ruach chadasha etayn b'kirbachem." Sh'kol tevilah
yehiyeh zecher l'yom zeh v'siman le-tse-eh-tsa-eha ha-atidoot lavoh.
B'schar zot El chai tzoraynoo tzaveh lehatzil yedidoot she-ey-renu
mishachat. Lema'an brit mikvah asher tavalnoo tapaynoo. Baruch
Atah Adonai koret habrit.*

Blessed are You, Lord our God, Creator of the universe, who did
sanctify the well-beloved from the womb, and established this
covenant with Your people Israel, as it is written: "And I will sprinkle clean water upon you and you shall be clean ... A new heart
also will I give you, and a new spirit will I put within you...."
(Ezekiel 36:25–26)

That every immersion shall be a remembrance of this day, and a sign of future generations. On this account, O living God our rock, give command to deliver from destruction your beloved people, for the sake of the covenant of *mikvah* for which we have immersed our children. Blessed are You, Lord our God, who establishes the covenant.

Continue to the naming part of the ceremony. The baby's mother or father says:

She is transformed, named, given tribe and history, roots, purpose, baggage, and wings. And as she is transformed, so are we, the community gathered for the ritual, who have relived again the biblical stories of our ancestors and the messianic promise of our redemption, in the process of welcoming another Jew into our covenantal community.

מִי שֶׁבֵּרַךְ אִמּוֹתֵינוּ שָׂרָה רִבְקָה רָחֵל וְלֵאָה וּמִרְיָם הַנְּבִיאָה וַאֲבִיגַיִל וְאֶסְתֵּר הַמַּלְכָּה בַּת אֲבִיחַיִל. הוּא יְבָרֵךְ אֶת הַנַּעֲרָה הַנְּעִימָה הַזֹּאת וְיִקָּרֵא שְׁמָהּ בְּיִשְׂרָאֵל _____ בְּמַזָּל טוֹב וּבְשָׁעַת בְּרָכָה. וְיִגְדְּלָהּ בִּבְרִיאוּת שָׁלוֹם וּמְנוּחָה לְתוֹרָה וּלְחֻפָּה וּלְמַעֲשִׂים טוֹבִים. וִיזַכֶּה אֶת אָבִיהָ וְאֶת אִמָּהּ לִרְאוֹת בְּשִׂמְחָתָהּ בְּבָנִים וּבָנוֹת עֹשֶׁר וְכָבוֹד דְּשֵׁנִים וְרַעֲנַנִּים יְנוּבוּן בְּשֵׂיבָה וְכֵן יְהִי רָצוֹן וְנֹאמַר אָמֵן.

Mi she-beyrach imoteynoo Sarah, Rivkah, Rachel v'Leah oo-Miriam ha-neviyah v'Avigayil v'Esther ha-malkah. Who yivarech et ha-na'arah ha'na'imah hazot v'yikarah shem-ah b'Yisrael _____. B'mazal tov oo-v'sha'aht bracha. V'yigadlah b'vrioot shalom oo-menoocha l'Torah oo-l'chuppah oo-l'ma'asim tovim. V'yizakeh et avi-ha, v'et eem-ah lirot b'simchata b'vanim oo-vanot osher v'chavod d'shenim v'ra'ananim yinoovoon b'seva v'chen yihi ratzon v'nomar amen.

May God who blessed our mothers Sarah, Rivkah, Rachel and Leah, Miriam the prophet, Avigail, and Queen Esther, bless this lovely girl _____, daughter of

_____ and _____ at this favorable and blessed hour.

May she grow in health, peace, and tranquillity and be raised to a life of Torah, the wedding canopy, and good deeds. May her parents merit to see her joyful, blessed with children, prosperity and honor, bringing fulfillment and refreshment to their old age. May this be God's will. Amen.

Then the baby's parents discuss the significance of their daughter's name. A grandparent or other loved one may recite:

The Gift of Gratitude
MARCIA FALK, FROM *THE BOOK OF BLESSINGS*

בְּפֶה מָלֵא שִׁירָה
וּבְלָשׁוֹן שׁוֹפַעַת רִנָּה —

נְבָרֵךְ אֶת עֵין הַחַיִּים
וְכֹה נִתְבָּרֵךְ.

B'feh maley shirah
uvlashon shofa'at rinah—
N'vareykh et eyn hahayim
v'khoh nitbareykh.

Our mouths filled with song,
our tongues overflowing with joy—

We bless the source of life
and so we are blessed.

Then everyone joins together to sing a closing song:

L'chi Lach
DEBBIE FRIEDMAN

L'chi lach to a land that I will show you
Lech l'cha to a place you do not know

L'chi lach, on your journey I will bless you.
And you shall be a blessing, you shall be a blessing
You shall be a blessing, *I'chi lach.*

L'chi lach, and I shall make your name great
Lech I'cha, and all shall praise your name
L'chi lach, to the place that I will show you
L'simchat chochma, I'simchat chayim
L'simchat chayim, L'chi lach.
And you shall be a blessing, you shall be a blessing
You shall be a blessing, *L'chi lach.*

Finally, the parents or honored guests recite the blessings over wine
(or grape juice) and challah.

A Humanism-Based Ceremony

This sample welcoming ceremony focuses more on universal desires
for our daughters and less on the particular concept of covenant,
but still retains the essential form of a Jewish welcoming ceremony
and its feeling.

The baby is carried into the room by her grandmother, godmother, or other honored female guest, while the others gathered
say, strongly, "Welcome! *Brucha haba'ah!*"

The baby is then handed to her mother, who says:

Blessed are You, Source of all creation, who in bestowing goodness
upon humankind has dealt graciously with me.

The baby is handed to her father, who recites:

Blessing of Creation

MARCIA FALK, FROM *THE BOOK OF BLESSINGS*

נְבָרֵךְ אֶת עֵין הַחַיִּים,
מְקוֹר הַחֹשֶׁךְ וְהָאוֹר,
מְקוֹר הַשְּׁלֵמוּת וְהַתֹּהוּ,
מְקוֹר הַטּוֹב וְהָרָע,
מְקוֹר כָּל יְצִירָה.

N'vareykh et eyn hahayim,
m'kor hahoshekh v'ha'or,
m'kor hash'leymut v'hatohu,
m'kor hatov v'hara,
m'kor kol y'tzirah.

Let us bless the source of life,
source of darkness and light,
heart of harmony and chaos,
creativity and creation.

An honored guest reads:

For Each Child That's Born

YSAYE MARIA BARNWELL

For each child that's born
a morning star rises and sings to the universe
who we are

We are our grandfather's prayers
We are our grandmother's dreamings
We are the breath of the ancestors
We are the spirit of God.

We are
Mothers of courage
Fathers of time
Daughters of dust

The sons of great visions
Brothers of love
Lovers of life
Builders of nations
Seekers of truth
Keepers of faith
Makers of peace
Wisdom of ages …

Another honored guest reads:

Your Children Are Not Your Children

FROM *THE PROPHET* BY KAHLIL GIBRAN

Your children are not your children.
They are the sons and daughters of Life's longing for itself.
They come through you but not from you,
And though they are with you, yet they belong not to you.

You may give them your love but not your thoughts,
For they have their own thoughts.
You may house their bodies but not their souls,
For their souls dwell in the house of tomorrow, which you cannot
    visit, not even in your dreams.

You may strive to be like them, but seek not to make them like
    you.
For life goes not backward nor tarries with yesterday.
You are the bows from which your children as living arrows are
    sent forth.
The archer sees the mark upon the path of the infinite, and He
    bends you with His might that His arrows may go swift and far.

Let your bending in the archer's hand be for gladness;
For even as He loves the arrow that flies, so He loves also the bow
    that is stable.

At this point, those who wish to should approach the parents and the new baby at the front of the room to offer the new daughter a gift of some Jewish ceremonial item or other meaningful object, and to offer the family their thoughts, blessings, and poems.

An honored guest may read:

With Every Child Born

ADAPTED FROM ABRAHAM JOSHUA HESCHEL

With every child born a new experience enters the world. She encounters not only flowers and stars, mountains and walls, but a sublime expectation, a waiting for, when something is asked of you. Meaning is found in responding to the demand, meaning is found in sensing the demand.

May you remember that every deed counts, that every word has power, and that we can all do our share to redeem the world in spite of all the absurdities and all the frustrations and disappointments. Above all, remember to build a life as if it were a work of art.

You are unique, exceedingly precious, not to be exchanged for anything else.

No one will live your life for you, _____, no one will think your thoughts for you or dream your dreams.

Then an honored guest, like a grandparent, may read this prayer:

Let _____ be a person whose heart will be clear, whose goals will be high, a person who will master herself before she seeks to master others, one who will learn to laugh, yet never forget how to weep, one who will reach into the future, yet never forget the past. After all these things are hers, this we pray, enough sense of humor that she may always be serious but never take herself too seriously. Give her humility so that she may always remember the simplicity of true greatness, the open mind of true wisdom, the meekness of true strength. Then we, her family and friends, will dare to whisper that we, too, have been enriched.

Next, the parents may read this, alternating lines:

Parents' Prayer
RABBI SANDY EISENBERG SASSO

What I/we wish for _____ , I/we wish for all children. I/we wish for you to be a person of character, strong but not tough, gentle but not weak.

I/we wish for you to be righteous but not self-righteous, honest but not unforgiving.

Whenever you journey, may your steps be firm and may you walk in just paths and not be afraid.

Whenever you speak, may your words be words of wisdom and friendship.

May your hands build, and your heart preserve what is good and beautiful in our world.

May the voices of the generations of our people move through you, and may the God of our ancestors be your God as well.

May you know that there is a people, a rich heritage to which you belong, and from that sacred place you are connected to all who dwell on earth.

May the stories of our people be upon your heart, and the grace of the Torah rhythm dance in your soul.

For the naming part of the ceremony, a parent or honored guest may read:

Adapted from 1 Samuel 25:25
Like her name, so is she.

There Are Three Names
ADAPTED FROM *MIDRASH TANHUMA, PARASHAT VAYIKAHAL*

There are three names by which a person is called:
One which her father and mother call her,
And one which people call her,
And one which she earns for herself.
The best one of these is the one that she earns for herself.

The ceremony leader or honored guest says to the parents:

> Friends, may you dedicate yourselves to give your holiest gifts—love and respect—to this new person, whom you have brought to be named, and may you ever give freely of yourselves so that in time's fullness your love will bestow upon this child the gift of freedom. May joy ever accompany such giving and receiving.

The s/he says to the child:

> Now, in the presence of loved ones, we give to you the name _____, daughter of _____ and of _____. Let it become a name honored and respected for wisdom and good deeds. _____, we commit ourselves to the unfolding of your promise; may you walk the path of goodness, beauty, and truth. Do justly and love mercy, and be humble before the mystery of life and the grandeur of the universe into which you have been born.
>
> May God's blessing rest on you now and always:

יְבָרֶכְךָ יהוה וְיִשְׁמְרֶךָ, יָאֵר יהוה פָּנָיו אֵלֶיךָ וִיחֻנֶּךָ. יִשָּׂא יהוה פָּנָיו אֵלֶיךָ וְיָשֵׂם לְךָ שָׁלוֹם.

> *Y'varech'cha Adonai v'yishm'recha. Ya'er Adonai panav aylecha vichunekka. Yissa Adonai panav eilecha v'yahsem lecha shalom.*
>
> May God bless you and keep you. May God look kindly upon you and be gracious to you. May God reach out to you in tenderness, and give you peace.

Then the parents may continue, saying:

> *Mother:* When I look upon you, _____, the child we have made, there are no limitations or longings. I am looking with perfect love. As I experience the perfection of motherhood, the rest of the world is remade before my eyes. I feel something in the world that is more important than I am. I know every other person with different eyes. I know a new kind of love that is devoid of self-interest and desire. Motherhood, like marriage, is a constant

struggle against one's limitations and self-interests. But the urge to be the perfect mother is there, because our child is the perfect gift.

Father: To be your father is the greatest honor I have ever received. It has allowed me to touch mystery for a moment, and to see my love made flesh. If I could have but one wish, it would be for you to pass that love along. After all, there is not much more to life than that.

Mother: My daughter, my child, you are as dear to me as my own breath. May I hold you gently now with the love to keep you close and with the strength to let you grow.

Father: My daughter, my child, a piece of my life is you. You have grown to life apart from me, but now I hold you close to my heart and cradle you in my arms with love.

Parents, together: We have been blessed with the gift of a new life. We have shared love and pain and joy in bringing our daughter into life. By the way we live, we aspire to teach our daughter to become a loving and caring person. God of our ancestors, we pray for love, for life, for good. Keep us strong together and bring us into the shelter of Your presence with a gentle love. Blessed is the Holy Source of Life who causes parents to rejoice with their children.

NOTES

Chapter 1

1. Judith Plaskow, *Standing Again at Sinai: Judaism From a Feminist Perspective* (San Francisco: Harper & Row, 1990), p. xvi.

2. Rabbi Michael Strassfeld, interview with author, July 8, 1999. See also Sharon Strassfeld and Michael Strassfeld, eds., *The Second Jewish Catalog* (Philadelphia: Jewish Publication Society, 1976), pp. 36–37.

3. Rabbi Nina Beth Cardin, interview with author, July 27, 1999.

4. Joseph Kaplan, interview with author, April 2000.

5. Nadine Brozan, "A Share For Girls in Jewish Birthright," *The New York Times*, March 14, 1977.

6. Judy Petsonk, *Taking Judaism Personally: Creating a Meaningful Spiritual Life* (New York: The Free Press, 1996), p. 142.

Chapter 2

1. Rabbi Zevulun Lieberman, interview with author, June 29, 1999.

2. Rabbi Marc Angel, spiritual leader of Manhattan's Congregation Shearith Israel, known as the Spanish and Portuguese Synagogue, interview with author, February 8, 2000.

3. Michele Klein, *A Time to Be Born: Customs and Folklore of Jewish Birth* (Philadelphia: Jewish Publication Society, 1998), p. 180.

4. Angel, interview.

5. *The Orthodox Jewish Woman and Ritual: Options and Opportunities—Birth* (New York: The Jewish Orthodox Feminist Alliance, 1999), p. 3.

6. Klein, *A Time to Be Born,* p. 190.

7. Nikos Stavroulakis, interview with author, July 2000

Chapter 3

1. Rabbi Avi Shafran, interview with author, July 30, 1999.

Chapter 4

1. Rabbi Yoel Kahn in a paper about new life-cycle ceremonies presented to the annual convention of the Reform movement's rabbinical organization, the Central Conference of American Rabbis, in 1992.

Chapter 5

1. *The Orthodox Jewish Woman and Ritual,* p. 11.

2. Chaim Stern, ed., *On the Doorposts of Your House: Prayers and Ceremonies for the Jewish Home* (New York: Central Conference of American Rabbis, 1994), p. 110.

3. From *Moreh Derekh: The Rabbinical Assembly Rabbi's Manual* (New York: The Rabbinical Assembly, 1998), p. A-11.

4. From the welcoming ceremony of Bonnie Lauren Schwartz, in 1996, cited in *The Orthodox Jewish Woman and Ritual,* p. 14.

Chapter 7

1. Rabbis Sandy Eisenberg Sasso and Dennis Sasso in "*B'rit B'not Yisrael:* Covenant for the Daughters of Israel," *Moment,* May/June 1975 (inaugural issue).

Chapter 8

1. *Babylonian Talmud, Gittin 57A.*

2. Rabbi Debra Orenstein, ed., *Lifecycles, Vol. 1: Jewish Women on Life Passages & Personal Milestones* (Woodstock, Vt.: Jewish Lights Publishing, 1994), p. 76.

Chapter 9

1. From *Moreh Derekh*, p. A-30.

2. Adapted from *Moreh Derekh*, p. A-35.

3. Adapted from *On the Doorposts of Your House*, p. 116.

4. From the introduction to Kayla Strassfeld's welcoming ceremony in 1973, written by her parents, Michael Strassfeld and Sharon Strassfeld.

5. Excerpted from an unpublished paper on *brit melach*, by Alana Susskin, a rabbinical student at the University of Judaism in Los Angeles. She suggests starting the ritual by reciting Psalms 135 and 148, followed by a number of other prayers. To get a copy of her extensive ritual, contact asusskin@uj.edu.

6. Said by Ruth Seligman and Jonathan Mark during the welcoming ceremony for their daughter, Sara Noa Nechama Mark, in 1992.

7. Adapted from *Moreh Derekh*, p. A-38.

8. From *On the Doorposts of Your House*, p. 120.

9. From *Kol Haneshama: Songs, Blessings and Rituals for the Home* (Wyncote, Pa.: The Reconstructionist Press, 1991).

Chapter 10

1. Dr. David De Sola Pool, ed. *Daily and Sabbath Prayerbook* (New York: Union of Sephardic Congregations, 1983), p. 417.

2. From the welcoming party for Shoshana Meira Lambert-Caplan, December 4, 1994, in Baltimore, Md.

RESOURCES

Books

Abramowitz, Yosef, and Rabbi Susan Silverman. *Jewish Family & Life Traditions, Holidays and Values for Today's Parents and Children.* New York: Golden Books, 1997.

Birnbaum, Philip, ed. *Ha-Siddur Ha-Shalem: Daily Prayer Book.* New York: Hebrew Publishing Company, 1949.

Breger, Lisa, and Lisa Schlaff, eds. *The Orthodox Jewish Woman and Ritual: Options and Opportunities—Birth.* New York: The Jewish Orthodox Feminist Alliance, 2000.

Diamant, Anita. *The New Jewish Baby Book: Names, Ceremonies, Customs—A Guide for Today's Families.* Woodstock, Vt.: Jewish Lights Publishing, 1993.

Falk, Marcia. *The Book of Blessings: New Jewish Prayers for Daily Life, the Sabbath and the New Moon Festival.* New York: HarperSanFrancisco, 1996.

Fishbein Reifman, Toby, ed. *Blessing the Birth of a Daughter: Jewish Naming Ceremonies for Girls.* New York: Ezrat Nashim, 1978.

Frymer-Kensky, Tikvah. *Motherprayer: The Pregnant Woman's Spiritual Companion.* New York: Riverhead Books, 1995.

Geffen, Rela M. *Celebration and Renewal: Rites of Passage in Judaism.* Philadelphia: The Jewish Publication Society, 1993.

Janner-Klausner, Laura, ed. *Neshama Hadasha/A New Life: An Anthology of New Birth Celebrations from Kehilat Kol Haneshamah.* Jerusalem: Kehilat Kol Haneshama, 1999.

Klein, Michele. *A Time to Be Born: Customs and Folklore of Jewish Birth.* Philadelphia: The Jewish Publication Society, 1998.

Moreh Derekh: The Rabbinical Assembly Rabbi's Manual. New York: The Rabbinical Assembly, 1998.

Orenstein, Rabbi Debra, ed. *Lifecycles, Vol. 1: Jewish Women on Life Passages & Personal Milestones.* Woodstock, Vt.: Jewish Lights Publishing, 1994.

Pleck, Elizabeth H. *Celebrating the Family: Ethnicity, Consumer Culture, and Family Rituals.* Cambridge, Mass.: Harvard University Press, 2000.

Shepard Kraemer, Ross. *Her Share of the Blessings: Women's Religions Among Pagans, Jews and Christians in the Greco-Roman World.* New York: Oxford University Press, 1992.

Stern, Chaim, ed. *On the Doorposts of Your House: Prayers and Ceremonies for the Jewish Home.* New York: The Central Conference of American Rabbis, 1994.

Strassfeld, Sharon, and Michael, eds. *The Second Jewish Catalog.* Philadelphia: The Jewish Publication Society of America, 1976.

Teutsch, Rabbi David, ed. *Kol Haneshamah: Songs, Blessings and Rituals for the Home.* Wyncote, Penn.: The Reconstructionist Press, 1991.

Weidman Schneider, Susan. *Jewish and Female: A Guide and Sourcebook for Today's Jewish Woman.* New York: Simon & Schuster, 1984.

Wolowelsky, Joel. *Women, Jewish Law and Modernity: New Opportunities in a Post-Feminist Age.* Hoboken, N.J.: KTAV Publishing House, 1997.

Websites

www.jewishlights.com Jewish Lights Publishing. For books and other resources. 800-962-4544.

www.jewishmusic.com Tara Publications. For recordings and sheet music by Rabbi Shlomo Carlebach, Debbie Friedman, and Esta

Cassway, among many others. The website also carries a wide range of Jewish videos, software, and books. 800-TARA-400.

www.soundswrite.com SoundsWrite Productions. For recordings, videos, and sheet music by Debbie Friedman. 800-9-SOUND-9 or 800-976-8639.

www.jmwc.org Jewish Music Web Center. An academic focus on Jewish music.

www.haruth.com/JewishMusic A great resource to view and hear traditional, Yiddish, Sephardic, and American popular Jewish music.

www.ritualwell.org A website run jointly by the Jewish feminist groups Ma'yan and Kolot, with information on innovative Jewish rituals including welcoming ceremonies for girls and for boys.

www.Jewish.com A front door into many things Jewish: news, columnists, shopping, and chat.

www.womenandorthodoxy.com An interesting discussion of issues related to women and Orthodoxy on a website sponsored by the Orthodox Caucus, a modern Orthodox leadership group.

www.youngleadership.org A website sponsored by the youngleadership division of UJA–Federation of New York with some information relevant to planning a *simchat bat*.

www.emoil.com A full-service website by Cantor Phillip Sherman, a very popular mohel based in New York who has appeared in an article in the *New Yorker* magazine. His website provides contact information for him as well as a fairly extensive discussion of *brit milah* for boys and welcoming ceremonies for girls. He also addresses a variety of family constellations.

www.arepublishing.com A place to buy a certificate to hang in your home commemorating your daughter's welcoming ceremony.

www.uscj.org The website run by the United Synagogue of Conservative Judaism, with some information on *simchat bat*.

GLOSSARY

Adonai: One of the names for God.

aliyah: Literally, ascent. It is also the name for the honor of being called to bless the Torah before it is read out loud, in synagogue.

Ashkenazic: Jews of Central and Eastern European ancestry.

Avigail: A wife of King David who was known for her beauty and intelligence.

bimah: Raised platform at the front of a synagogue from where services are led.

brit: Covenant.

brit bat: Covenant of a daughter.

brit milah: Commanded covenant of circumcision. Also *bris*.

chuppah: Jewish wedding canopy.

Elijah: The prophet whose presence foretells the messianic age, according to Jewish tradition.

Hollekreisch: The traditional welcoming ritual for German Jewish babies.

kiddush: Blessing over wine; also the name of the reception, with food and drink, following Sabbath synagogue services.

kvatter/kvatterin: Yiddish terms for godfather/godmother (in

Hebrew, *sandek/sandeket*); those with an important role during the rituals of *brit milah* and *simchat bat,* usually carrying in or holding the baby.

Las Fadas: Name of Sephardic home-based welcoming ceremony for Jewish girls.

ma'asim tovim: Good deeds.

midrash: An interpretative commentary on the Torah text.

mikvah: Pool of collected natural water in which Jewish women ritually immerse.

Miriam: A prophetess whose brothers were Moses and Aaron.

mishebeyrach: Prayer of petition for good health and well-being.

mohel: Ritual circumciser.

mohelet: Female ritual circumciser.

niggun/im: Religious song/s without words that is hummed or chanted.

ruach: Spirit, or wind.

sandek/sandeket: Godfather or godmother who has the honor of holding the baby during the *brit milah* or *simchat bat.*

Sephardic: Jews of Spanish and Middle Eastern ancestry.

shehechiyanu: Prayer of thanks said when something good happens.

simcha: Celebration.

Simchat Bat: Celebration of a daughter.

Talmud: Compilation of rabbinic commentaries on the Bible.

Torah: The Bible, the central text of the Jewish people.

Yisrael: A Hebrew term for the people of Israel.

zeved habat: Name of the traditional Sephardic welcoming ceremony for girls.

About JEWISH LIGHTS Publishing

People of all faiths and backgrounds yearn for books that attract, engage, educate and spiritually inspire.

Our principal goal is to stimulate thought and help all people learn about who the Jewish People are, where they come from, and what the future can be made to hold. While people of our diverse Jewish heritage are the primary audience, our books speak to people in the Christian world as well and will broaden their understanding of Judaism and the roots of their own faith.

We bring to you authors who are at the forefront of spiritual thought and experience. While each has something different to say, they all say it in a voice that you can hear.

Our books are designed to welcome you and then to engage, stimulate and inspire. We judge our success not only by whether or not our books are beautiful and commercially successful, but by whether or not they make a difference in your life.

We at Jewish Lights take great care to produce beautiful books that present meaningful spiritual content in a form that reflects the art of making high quality books. Therefore, we want to acknowledge those who contributed to the production of this book.

Stuart M. Matlins, Publisher

PRODUCTION
Marian B. Wallace & Bridgett Taylor

EDITORIAL
Sandra Korinchak, Emily Wichland,
Martha McKinney & Amanda Dupuis

COVER DESIGN
Kathryn Kunz Finney, Des Moines, Iowa

TEXT DESIGN & TYPESETTING
Chelsea Cloeter, Chelsea Designs, Scotia, New York

COVER / TEXT PRINTING & BINDING
Versa Press, East Peoria, Illinois

The Way Into... Series

A major 14-volume series to be completed over the next several years, *The Way Into...* provides an accessible and usable "guided tour" of the Jewish faith, its people, its history and beliefs—in total, an introduction to Judaism for adults that will enable them to understand and interact with sacred texts. Each volume is written by a major modern scholar and teacher, and is organized around an important concept of Judaism.

The Way Into... will enable all readers to achieve a real sense of Jewish cultural literacy through guided study. Available volumes include:

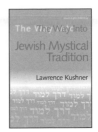

The Way Into Torah

by *Dr. Norman J. Cohen*

What is "Torah"? What are the different approaches to studying Torah? What are the different levels of understanding Torah? For whom is the study intended? Explores the origins and development of Torah, why it should be studied and how to do it.

6 x 9, 176 pp, HC, ISBN 1-58023-028-8 **$21.95**

The Way Into Jewish Prayer

by *Dr. Lawrence A. Hoffman*

Opens the door to 3,000 years of the Jewish way to God by making available all you need to feel at home in Jewish worship. Provides basic definitions of the terms you need to know as well as thoughtful analysis of the depth that lies beneath Jewish prayer.

6 x 9, 224 pp, HC, ISBN 1-58023-027-X **$21.95**

The Way Into Encountering God in Judaism

by *Dr. Neil Gillman*

Explains how Jews have encountered God throughout history—and today—by exploring the many metaphors for God in Jewish tradition. Explores the Jewish tradition's passionate but also conflicting ways of relating to God as Creator, relational partner, and a force in history and nature.

6 x 9, 240 pp, HC, ISBN 1-58023-025-3 **$21.95**

The Way Into Jewish Mystical Tradition

by *Rabbi Lawrence Kushner*

Explains the principles of Jewish mystical thinking, their religious and spiritual significance, and how they relate to our lives. A book that allows us to experience and understand the Jewish mystical approach to our place in the world.

6 x 9, 224 pp, HC, ISBN 1-58023-029-6 **$21.95**

Or phone, fax, mail or e-mail to: **JEWISH LIGHTS Publishing**

Sunset Farm Offices, Route 4 • P.O. Box 237 • Woodstock, Vermont 05091

Tel: (802) 457-4000 • Fax: (802) 457-4004 • www.jewishlights.com

Credit card orders: **(800) 962-4544** (9AM–5PM ET Monday–Friday)

Generous discounts on quantity orders. SATISFACTION GUARANTEED. Prices subject to change.

Spirituality

My People's Prayer Book: *Traditional Prayers, Modern Commentaries*
Ed. by *Dr. Lawrence A. Hoffman*

Provides a diverse and exciting commentary to the traditional liturgy, helping modern men and women find new wisdom in Jewish prayer, and bring liturgy into their lives. Each book includes Hebrew text, modern translation, and commentaries *from all perspectives* of the Jewish world.

Vol. 1—*The Sh'ma and Its Blessings*, 7 x 10, 168 pp, HC, ISBN 1-879045-79-6 **$23.95**
Vol. 2—*The Amidah*, 7 x 10, 240 pp, HC, ISBN 1-879045-80-X **$23.95**
Vol. 3—*P'sukei D'zimrah* (Morning Psalms), 7 x 10, 240 pp, HC, ISBN 1-879045-81-8 **$23.95**
Vol. 4—*Seder K'riat Hatorah* (The Torah Service), 7 x 10, 264 pp, ISBN 1-879045-82-6 **$23.95**
Vol. 5—*Birkhot Hashachar* (Morning Blessings), 7 x 10, 240 pp (est), ISBN 1-879045-83-4 **$24.95**
(Avail. Fall 2001)

   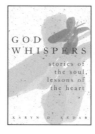 

Becoming a Congregation of Learners
Learning as a Key to Revitalizing Congregational Life by Isa Aron, Ph.D.;
Foreword by Rabbi Lawrence A. Hoffman, Co-Developer, Synagogue 2000
6 x 9, 304 pp, Quality PB, ISBN 1-58023-089-X **$19.95**

Self, Struggle & Change
Family Conflict Stories in Genesis and Their Healing Insights for Our Lives
by Dr. Norman J. Cohen 6 x 9, 224 pp, Quality PB, ISBN 1-879045-66-4 **$16.95**;
HC, ISBN 1-879045-19-2 **$21.95**

Voices from Genesis: *Guiding Us through the Stages of Life*
by Dr. Norman J. Cohen 6 x 9, 192 pp, Quality PB, ISBN 1-58023-118-7 **$16.95**;
HC, ISBN 1-879045-75-3 **$21.95**

God Whispers: *Stories of the Soul, Lessons of the Heart*
by Rabbi Karyn D. Kedar 6 x 9, 176 pp, Quality PB, ISBN 1-58023-088-1 **$15.95**

The Business Bible: *10 New Commandments for Bringing Spirituality &
Ethical Values into the Workplace*
by Rabbi Wayne Dosick 5½ x 8½, 208 pp, Quality PB, ISBN 1-58023-101-2 **$14.95**

Being God's Partner: *How to Find the Hidden Link Between Spirituality and Your Work*
by Rabbi Jeffrey K. Salkin; Intro. by Norman Lear AWARD WINNER!
6 x 9, 192 pp, Quality PB, ISBN 1-879045-65-6 **$16.95**; HC, ISBN 1-879045-37-0 **$19.95**

God & the Big Bang
Discovering Harmony Between Science & Spirituality AWARD WINNER!
by Daniel C. Matt
6 x 9, 224 pp, Quality PB, ISBN 1-879045-89-3 **$16.95**

Soul Judaism: *Dancing with God into a New Era*
by Rabbi Wayne Dosick 5½ x 8½, 304 pp, Quality PB, ISBN 1-58023-053-9 **$16.95**

Finding Joy: *A Practical Spiritual Guide to Happiness* AWARD WINNER!
by Rabbi Dannel I. Schwartz with Mark Hass
6 x 9, 192 pp, Quality PB, ISBN 1-58023-009-1 **$14.95**; HC, ISBN 1-879045-53-2 **$19.95**

Spirituality/Jewish Meditation

Discovering Jewish Meditation
Instruction & Guidance for Learning an Ancient Spiritual Practice
by *Nan Fink Gefen*

Gives readers of any level of understanding the tools to learn the practice of Jewish meditation on your own, starting you on the path to a deep spiritual and personal connection to God and to greater insight about your life. 6 x 9, 208 pp, Quality PB, ISBN 1-58023-067-9 **$16.95**

Entering the Temple of Dreams: *Jewish Prayers, Movements, and Meditations for the End of the Day* by *Tamar Frankiel* and *Judy Greenfeld*

Nighttime spirituality is much more than bedtime prayers! Here, you'll uncover deeper meaning to familiar nighttime prayers—and learn to combine the prayers with movements and meditations to enhance your physical and psychological well-being.
7 x 10, 192 pp, Quality PB, Illus., ISBN 1-58023-079-2 **$16.95**

One God Clapping: *The Spiritual Path of a Zen Rabbi* AWARD WINNER!
by *Alan Lew* & *Sherril Jaffe*

A fascinating personal story of a Jewish meditation expert's roundabout spiritual journey from Zen Buddhist practitioner to rabbi. 5½ x 8½, 336 pp, Quality PB, ISBN 1-58023-115-2 **$16.95**

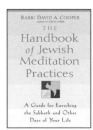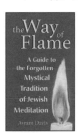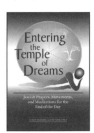

The Handbook of Jewish Meditation Practices
A Guide for Enriching the Sabbath and Other Days of Your Life
by *Rabbi David A. Cooper*

Gives us ancient and modern Jewish tools—Jewish practices and traditions, easy-to-use meditation exercises, and contemplative study of Jewish sacred texts. 6 x 9, 208 pp, Quality PB, ISBN 1-58023-102-0 **$16.95**

Stepping Stones to Jewish Spiritual Living: *Walking the Path Morning, Noon, and Night*
by Rabbi James L. Mirel & Karen Bonnell Werth
6 x 9, 240 pp, Quality PB, ISBN 1-58023-074-1 **$16.95**

Meditation from the Heart of Judaism
Today's Teachers Share Their Practices, Techniques, and Faith
Ed. by Avram Davis 6 x 9, 256 pp, Quality PB, ISBN 1-58023-049-0 **$16.95**;
HC, ISBN 1-879045-77-X **$21.95**

The Way of Flame: *A Guide to the Forgotten Mystical Tradition of Jewish Meditation*
by Avram Davis 4½ x 8, 176 pp, Quality PB, ISBN 1-58023-060-1 **$15.95**

Minding the Temple of the Soul: *Balancing Body, Mind, and Spirit through Traditional Jewish Prayer, Movement, and Meditation*
by Tamar Frankiel and Judy Greenfeld 7 x 10, 184 pp, Quality PB, Illus.,
ISBN 1-879045-64-8 **$16.95**; Audiotape of the Blessings and Meditations (60-min. cassette), JN01 **$9.95**; Videotape of the Movements and Meditations (46-min.), S507 **$20.00**

Life Cycle/Grief

Against the Dying of the Light
A Father's Journey through Loss
by *Leonard Fein*

The sudden death of a child. A personal tragedy beyond description. Rage and despair deeper than sorrow. What can come from it? Raw wisdom and defiant hope. In this unusual exploration of heartbreak and healing, Fein chronicles the sudden death of his 30-year-old daughter and reveals what the progression of grief can teach each one of us.
5½ x 8½, 176 pp, HC, ISBN 1-58023-110-1 **$19.95**

Mourning & Mitzvah: *A Guided Journal for Walking the Mourner's Path through Grief to Healing* with *Over 60 Guided Exercises*
by *Anne Brener, L.C.S.W.*

For those who mourn a death, for those who would help them, for those who face a loss of any kind, Brener teaches us the power and strength available to us in the fully experienced mourning process. 7½ x 9, 288 pp, Quality PB, ISBN 1-879045-23-0 **$19.95**

Tears of Sorrow, Seeds of Hope
A Jewish Spiritual Companion for Infertility and Pregnancy Loss
by Rabbi Nina Beth Cardin   6 x 9, 192 pp, HC, ISBN 1-58023-017-2 **$19.95**

Grief in Our Seasons: *A Mourner's Kaddish Companion*
by Rabbi Kerry M. Olitzky   4½ x 6½, 448 pp, Quality PB, ISBN 1-879045-55-9 **$15.95**

A Time to Mourn, A Time to Comfort
A Guide to Jewish Bereavement and Comfort
by Dr. Ron Wolfson   7 x 9, 336 pp, Quality PB, ISBN 1-879045-96-6 **$18.95**

When a Grandparent Dies
A Kid's Own Remembering Workbook for Dealing with Shiva and the Year Beyond
by Nechama Liss-Levinson, Ph.D.
8 x 10, 48 pp, HC, Illus., 2-color text, ISBN 1-879045-44-3 **$15.95**

Spirituality & More

The Jewish Lights Spirituality Handbook
A Guide to Understanding, Exploring & Living a Spiritual Life
Ed. by *Stuart M. Matlins, Editor-in-Chief, Jewish Lights Publishing*
Rich, creative material from over 50 spiritual leaders on every aspect of Jewish spirituality today: prayer, meditation, mysticism, study, rituals, special days, the everyday, and more.
6 x 9, 304 pp, Quality PB, ISBN 1-58023-093-8 **$16.95**; HC, ISBN 1-58023-100-4 **$24.95**

Six Jewish Spiritual Paths: *A Rationalist Looks at Spirituality*
by *Rabbi Rifat Sonsino*
The quest for spirituality is universal, but which path to spirituality is right *for you*? A straightforward, objective discussion of the many ways—each valid and authentic—for seekers to gain a richer spiritual life within Judaism. 6 x 9, 208 pp, HC, ISBN 1-58023-095-4 **$21.95**

Restful Reflections: *Nighttime Inspiration to Calm the Soul,*
Based on Jewish Wisdom by *Rabbi Kerry M. Olitzky* and *Rabbi Lori Forman*
Wisdom to "sleep on." For each night of the year, an inspiring quote from a Jewish source and a personal reflection on it from an insightful spiritual leader help you to focus on your spiritual life and the lessons your day has offered. The companion to *Sacred Intentions: Daily Inspiration to Strengthen the Spirit, Based on Jewish Wisdom* (see below).
4½ x 6½, 448 pp, Quality PB, ISBN 1-58023-091-1 **$15.95**

 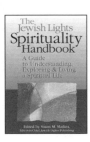 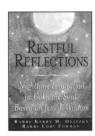 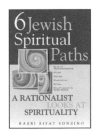 

Sacred Intentions: *Daily Inspiration to Strengthen the Spirit, Based on Jewish Wisdom*
by Rabbi Kerry M. Olitzky and Rabbi Lori Forman
4½ x 6½, 448 pp, Quality PB, ISBN 1-58023-061-X **$15.95**

The Enneagram and Kabbalah: *Reading Your Soul*
by Rabbi Howard A. Addison   6 x 9, 176 pp, Quality PB, ISBN 1-58023-001-6 **$15.95**

Embracing the Covenant: *Converts to Judaism Talk About Why & How*
Ed. and with Intros. by Rabbi Allan L. Berkowitz and Patti Moskovitz
6 x 9, 192 pp, Quality PB, ISBN 1-879045-50-8 **$15.95**

Mystery Midrash: *An Anthology of Jewish Mystery & Detective Fiction*   AWARD WINNER!
Ed. by Lawrence W. Raphael   6 x 9, 304 pp, Quality PB, ISBN 1-58023-055-5 **$16.95**

Wandering Stars: *An Anthology of Jewish Fantasy & Science Fiction* Ed. by Jack Dann; Intro. by Isaac Asimov   6 x 9, 272 pp, Quality PB, ISBN 1-58023-005-9 **$16.95**

Israel—A Spiritual Travel Guide AWARD WINNER!
A Companion for the Modern Jewish Pilgrim
by Rabbi Lawrence A. Hoffman   4¾ x 10, 256 pp, Quality PB, ISBN 1-879045-56-7 **$18.95**

Theology/Philosophy

A Heart of Many Rooms: *Celebrating the Many Voices within Judaism*
by *Dr. David Hartman* **AWARD WINNER!**
From the perspective of traditional Judaism, Hartman shows that commitment to both Jewish tradition and to pluralism can create understanding between people of different religious convictions. 6 x 9, 352 pp, HC, ISBN 1-58023-048-2 **$24.95**

These Are the Words: *A Vocabulary of Jewish Spiritual Life*
by *Arthur Green*
What are the most essential ideas, concepts and terms that an educated person needs to know about Judaism? From *Adonai* (My Lord) to *zekhut* (merit), this enlightening and entertaining journey through Judaism teaches us the 149 core Hebrew words that constitute the basic vocabulary of Jewish spiritual life. 6 x 9, 304 pp, Quality PB, ISBN 1-58023-107-1 **$18.95**

Broken Tablets: *Restoring the Ten Commandments and Ourselves*
Ed. by *Rabbi Rachel S. Mikva*; Intro. by *Rabbi Lawrence Kushner* **AWARD WINNER!**
Twelve outstanding spiritual leaders each share profound and personal thoughts about these biblical commands and why they have such a special hold on us.
6 x 9, 192 pp, HC, ISBN 1-58023-066-0 **$21.95**

A Living Covenant: *The Innovative Spirit in Traditional Judaism* **AWARD WINNER!**
by Dr. David Hartman 6 x 9, 368 pp, Quality PB, ISBN 1-58023-011-3 **$18.95**

Evolving Halakhah: *A Progressive Approach to Traditional Jewish Law*
by Rabbi Dr. Moshe Zemer 6 x 9, 480 pp, HC, ISBN 1-58023-002-4 **$40.00**

The Death of Death: *Resurrection and Immortality in Jewish Thought* **AWARD WINNER!**
by Dr. Neil Gillman 6 x 9, 336 pp, Quality PB, ISBN 1-58023-081-4 **$18.95**;
HC, ISBN 1-879045-61-3 **$23.95**

The Last Trial: *On the Legends and Lore of the Command to Abraham to Offer Isaac as a Sacrifice* by Shalom Spiegel; New Preface by Judah Goldin
6 x 9, 208 pp, Quality PB, ISBN 1-879045-29-X **$17.95**

Tormented Master: *The Life and Spiritual Quest of Rabbi Nahman of Bratslav*
by Dr. Arthur Green 6 x 9, 416 pp, Quality PB, ISBN 1-879045-11-7 **$18.95**

The Earth Is the Lord's: *The Inner World of the Jew in Eastern Europe*
by Abraham Joshua Heschel 5½ x 8, 112 pp, Quality PB, ISBN 1-879045-42-7 **$13.95**

A Passion for Truth: *Despair and Hope in Hasidism* by Abraham Joshua Heschel
5½ x 8, 352 pp, Quality PB, ISBN 1-879045-41-9 **$18.95**

Your Word Is Fire: *The Hasidic Masters on Contemplative Prayer*
Ed. and Trans. with a New Introduction by Dr. Arthur Green and Dr. Barry W. Holtz
6 x 9, 160 pp, Quality PB, ISBN 1-879045-25-7 **$14.95**

Healing/Wellness/Recovery

Jewish Pastoral Care
A Practical Handbook from Traditional and Contemporary Sources
Ed. by *Rabbi Dayle A. Friedman*

Gives today's Jewish pastoral counselors practical guidelines based in the Jewish tradition.
6 x 9, 464 pp, HC, ISBN 1-58023-078-4 **$35.00**

Healing of Soul, Healing of Body
Spiritual Leaders Unfold the Strength & Solace in Psalms
Ed. by *Rabbi Simkha Y. Weintraub*, CSW, for The National Center for Jewish Healing

A source of solace for those who are facing illness, as well as those who care for them. Provides a wellspring of strength with inspiring introductions and commentaries by eminent spiritual leaders reflecting all Jewish movements.
6 x 9, 128 pp, Quality PB, Illus., 2-color text, ISBN 1-879045-31-1 **$14.95**

Jewish Paths toward Healing and Wholeness
A Personal Guide to Dealing with Suffering
by *Rabbi Kerry M. Olitzky*; Foreword by *Debbie Friedman*

Why me? Why do we suffer? How can we heal? Grounded in personal experience with illness and Jewish spiritual traditions, this book provides healing rituals, psalms and prayers that help readers initiate a dialogue with God, to guide them along the complicated path of healing and wholeness.
6 x 9, 192 pp, Quality PB, ISBN 1-58023-068-7 **$15.95**

Twelve Jewish Steps to Recovery: *A Personal Guide to Turning from Alcoholism & Other Addictions . . . Drugs, Food, Gambling, Sex . . .* by Rabbi Kerry M. Olitzky & Stuart A. Copans, M.D. Preface by Abraham J. Twerski, M.D.; Intro. by Rabbi Sheldon Zimmerman; "Getting Help" by JACS Foundation 6 x 9, 144 pp, Quality PB, ISBN 1-879045-09-5 **$13.95**

One Hundred Blessings Every Day: *Daily Twelve Step Recovery Affirmations, Exercises for Personal Growth & Renewal Reflecting Seasons of the Jewish Year* by Rabbi Kerry M. Olitzky 4½ x 6½, 432 pp, Quality PB, ISBN 1-879045-30-3 **$14.95**

Recovery from Codependence: *A Jewish Twelve Steps Guide to Healing Your Soul* by Rabbi Kerry M. Olitzky 6 x 9, 160 pp, Quality PB, ISBN 1-879045-32-X **$13.95**; HC, ISBN 1-879045-27-3 **$21.95**

Renewed Each Day: *Daily Twelve Step Recovery Meditations Based on the Bible* by Rabbi Kerry M. Olitzky & Aaron Z. *Vol. I: Genesis & Exodus; Vol. II: Leviticus, Numbers and Deuteronomy*
Vol. I: 6 x 9, 224 pp, Quality PB, ISBN 1-879045-12-5 **$14.95**
Vol. II: 6 x 9, 280 pp, Quality PB, ISBN 1-879045-13-3 **$14.95**

Spirituality—The Kushner Series
Books by Lawrence Kushner

The Way Into Jewish Mystical Tradition

Explains the principles of Jewish mystical thinking, their religious and spiritual significance, and how they relate to our lives. A book that allows us to experience and understand the Jewish mystical approach to our place in the world. 6 x 9, 224 pp, HC, ISBN 1-58023-029-6 **$21.95**

Eyes Remade for Wonder
The Way of Jewish Mysticism and Sacred Living
A Lawrence Kushner Reader Intro. by *Thomas Moore*

Whether you are new to Kushner or a devoted fan, you'll find inspiration here. With samplings from each of Kushner's works, and a generous amount of new material, this book is to be read and reread, each time discovering deeper layers of meaning in our lives.
6 x 9, 240 pp, Quality PB, ISBN 1-58023-042-3 **$16.95**; HC, ISBN 1-58023-014-8 **$23.95**

Because Nothing Looks Like God

by *Lawrence and Karen Kushner*; Full-color illus. by *Dawn W. Majewski*

What is God like? The first collaborative work by husband-and-wife team Lawrence and Karen Kushner introduces children to the possibilities of spiritual life with three poetic spiritual stories. Real-life examples of happiness and sadness—from goodnight stories, to the hope and fear felt the first time at bat, to the closing moments of life—invite us to explore, together with our children, the questions we all have about God, no matter what our age. **For ages 4 & up**
11 x 8½, 32 pp, HC, Full-color illus., ISBN 1-58023-092-X **$16.95**

   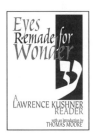 

Invisible Lines of Connection: *Sacred Stories of the Ordinary* **AWARD WINNER!**
6 x 9, 160 pp, Quality PB, ISBN 1-879045-98-2 **$15.95**; HC, ISBN 1-879045-52-4 **$21.95**

Honey from the Rock SPECIAL ANNIVERSARY EDITION
An Introduction to Jewish Mysticism 6 x 9, 176 pp, Quality PB, ISBN 1-58023-073-3 **$15.95**

The Book of Letters: *A Mystical Hebrew Alphabet* AWARD WINNER!
Popular HC Edition, 6 x 9, 80 pp, 2-color text, ISBN 1-879045-00-1 **$24.95**; *Deluxe Gift Edition,* 9 x 12, 80 pp, HC, 2-color text, ornamentation, slipcase, ISBN 1-879045-01-X **$79.95**; *Collector's Limited Edition,* 9 x 12, 80 pp, HC, gold-embossed pages, hand-assembled slipcase. With silkscreened print. Limited to 500 signed and numbered copies, ISBN 1-879045-04-4 **$349.00**

The Book of Words: *Talking Spiritual Life, Living Spiritual Talk* AWARD WINNER!
6 x 9, 160 pp, Quality PB, 2-color text, ISBN 1-58023-020-2 **$16.95**;
152 pp, HC, ISBN 1-879045-35-4 **$21.95**

God Was in This Place & I, i Did Not Know
Finding Self, Spirituality and Ultimate Meaning
6 x 9, 192 pp, Quality PB, ISBN 1-879045-33-8 **$16.95**

The River of Light: *Jewish Mystical Awareness* SPECIAL ANNIVERSARY EDITION
6 x 9, 192 pp, Quality PB, ISBN 1-58023-096-2 **$16.95**

Ecology/Women's Spirituality

Torah of the Earth: *Exploring 4,000 Years of Ecology in Jewish Thought*
In 2 Volumes Ed. by *Rabbi Arthur Waskow*

Major new resource offering us an invaluable key to understanding the intersection of ecology and Judaism. Leading scholars provide us with a guided tour of ecological thought from four major Jewish viewpoints.
Vol. 1: *Biblical Israel & Rabbinic Judaism,* 6 x 9, 272 pp, Quality PB, ISBN 1-58023-086-5 **$19.95**
Vol. 2: *Zionism & Eco-Judaism,* 6 x 9, 336 pp, Quality PB, ISBN 1-58023-087-3 **$19.95**

Ecology & the Jewish Spirit: *Where Nature & the Sacred Meet* Ed. and with Intros. by Ellen Bernstein 6 x 9, 288 pp, Quality PB, ISBN 1-58023-082-2 **$16.95**;
HC, ISBN 1-879045-88-5 **$23.95**

The Jewish Gardening Cookbook: *Growing Plants & Cooking for Holidays & Festivals*
by Michael Brown 6 x 9, 224 pp, Illus., Quality PB, ISBN 1-58023-116-0 **$16.95**;
HC, ISBN 1-58023-004-0 **$21.95**

Moonbeams: *A Hadassah Rosh Hodesh Guide*

Ed. by *Carol Diament, Ph.D.*

This hands-on "idea book" focuses on *Rosh Hodesh*, the festival of the new moon, as a source of spiritual growth for Jewish women. A complete sourcebook that will initiate or rejuvenate women's study groups, it is also perfect for women preparing for *bat mitzvah*, or for anyone interested in learning more about *Rosh Hodesh* observance and what it has to offer. 8½ x 11, 240 pp, Quality PB, ISBN 1-58023-099-7 **$20.00**

The Women's Torah Commentary: *New Insights from Women Rabbis on the 54 Weekly Torah Portions* Ed. by *Rabbi Elyse Goldstein*

For the first time, women rabbis provide a commentary on the entire Five Books of Moses. More than 25 years after the first woman was ordained a rabbi in America, these inspiring teachers bring their rich perspectives to bear on the biblical text. In a week-by-week format; a perfect gift for others, or for yourself. 6 x 9, 496 pp, HC, ISBN 1-58023-076-8 **$34.95**

Lifecycles, in Two Volumes AWARD WINNERS!
V. 1: *Jewish Women on Life Passages & Personal Milestones*
Ed. and with Intros. by Rabbi Debra Orenstein
V. 2: *Jewish Women on Biblical Themes in Contemporary Life*
Ed. and with Intros. by Rabbi Debra Orenstein and Rabbi Jane Rachel Litman
V. 1: 6 x 9, 480 pp, Quality PB, ISBN 1-58023-018-0 **$19.95**; HC, ISBN 1-879045-14-1 **$24.95**
V. 2: 6 x 9, 464 pp, Quality PB, ISBN 1-58023-019-9 **$19.95**

ReVisions: *Seeing Torah through a Feminist Lens* AWARD WINNER!
by Rabbi Elyse Goldstein 5½ x 8½, 224 pp, Quality PB, ISBN 1-58023-117-9 **$16.95**;
208 pp, HC, ISBN 1-58023-047-4 **$19.95**

The Year Mom Got Religion: *One Woman's Midlife Journey into Judaism*
by Lee Meyerhoff Hendler 6 x 9, 208 pp, Quality PB, ISBN 1-58023-070-9 **$15.95**

Children's Spirituality

God Said Amen
by *Sandy Eisenberg Sasso*
Full-color illus. by *Avi Katz*

For ages 4 & up

A warm and inspiring tale of two kingdoms: one overflowing with water but without oil to light its lamps; the other blessed with oil but no water to grow its gardens. The kingdoms' rulers ask God for help but are too stubborn to ask each other. It takes a minstrel, a pair of royal riding-birds and their young keepers, and a simple act of kindness to show that they need only reach out to each other to find God's answer to their prayers.

9 x 12, 32 pp, HC, Full-color illus., ISBN 1-58023-080-6 **$16.95**

For Heaven's Sake
by *Sandy Eisenberg Sasso*; Full-color illus. by *Kathryn Kunz Finney*

For ages 4 & up

Everyone talked about heaven: "Thank heavens." "Heaven forbid." "For heaven's sake, Isaiah." But no one would say what heaven was or how to find it. So Isaiah decides to find out, by seeking answers from many different people.
9 x 12, 32 pp, HC, Full-color illus., ISBN 1-58023-054-7 **$16.95**

But God Remembered
Stories of Women from Creation to the Promised Land

For ages 8 & up

by *Sandy Eisenberg Sasso*; Full-color illus. by *Bethanne Andersen*

A fascinating collection of four different stories of women only briefly mentioned in biblical tradition and religious texts. Vibrantly brings to life courageous and strong women from ancient tradition; all teach important values through their actions and faith.
9 x 12, 32 pp, HC, Full-color illus., ISBN 1-879045-43-5 **$16.95**

God in Between
by *Sandy Eisenberg Sasso*; Full-color illus. by *Sally Sweetland*

For ages 4 & up

If you wanted to find God, where would you look? A magical, mythical tale that teaches that God can be found where we are: within all of us and the relationships between us.
9 x 12, 32 pp, HC, Full-color illus., ISBN 1-879045-86-9 **$16.95**

For ages 4 & up

A Prayer for the Earth: The Story of Naamah, Noah's Wife
by *Sandy Eisenberg Sasso;* Full-color illus. by *Bethanne Andersen* **AWARD WINNER!**

This new story, based on an ancient text, opens readers' religious imaginations to new ideas about the well-known story of the Flood. When God tells Noah to bring the animals of the world onto the ark, God also calls on Naamah, Noah's wife, to save each plant on Earth.
9 x 12, 32 pp, HC, Full-color illus., ISBN 1-879045-60-5 **$16.95**

Children's Spirituality

In Our Image
God's First Creatures
by *Nancy Sohn Swartz*
Full-color illus. by *Melanie Hall*

For ages
4 & up

A playful new twist on the Creation story—from the perspective of the animals. Celebrates the interconnectedness of nature and the harmony of all living things. "The vibrantly colored illustrations nearly leap off the page in this delightful interpretation." —*School Library Journal*

9 x 12, 32 pp, HC, Full-color illus., ISBN 1-879045-99-0 **$16.95**

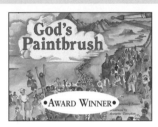 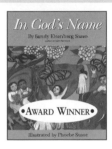 

God's Paintbrush

For ages
4 & up

by *Sandy Eisenberg Sasso*; Full-color illus. by *Annette Compton*

Invites children of all faiths and backgrounds to encounter God openly in their own lives. Wonderfully interactive; provides questions adult and child can explore together at the end of each episode.

11 x 8½, 32 pp, HC, Full-color illus., ISBN 1-879045-22-2 **$16.95**

Also available: A Teacher's Guide: **A Guide for Jewish & Christian Educators and Parents**
8½ x 11, 32 pp, PB, ISBN 1-879045-57-5 **$6.95**

God's Paintbrush Celebration Kit 9½ x 12, HC, Includes 5 sessions/40 full-color Activity Sheets and Teacher Folder with complete instructions, ISBN 1-58023-050-4 **$21.95**

In God's Name

For ages
4 & up

by *Sandy Eisenberg Sasso*; Full-color illus. by *Phoebe Stone*

Like an ancient myth in its poetic text and vibrant illustrations, this award-winning modern fable about the search for God's name celebrates the diversity and, at the same time, the unity of all the people of the world.

9 x 12, 32 pp, HC, Full-color illus., ISBN 1-879045-26-5 **$16.95**

What Is God's Name? (A Board Book)

For ages
0–4

An abridged board book version of the award-winning *In God's Name*.

5 x 5, 24 pp, Board, Full-color illus., ISBN 1-893361-10-1 **$7.95** A SKYLIGHT PATHS Book

The 11th Commandment: Wisdom from Our Children

For
all ages

by *The Children of America*

"If there were an Eleventh Commandment, what would it be?" Children of many religious denominations across America answer this question—in their own drawings and words. "A rare book of spiritual celebration for all people, of all ages, for all time."—*Bookviews*

8 x 10, 48 pp, HC, Full-color illus., ISBN 1-879045-46-X **$16.95**

Children's Spirituality

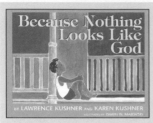

Because Nothing Looks Like God
by *Lawrence and Karen Kushner*
Full-color illus. by *Dawn W. Majewski*

For ages 4 & up

MULTICULTURAL, NONDENOMINATIONAL, NONSECTARIAN

What is God like? The first collaborative work by husband-and-wife team Lawrence and Karen Kushner introduces children to the possibilities of spiritual life. Real-life examples of happiness and sadness—from goodnight stories, to the hope and fear felt the first time at bat, to the closing moments of life—invite us to explore, together with our children, the questions we all have about God, no matter what our age.

11 x 8½, 32 pp, HC, Full-color illus., ISBN 1-58023-092-X **$16.95**

Where Is God? (A Board Book)
by *Lawrence and Karen Kushner*; Full-color illus. by *Dawn W. Majewski*

For ages 0–4

Gently invites children to become aware of God's presence all around them. Abridged from *Because Nothing Looks Like God* by Lawrence and Karen Kushner.
5 x 5, 24 pp, Board, Full-color illus., ISBN 1-893361-17-9 **$7.95** A SKYLIGHT PATHS Book

Sharing Blessings
Children's Stories for Exploring the Spirit of the Jewish Holidays
by *Rahel Musleah* and *Rabbi Michael Klayman*
Full-color illus. by *Mary O'Keefe Young*

For ages 6 & up

What is the spiritual message of each of the Jewish holidays? How do we teach it to our children? Many books tell children about the historical significance and customs of the holidays. Through stories about one family's preparation, *Sharing Blessings* explores ways to get into the *spirit* of 13 different holidays.
8½ x 11, 64 pp, HC, Full-color illus., ISBN 1-879045-71-0 **$18.95**

The Book of Miracles
A Young Person's Guide to Jewish Spiritual Awareness
by *Lawrence Kushner*

For ages 9 & up

Introduces kids to a way of everyday spiritual thinking to last a lifetime. Kushner, whose award-winning books have brought spirituality to life for countless adults, now shows young people how to use Judaism as a foundation on which to build their lives.
6 x 9, 96 pp, HC, 2-color illus., ISBN 1-879045-78-8 **$16.95**

Life Cycle & Holidays

How to Be a Perfect Stranger, 2nd. Ed. In 2 Volumes
A Guide to Etiquette in Other People's Religious Ceremonies
Ed. by *Stuart M. Matlins* & *Arthur J. Magida* AWARD WINNER!

What will happen? What do I do? What do I wear? What do I say? What are their basic beliefs? Should I bring a gift? Explains the rituals and celebrations of America's major religions/denominations, helping an interested guest to feel comfortable. *Not* presented from the perspective of any particular faith. A SKYLIGHT PATHS Book

Vol. 1: *North America's Largest Faiths,* 6 x 9, 432 pp, Quality PB, ISBN 1-893361-01-2 **$19.95**
Vol. 2: *Other Faiths in North America,* 6 x 9, 416 pp, Quality PB, ISBN 1-893361-02-0 **$19.95**

Celebrating Your New Jewish Daughter
Creating Jewish Ways to Welcome Baby Girls into the Covenant— New and Traditional Ceremonies
by *Debra Nussbaum Cohen*; Foreword by *Rabbi Sandy Eisenberg Sasso*

Features everything families need to plan a celebration that reflects Jewish tradition, including a how-to guide to new and traditional ceremonies, and practical guidelines for planning the joyous event. 6 x 9, 272 pp, Quality PB, ISBN 1-58023-090-3 **$18.95**

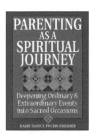    

The New Jewish Baby Book AWARD WINNER!
Names, Ceremonies & Customs—A Guide for Today's Families
by Anita Diamant 6 x 9, 336 pp, Quality PB, ISBN 1-879045-28-1 **$18.95**

Parenting As a Spiritual Journey
Deepening Ordinary & Extraordinary Events into Sacred Occasions
by Rabbi Nancy Fuchs-Kreimer 6 x 9, 224 pp, Quality PB, ISBN 1-58023-016-4 **$16.95**

Putting God on the Guest List, 2nd Ed. AWARD WINNER!
How to Reclaim the Spiritual Meaning of Your Child's Bar or Bat Mitzvah
by Rabbi Jeffrey K. Salkin 6 x 9, 224 pp, Quality PB, ISBN 1-879045-59-1 **$16.95**

For Kids—Putting God on Your Guest List
How to Claim the Spiritual Meaning of Your Bar or Bat Mitzvah
by Rabbi Jeffrey K. Salkin 6 x 9, 144 pp, Quality PB, ISBN 1-58023-015-6 **$14.95**

Bar/Bat Mitzvah Basics: *A Practical Family Guide to Coming of Age Together*
Ed. by Cantor Helen Leneman 6 x 9, 240 pp, Quality PB, ISBN 1-879045-54-0 **$16.95**

Hanukkah: The Art of Jewish Living
by Dr. Ron Wolfson 7 x 9, 192 pp, Quality PB, Illus., ISBN 1-879045-97-4 **$16.95**

The Shabbat Seder: The Art of Jewish Living
by Dr. Ron Wolfson 7 x 9, 272 pp, Quality PB, Illus., ISBN 1-879045-90-7 **$16.95**

The Passover Seder: The Art of Jewish Living
by Dr. Ron Wolfson 7 x 9, 352 pp, Quality PB, Illus., ISBN 1-879045-93-1 **$16.95**

Spirituality

Does the Soul Survive?

A Jewish Journey to Belief in Afterlife, Past Lives & Living with Purpose

by *Rabbi Elie Kaplan Spitz*; Foreword by *Brian L. Weiss*, M.D.

Do we have a soul that survives our earthly existence? To know the answer is to find greater understanding, comfort and purpose in our lives. Spitz relates his own experiences and those shared with him by people he has worked with as a rabbi, and shows us that belief in afterlife and past lives, so often approached with reluctance, is in fact true to Jewish tradition.
6 x 9, 288 pp, HC, ISBN 1-58023-094-6 **$21.95**

The Women's Torah Commentary: *New Insights from Women Rabbis on the 54 Weekly Torah Portions* Ed. by *Rabbi Elyse Goldstein*

For the first time, women rabbis provide a commentary on the entire Torah. More than 25 years after the first woman was ordained a rabbi in America, these inspiring teachers bring their rich perspectives to bear on the biblical text. In a week-by-week format; a perfect gift for others, or for yourself. 6 x 9, 496 pp, HC, ISBN 1-58023-076-8 **$34.95**

Bringing the Psalms to Life

How to Understand and Use the Book of Psalms by *Rabbi Daniel F. Polish*

The most beloved—and least understood—part of the Bible comes alive. This simultaneously insightful and practical guide shows how the psalms address a myriad of spiritual issues in our lives: feeling abandoned, overcoming illness, dealing with anger, and more.
6 x 9, 208 pp, HC, ISBN 1-58023-077-6 **$21.95**

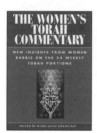    

The Empty Chair: *Finding Hope and Joy—Timeless Wisdom from a Hasidic Master, Rebbe Nachman of Breslov* AWARD WINNER!
4 x 6, 128 pp, Deluxe PB, 2-color text, ISBN 1-879045-67-2 **$9.95**

The Gentle Weapon: *Prayers for Everyday and Not-So-Everyday Moments*
Adapted from the Wisdom of Rebbe Nachman of Breslov
4 x 6, 144 pp, Deluxe PB, 2-color text, ISBN 1-58023-022-9 **$9.95**

Ancient Secrets: *Using the Stories of the Bible to Improve Our Everyday Lives*
by Rabbi Levi Meier, Ph.D. 5½ x 8½, 288 pp, Quality PB, ISBN 1-58023-064-4 **$16.95**

Or phone, fax, mail or e-mail to: **JEWISH LIGHTS** Publishing
Sunset Farm Offices, Route 4 • P.O. Box 237 • Woodstock, Vermont 05091
Tel: (802) 457-4000 • Fax: (802) 457-4004 • www.jewishlights.com
Credit card orders: **(800) 962-4544** (9AM–5PM ET Monday–Friday)
Generous discounts on quantity orders. SATISFACTION GUARANTEED. Prices subject to change.

PRAYING TWICE

THE MUSIC AND WORDS
OF CONGREGATIONAL SONG

Brian Wren

Westminster John Knox Press
Louisville, Kentucky

For Susan

"JSB"

Scripture quotations, unless otherwise indicated, are from the New Revised Standard Version of the Bible, copyright © 1989 by the Division of Christian Education of the National Council of the Churches of Christ in the U.S.A., and are used by permission. Scripture quotations marked REB are taken from *The Revised English Bible,* © Oxford University Press and Cambridge University Press, 1989. Used by permission.

Book design by Sharon Adams
Cover design by Night & Day Design

First edition
Published by Westminster John Knox Press
Louisville, Kentucky

This book is printed on acid-free paper that meets the American National Standards Institute Z39.48 standard. ♾

PRINTED IN THE UNITED STATES OF AMERICA

00 01 02 03 04 05 06 07 08 09 — 10 9 8 7 6 5 4 3 2 1

Library of Congress Cataloging-in-Publication Data

Wren, Brian A., 1936–
    Praying twice : the music and words of congregational song / Brian Wren.—1st ed.
        p. cm.
    Includes bibliographical references (p.) and index.
    ISBN 0-664-25670-8 (alk. paper)
    1. Church music. 2. Hymns, English—History and criticism. I. Title.
ML3270 .W74 2000
264′.23—dc21   99-088810